"A breathtaking and propulsive portrait of an illicit global trade—and a compassionate testament to a most peculiar accomplice."

—John D'Agata

"There is no living essayist better at weaving wildly disparate worlds into a single, gorgeously lyrical whole. *Flight of the Diamond Smugglers* finds meaning in pigeons, diamonds, murder, love, and lost pregnancies. It is a journey with its own wild logic."

—Kerry Howley, author of *Thrown*

Flight of the Diamond Smugglers

Other books by Matthew Gavin Frank

Flight of the
Diamond
Smugglers

*A Tale of Pigeons,
Obsession, and Greed Along
Coastal South Africa*

Matthew Gavin Frank

Liveright Publishing Corporation
A Division of W. W. Norton & Company

For information about permission to reproduce selections from this book,
write to Permissions, Liveright Publishing Corporation, a division of
W. W. Norton & Company, Inc., 500 Fifth Avenue, New York, NY 10110

For information about special discounts for bulk purchases, please contact
W. W. Norton Special Sales at specialsales@wwnorton.com or 800-233-4830

Manufacturing by Lake Book Manufacturing
Production manager: Beth Steidle

Library of Congress Cataloging-in-Publication Data

Names: Frank, Matthew Gavin, author.
Title: Flight of the diamond smugglers : a tale of pigeons, obsession, and greed along
coastal South Africa / Matthew Gavin Frank.
Description: First edition. | New York : Liveright Publishing Corporation, 2021. |
Includes bibliographical references.
Identifiers: LCCN 2020028156 | ISBN 9781631496028 (hardcover) |
ISBN 9781631496035 (epub)
Subjects: LCSH: Diamond smuggling—South Africa. | Diamond mines and mining—
South Africa. | Homing pigeons—South Africa.
Classification: LCC HJ7104.5.Z5 F63 2021 | DDC 364.13360968—dc23
LC record available at https://lccn.loc.gov/2020028156

Liveright Publishing Corporation, 500 Fifth Avenue, New York, N.Y. 10110
www.wwnorton.com

W. W. Norton & Company Ltd., 15 Carlisle Street, London W1D 3BS

1 2 3 4 5 6 7 8 9 0

For Fava

If we view ourselves from a great height, it is frightening to realize how little we know about our species, our purpose and our end, I thought, as we crossed the coastline and flew out over the jelly-green sea.

—W. G. SEBALD

Contents

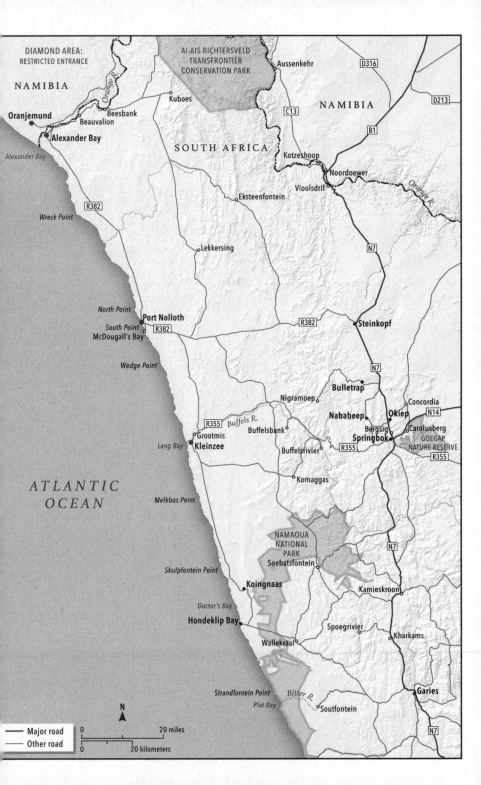

Author's Note

WITH THE EXCEPTION OF HISTORICAL FIGURES, PUBLIC FIGURES, AND my partner, Louisa, all names have been changed. Certain quotes have been reconstructed from memory, to the best of my ability.

Prologue

AFTER OUR SIXTH MISCARRIAGE, MY PARTNER, LOUISA, AND I DECIDED that we could no longer endure another attempt at conceiving a child. In the nights that followed, we slept little, often waking in the middle of the night to sit up together in bed, stretch our hands out in front of us, fingers splayed. We did these exercises according to the ob-gyn's instructions, to stimulate blood flow, to decrease the chance of Louisa cramping in sleep, decrease her dependency on the pain pills. We would neurotically peruse my nightstand notebook in which we had recorded pages of potential baby names over the last few years. We would comment on how the name ideas had changed, evolved, doubled back on themselves—a sad little record of our personalities in microcosm over that period. Each of these names was a ghost, we told ourselves.

In the middle of the night, we started reciting—aloud, as if in mantra or lullaby—the names of these ghosts, of each distinctive personality Louisa and I almost had the shot at spending our lives with. Next to me was the rectangle of bare nightstand wood, framed in dust, where my *Dad's Pregnant Too* book once rested. The farrago of loneliness was insidious and unevolving—hard, unholdable, unrockable, unfeedable fact. We feared all this love we had inside of us would ever remain stupidly, perfectly unrequited.

"I need to be around my family . . . soon," Louisa began repeating. And so, soon after the loss, we traveled to South Africa, Louisa's home country, in order to seek solace with her family and to conduct a funeral ceremony of sorts at the Big Hole in Kimberley. A gaping open-pit and underground diamond mine that was active from 1871 to 1914, the Big Hole is a man-made Grand Canyon. Nearly fifty years after mining operations ceased, Kimberley's city council, in an effort to boost the town's economy, decided to rebrand the Big Hole as a tourist attraction. They built a museum and, in this new context, what had previously been dismissed as old rusty mining junk now became "important historical relics." It has been drawing curious travelers since the mid-1960s, and some of Louisa's happiest childhood memories—into which she would often retreat as part of the grieving process—involve her long-ago family vacations there.

With a thermos of ashes, we squatted at sunset beneath the Big Hole's red observation deck, and stared into what is often claimed to be the biggest hole excavated by hand in the world. We listened to the vibrations above us as other tourists stepped onto the deck, their bodies suspended to take their panoramic photos.

We tried not to name this one. I recited the Jewish mourner's Kaddish there at the threshold—all 42 acres of its surface area, 1,519 feet of its width, all 22,500,000 tons of excavated, missing earth, and Louisa's contribution was the final "Amen." Her syllables echoed downward through the shaft, from basalt to melaphyre to quartzite to quartz porphyry, to the Vaal River conglomerate, to deeply impacted and ancient granite gneiss. We watched the burnt bridal veil-ness of the scattering, the arching of this tiny atomized body all 790 feet down to the floor of this abyss that once revealed to us the stories of rocks and the burden of 6,000 pounds of diamonds.

In order to contextualize my grief—however inadequately, but essentially—I became obsessed with the history of the Big Hole, which was, after all, the *actual* context and physical space into which we decided to embed the ashes of our final miscarriage, and, in turn, this phase in our lives. I desperately wanted to know what the Big Hole, and all of the other stories it contained, could tell us about the parameters of our own—to find out, in part, what our grief was made of.

In order to foster this conversation between our lives and this larger history, I began to consider diamonds, and the industry they birthed. Pretty soon, I found pigeons.

Like many who carry a childish sort of curiosity into adulthood, I am attracted to forbidden places. I trespass. When I heard that a portion of South Africa's West Coast was owned by the De Beers conglomerate and had been officially closed off to the public for the better part of eighty years (the heyday of diamond exploration and mining in the area), plunging the local communities into a mysterious isolation, I became infatuated with the idea of visiting the place. During this "heyday," everyone in Die Sperrgebiet (the Forbidden Zone), as it was called, labored for De Beers; no one was allowed to leave the area. De Beers kept the residents distracted with trucked-in luxuries and social programs. Fully furnished and well-stocked houses were provided. Sundries were provided, and regularly replaced. De Beers set up their own school system for the children, and provided various entertainments and recreational clubs. De Beers even had a shadowy agreement with satellite companies to redact images of the Forbidden Zone from their recorded files. It was, officially, an erasure from the earth: terra incognita meets planned community. Heavily armed security forces guarded (and still guard) its borders.

Beginning in 2007, De Beers deemed portions of this land "overmined," and as they began to withdraw their interests in the ensuing years, the doors to some of these towns slowly began opening to the public for the first time. Though De Beers still controls the area, and though signs threatening trespassers with imprisonment and/or death still proliferate roadside, restricted public entry is now possible.

I badly wanted to listen to the stories of those who live there. Eventually, I navigated the hoops necessary for a visit (replete with the sending of various copies of my passport and other identifying documents in advance, and subsequent background checks).

My journey brought me to the mining towns of Alexander Bay, Port Nolloth, and Kleinzee on South Africa's notorious Diamond Coast. Once there on the ground, the story that began to haunt me most, and focused my inquiries, was the one told to me one afternoon by a diamond digger and diver (and curator of the ramshackle Port Nolloth Museum). His story was about the various ingenious methods employed by those who participate in the thriving and ancillary "industry" of "illicit" diamond smuggling, of which he admitted he was a part. One such method involved the sneaking of trained carrier pigeons onto the mine property, affixing diamonds to the birds, and sending them into the air to fly from the mine to the workers' homes. When overeager laborers began affixing too many diamonds to the birds, though, the exhausted and overloaded pigeons began to falter, and landed at random along the beaches of the Diamond Coast.

De Beers officials caught wind of this and, having infiltrated the local governments, had it declared illegal to raise pigeons in the region. In fact, in 1998, a local lawmaker made it illegal to *not* shoot a pigeon on sight, should one have the means to do so. Still, many here raise pigeons in secret, and sometimes successfully smuggle diamonds using this method. But those who are caught suffer various consequences— official and unofficial. Sometimes, those suspected of raising pigeons (and subsequently smuggling diamonds) simply disappear.

I began to wonder what these stories might mean. What these stories might reveal when told in conjunction with other, seemingly dissimilar stories. I wanted to speak to those who still raise pigeons in secret, who still smuggle in spite of the consequences. I wanted to speak to those who are charged with levying said consequences. I wanted to burrow into the hidden alleyways and natures of this big international business, using as a lens its impact on a handful of small, secluded towns on the Diamond Coast—the towns, one can argue, most directly and viscerally affected by this big international conglomerate. I wanted to find out about the industry policies—declared and undeclared, official and unofficial—that made such ingenuity (the likes of the "pigeon-method") necessary, possible, and still prevalent.

I found, strangely, that people were willing to open up to me—often eagerly and urgently—about the things they had seen and done, as a mere result of my anomalous presence there (which the local rumor mills rapidly circulated). A conversation with one person invariably led to a related conversation with another person. People, oftentimes wishing to unburden themselves of their stories, tended to find me, and together we whirled down the proverbial rabbit-hole. In order to situate these contemporary stories within a larger context, I soon began to investigate various mythologies across history and cultures, to find out where our stories of pigeons intersect with our stories of diamonds.

It may sound moony, but I became interested in the notion of carriage itself, and the language we lend to it; the act of loading and sometimes overloading a pigeon with cargo we deem valuable, and the benefits and consequences thereof; the ways in which the labors of the carrier pigeon connect, however lyrically and ephemerally, to problems with the act of carrying, to miscarriage.

In the aftermath of writing of this book, I try, and often fail, to take comfort in Gabriel García Márquez's admission, in the acknowledgments of his book *News of a Kidnapping*, with regard to the book's subjects: "My only frustration is knowing that none of them will find on paper more than a faded reflection of the horror they endured in their real lives . . . I share this sense of inadequacy [and] . . . To all the protagonists and my collaborators, I offer my eternal gratitude for not allowing this gruesome drama to sink into oblivion . . . with the hope that the story it tells will never befall us again." My sense of inadequacy here, too, remains overwhelming.

Chapter 1

Msizi and His Bird

IN MSIZI'S LUNGS, THE DIAMOND DUST EMBEDS ITSELF INTO THE pink muscle tissue, the sponge and the honeycomb. This is the dust that will, most assuredly, elicit the growth of collagenous nodules, making it difficult—for the rest of his life—for the child to breathe. In his hands, a pigeon named Bartholomew.

This is the pigeon, he believes, that will provide him reparations for his future medical issues, that will allow him, his mother, and his brother, their deserved riches. This is the pigeon that is not only a pet, but also an agent of smuggling, the pigeon that the mine bosses believe is an accessory to a quiet—but punishable—piracy. Bartholomew doesn't think of words like *weight* or *capacity*, or *weighed-down*, or *over-capacity*, but he knows what it's like to have too many diamonds tied to his feet.

Msizi is afraid of getting caught. He is afraid, and he is thirteen years old, and he is sitting cross-legged in the red dust and white sand, and Bartholomew coos as Msizi strokes the feathers with his good pinky, and Bartholomew wriggles like a liver when the child tightens his grip involuntarily as he coughs up his blood. When he stops coughing, he tells me, "I probably should not be showing you him," meaning the pigeon. "I don't want him to die."

"Why are you?" I ask.

Msizi takes one hand from Bartholomew, extends his index fin-

7

ger, and runs it along the skin of my forearm. "My mother says to," he answers. "She says you are probably safe." His voice is thin, but deep—too deep, it seems, for his age and slight frame. He smiles and begins to laugh a little, a laugh that quickly becomes another coughing fit. I confess that I do not know what his answer means, that all of my guesses are uneducated. When I ask him to clarify, he shrugs his shoulders, smiles again, and says nothing.

It's Sunday. We are on a beach just on the South African side of the Namibian border, on the outskirts of the restricted mining town of Oranjemund, sitting beneath a sun-bleached sign that reads "No Entry." Here, we are mere specks in the middle of the Namaqualand region, 444,000 square kilometers of arid desert that encompasses the western coasts of Namibia and South Africa. Sitting concealed against the lee of a dune, we are about a kilometer from where Msizi lives in a small house with his mother and brother. We can hear, but can't see, the ocean roaring. Msizi and I found each other this morning in the small dirt parking lot of the local multipurpose store, which sells an array of sundries from canned food to electronics. As he was wearing the palatinate blue overalls worn by those who labor in the diamond pits here, Louisa encouraged me to approach him and his mother, to tell them what, in part, I'm doing here. When I finished my spiel, his mother, disarmingly, urged Msizi, "Speak to him." The infant-sized sack of cornmeal shifted in her arms. We organized to meet here, this evening. It was his mother, he tells me, who told him to bring Bartholomew.

The sand at our backs is cooling, but still warm. This is the first stop along my planned route down the Diamond Coast, and I have been urged by the locals, Msizi's mother included, to be careful while driving here, as many of the roads are private—for diamond industry workers only. The guards patrolling the roads, apparently, are often directed to shoot first and ask no questions whatsoever. I catch myself staring at Msizi's lame pinky. The wind cakes my molars with dust.

He tells me of being lowered into pits and shafts by older and bulkier men, a thin rope cinched under his arms. He does not show me the scars at his armpits, but I have seen him scratching. Msizi is wearing his work uniform—the blue jumpsuit—even though it's his day off. It hangs loose over his body, and is sun-bleached and sand-softened, worn at the elbows and knees, cuffs and collar. It is speckled with faded orange stains that appear to be old blood. Msizi speaks of the digging required to fill burlap sacks with dirt, returning to the surface, rinsing and sifting through the contents for anything that catches the light and refracts it.

"Some days are good," he says, "and some days are bad. Some days, no stones. That's when they think I'm hiding something. I only use Bartholomew if I find a good amount, early in the day. I have to wait for when no one is looking at me." He smiles, and raises Bartholomew as if assessing his weight. "We are good at being invisible," he says, more to the bird than to me.

We don't speak of how a diamond is an allotrope of carbon, or of the stone's high refractive index of nearly 2.5. Nothing of how this measurement makes both physicists and brides-to-be salivate. Nothing of rainbows. On these issues, and others, the pigeon also stays quiet, searching for warmth in the hidden pockets of its own breast. Only when the circling vultures make their velociraptor screams does Bartholomew turn toward the sky. Msizi scratches at his dry scalp. His knuckles, too, are dry and cracking. His eyes are bloodshot and seem to be permanently so, as if they've taken in too much sand.

"I start at four," Msizi says, and I'm not sure if he's referring to his age when he began laboring in the diamond mines, or the morning hour at which he begins his shift. Though recent child labor laws in South Africa prohibit the hire of someone under the age of fifteen, the law is rarely enforced. According to a 2016 report by the Bureau of International Labor Affairs, "Gaps in labor law and criminal law enforcement remain. Children in South Africa [continue to] engage in the worst forms of child labor." According to the same report, the percentages of children between the ages of five and fourteen who work, who attend school, or who combine work and school are all "unavailable." One recent survey found that 46 percent of diamond miners were between the ages of five and sixteen.

The sun is down, but the red earth holds its light, makes it seem as if it's still up. Msizi and I listen out for voices or footsteps or the cocking of a gun, but all I can hear is the ocean and the wind, and the sand blowing against our bodies. I imagine the three of us as glimpsed through a sniper's scope, the crosshairs bobbing from Bartholomew to Msizi to me.

Msizi noses deeply into the feathers, knows that a feather stripped of barbs is bone. The code of the body. The positioning system in the synapses, the electric impulses, the capillaries, the heart. Like all of us, the bird knows something, but does not know how it knows it. The bird does not even coo. The bird, in fact, shows no outward signs of pleasure, or affection, at all.

"They'd probably kill me for talking to you," Msizi says, smiling.

"Who?" I ask, and Msizi shrugs. "Then why are you talking to me? Your mom said it was okay."

Msizi sniffs at Bartholomew's head. He laughs weakly; more of a dry heave than a laugh. "Can you run fast?" he asks.

"I can run fast."

He stops smiling. "They'd probably kill you also, for talking to me. And you're still talking to me."

I want to ask, "Who?" again, but I know this is a stupid question. There are so many answers to it. I begin to wonder why Msizi's mother chose to trust me. Surely, in these diamond towns, she's seen men who look like me break the bodies of children who look like Msizi.

Armed men are well paid to protect the rough diamond harvest at all costs—a harvest that can exceed 176 million carats per year. At 200 milligrams per carat, that amounts to 35,200,000 grams, or

77,603 pounds of diamonds produced for sale in a single year. To these armed men and those who employ them, Msizi and I are comparatively worthless.

*

DECORATING THIS NAMAQUALAND BEACH: A GOLD-PLATED NECK-lace, its pendant a broken heart; a dog-chewed doll, her stuffing breaching the cloth of her arms; a dog's red collar; a South African flag; many fish carcasses in various stages of decay, some eyeless, some with eyes watching the sky. A few times per year, confused pigeons with diamonds at their feet land on beaches such as this one, on the ribcages and caudal fins, faces and tails of the dead fish—fish named snoek and kingklip, slimeskate and catshark, puzzled toadfish and leaden labeo. Dime-sized horseflies whirl, and the pigeons land, confused because someone overloaded them with diamonds again. The pigeons will not make it to the miners' homes, to the spouses who expected to untie the stones, sell them on the black market, and get rich enough so that no one in their families will ever again have to work the mines.

When a carrier pigeon is overloaded with cargo, it loses its natural GPS, and this is what happens: a confetti of feathers and gems decorate the beach, and lovers stop kissing, and combers stop combing, and parents leave their children to the whimsy of the waves, and they yell and they point, and they fight, and they tear the diamonds from the pigeons' feet, sometimes tearing off the feet themselves, and, in the sand, no one can tell if it's the blood of the birds or the blood of the humans, but they fill their pockets, and their noses are running, and their children are underwater, and they are richer, and so they quiet one another. So no one else hears them, they quiet one another. At least one of the mine workers—maybe the culprit, maybe someone mistaken for the culprit—will have his pinky finger broken, or eye excised, or hands or ears or feet, or head, cut off.

When I ask Msizi about these punishments, and how and why and when and by whom they are administered, his voice goes quiet. He's not smiling anymore. He seems worried, and exasperated with me. Though we are clearly alone, he looks around the beach for eavesdroppers. He tells me that he is prohibited from talking about it—that if the mine security guards find out he has spoken to an outsider like me, they may call in the services of someone called Mr. Lester. As Msizi begins to describe Mr. Lester, his voice lowers in volume but increases in speed and pitch. His good fingers are nervously working Bartholomew's feathers. A strange clicking sound, like a time bomb, emanates from someplace within the bird. It seems to me, as Msizi speaks, that this Mr. Lester is probably just a fabricated threat, a tall tale meant to frighten the child workers and keep them obedient—but what do I know?

"But then why did your mom allow . . . ?" I begin again, but Msizi cuts me off, continuing to describe Mr. Lester. His voice grows shaky and ecstatic. He's almost whining.

Apparently, Mr. Lester is ten meters tall, breathes fire, has sharp teeth, no eyes, the wings of a raptor, and the ability to infiltrate one's dreams. Apparently, there's a good chance he knows all about our meeting here, and the content of the conversation we're having in real time. It's a small, insular community. Outsiders vividly stand out. People talk. Cameras and recording devices may be hidden just about anywhere. Freelance spies abound. Msizi is visibly upset as he divulges this to me, and he's squeezing Bartholomew, so I decide not to press further. I scribble *Mr. Lester* on the back of an old Engen gas station receipt, and tuck it into my jacket pocket. Bartholomew shifts uncomfortably, then settles down as Msizi's grip loosens.

The carrier pigeon's life is one of servitude and, thereby, mutilation. Of flight girdled. Msizi tells me that he has fashioned little smuggling bags out of old cornmeal sacks, and that, on a good day, Bartholomew can accommodate up to four of them: one cinched to each foot, one tied beneath each wing. Not all days are good—sometimes there is only one bag, sometimes none at all. Msizi tells me that Bartholomew's left foot is the stronger one, and that he only uses the wing bags on the most bountiful of days, as they can stifle the bird's air vents there. He tells me that he's more careful than most; that he usually doesn't try to sneak Bartholomew onto mine property more than once a week. If someone else gets caught smuggling, he tells me, he'll wait up to three weeks before trying to use the bird again.

These timelines aren't hard and fast. He admits that there have been occasions when he was feeling reckless or angry, or desperate, or lucky; nervous-excited times when he dared to sneak the bird onto mine property five days in one week. "Everybody does it. Or tries to do it," he tells me. "Everybody knows. So you have to be tricky. Sometimes, I'm the trickiest."

"Everybody knows?" I ask him.

Msizi waves his hand, and Bartholomew stretches his wings. Up close like this, they appear longer than I would have expected. "Yeah, you know. Ask anyone. You have to be tricky."

"So the guards know?"

"Of course. Go ask them. They're the best at taking away the diamonds."

"You mean, smuggling them?"

"Yeah, of course. Go ask them."

I scribble furiously on the back of another receipt. In the distance, the ocean sounds as if it's sizzling, boiling something alive. A pink crab spider emerges from a hole in the sand, tests the air, and decides to return to its lair.

"Do you ever deal with any of the guards? Sell to them, I mean? Are some of them middlemen, you know . . ."

"I can't, I can't," Msizi says.

"Who, for the most part, buys them from you?"

"Everyone. So many people. Not just one type. Everybody knows. It is very easy here. You just have to be tricky."

When I ask Msizi how much his family makes from the smuggled diamonds, he refuses to give me a figure. He smiles, shakes his head, slaps my shoulder, and says, "Nah . . ." When I press, he assures me that it's not much, but only slightly more per carat than he makes as the "legitimate" bonus that De Beers gives to diamond diggers—which is, according to Msizi, the equivalent of about 20 cents. When I question the accuracy of that figure, as it seems surprisingly low, Msizi confirms it.

In contrast to Msizi's makeshift smuggling bags, "official" trainers of carrier pigeons have designed tiny and expensive backpacks, fitted to the pigeons' bodies, to be filled with anything from confidential blueprints for spacecraft meant to land on Mars, to heroin meant for prison inmates, to declarations of love and war, to blood samples, to heart tissue, to diamonds—anything we secretly desire, or desire to keep secret. Our underbellies, our interior lives, our fetishes, our wishes. A clandestine network mapping the diagrams and fluctuations of our ids, tied to bird-backs and bird-feet, twining the air above us— the air we're so busy trying to dominate, to bring down to our level.

Bartholomew tries to get away, but Msizi traps him with his good hand. The pigeon, alarmed, makes a grunting sound.

When first lowered into an underground mine, Msizi tells me, it's ceremonial and superstitious to exhale voluminously and with bravado, leaving a portion of oneself, in breath form, behind on the surface. When he demonstrates this exhale for me, it begets another one of his terrible coughing fits. He spits pink saliva to the sand. He tells me that legend has it that the breath will lend luck to the subterranean body, wait for the corporeal form to return to the surface, and reclaim the air into the lungs in an exhausted sort of homecoming.

"It's like magic," he says.

Bartholomew opens his beak. The pigeon's exhale is a coo-cum-hiss. In the articulation of its jaw joint, concludes ornithologist Dr. Jeff Birdsley (yes), is the most "important vestige of the [pigeons'] ancestral relationship to reptiles." Their necks coil like snakes, but we can't see this when they're alive and well, fat-breasted and double-chinned as they are, loaded with secrets and jewels. We can see this best only when they're dead.

*

THAT NIGHT, LOUISA AND I TRY TO SLEEP ON THE HORRIBLE MAT-tress at the local caravan park. When I close my eyes, I see red sand and birds and thin men with fat guns. I see Msizi again, walking home from our meeting for supper along a seam where the sand had drifted into other sand. When I open them, I watch the shadows of the mosquitoes at our window screen, their bloodthirsty ballet. Louisa pats my ribcage, tries to calm me down, tells me that I need sleep. I try to take comfort in thoughts of more familiar places—of our mundane "real life," and our home back in the Midwestern U.S: our kitchen, our bedroom, our laundry room, our backyard. I envision us on our patio there, so far from any desert, lying on our matching chaise longues and sipping our whiskies at sundown, the fireflies just beginning to show themselves, the crickets beginning their songs. The mosquitoes back home are different than the mosquitoes here—ganglier and less inclined to bite, bored by the regional familiarity of our blood. The mosquitoes here are still excited to drain us.

The too-bright security lantern outside our dorm pops its orange over the walls. I can see where someone long ago soaked their brush with too much white paint. The walls of the place are comprised of a series of these arrested old drips, none having quite made it to the linoleum; arrested mid-wall, as if mid-air. Our middles dip nearly to the floor. They don't quite make it either.

I push my nose deeply into the feathers of my pillow, know that the soft downy stuff before the quill is known as the afterfeather. Something secondary. Louisa reaches for the nightstand—a down-turned basket—and takes another pain pill without water, says something about trying again in the new year, that some couples—like her sister-in-law and brother—successfully conceive only after losing a half-dozen, and when they're—like us—in their early forties. I want to believe that, like us, the pigeons roosting in the caravan park's eaves anticipate tomorrow's burdens, even if they are convinced that their sleep is squeegeeing clean their tiny brains.

Chapter 2

Isaac Newton & Co.

ISAAC NEWTON WAS BORN IN THE YEAR THAT GALILEO DIED: 1642. Christmas morning. Newton, born prematurely, was expected to die, and his mother, newly single (his father had died three months earlier), kept him warm in a one-quart copper saucepan. Copper was reputed to have healing properties—defending the body against infection by stimulating our red blood cells, myelin, melanin, collagen. In fact, copper plumbing originated with the ancient Egyptians, as they believed the metal destroyed water-borne pathogens.

Baby Isaac lived (for all we know, that saucepan saved his life), and as a child was sent away to a reputable grammar school in Grantham, where he slept in the back room of the town's apothecary and developed his obsession with chemicals. Later, in order to pay his way through university, Newton worked in taverns and restaurants, wiping rings of whisky from wooden tables. But when the plague hit Europe, and started infecting Cambridge in the summer of 1665, Newton, according to University of Virginia physicist Michael Fowler, "returned home."

Newton was captivated by pigeons. He would seek them out in the wild and sit in the tall grass watching them mill about, sometimes for hours. He would gaze upon their bodies, and contemplate their fluidity—how one part of their bodies compelled other parts to move. He became obsessed with connecting the movements of the pigeon with the movements of other things in nature, including the petals of the pasque flower, his favorite plant. Often, Newton would sit on a riverbank and stare at these purple flowers swaying in the wind. In their windblown petals he saw the movements of the pigeon's wing, and thought of each as interconnected engines, mechanisms, the sort that drive all machinery and all of nature. Without the pigeon, he thought, there could be no waterwheel. Without the pigeon, no telescope, no calculus, no gravity. Newton, in fact, contemplating the interconnectedness of engines both natural and synthetic, based his famed third law of motion ("For every action, there is an equal and opposite reaction") on the "magical" flight of a wooden pigeon.

Said flight occurred around 400 BC, when a Greek physicist named Archytas bemused and unnerved the citizens of Tarentum by employing principles of rocket propulsion, launching a wooden pigeon along a wire by heating water and using the power of the steam. The Great Flying Pigeon, as it became known, was, according to the Kotsanas Museum of Ancient Greek Technology, "the first autonomous volatile machine of antiquity," the world's first robot—and a great inspiration to young Newton. Eventually, this technology would be adapted in the service of war weaponry, and the information gleaned from this magical wooden pigeon would soon result in rocket artillery, lost limbs, the sort of war that yielded the lyrics of "The Star Spangled Banner," the sort of war whose end was announced to the masses by real pigeons with crumpled paper tied to their feet.

*

HAVING SPENT COUNTLESS HOURS CONSIDERING THE MOVEMENTS of the pigeon, Newton naturally became infatuated with the building blocks of those movements—their bones. Soon, he became so obsessed with bones in general that, when he was knighted in 1705 by Queen Anne, he chose as his coat of arms an X comprised of human tibiae. Newton began to consider the interaction between the shapes and functions of bones, and such musings began to play a role in his larger conceptions of space, and of various bodies (whether human, avian, or otherwise) traversing that space.

As Newton and future scientific luminaries would find, the pigeon's skeletal system is streamlined and tapered, planed, twisted and fluted to meet the axiological and spirited rigors of flight. The muscle mass responsible for animating the legs and wings is packed into the center of the pigeon's body. The power comes from its middle, which is not to say that the pigeon's power comes from its heart. Humerus depends on radius, which depends on pollex, carpometacarpus, ulnare, and ulna. These are the bones of the wing, which itself would be nothing without the vertebrae and the ribs, the pubis and all of those beautiful lobes. The ulna (Latin for elbow) carries for etymologists implications of *luna*, the moon, and of the Sanskrit term for the point of a needle. Bone, moon, needle—all of this sharp celestial whiteness hidden beneath the filthy feathers.

The bones of the pigeon are mineshafts—hollow, filled with dark air. They are leashed to the intricacies of the respiratory system, fed by the air slurped into toothless beaks.

Pigeons don't eat worms so much as French fries, pretzel salt, hand-me-down popcorn. Their ocular orbits are huge. They have monocular vision (as opposed to binocular), and as a result of their eyes being side-mounted, pigeons bob their heads to lend themselves the illusion of depth perception.

Anatomy dictates: when the pigeon steps forward, its head, for just a moment, is briefly left behind. The rest of the body enjoys a brief atmospheric future, waiting for the head to catch up. There's something buried both in their little backpacks and their anatomy. Diamonds, blood samples, bloodlines, codes. They deliver all of these things to our waiting hands.

*

THOUGH WE NOW UNDERSTAND MUCH OF A CARRIER PIGEON'S PHYS-
iology, we still know very little about its miraculous ability to find its
way, oftentimes over great distances, to its singular home. Soon after
liftoff, a pigeon wants only to land, roost, soothe her giant breast—
which constitutes one-third of her body. She doesn't wait for home
to present itself, but senses home—days and nights away—someplace
beyond sun, Andromeda, the rank marshes and fragrance factories
of our own expansive ant farm. She wants to calm her 600 heartbeats
per minute down to her resting rate—a reasonable 200. She needs no
sleep, or we think she needs no sleep. On an ounce of birdseed—the
caloric equivalent of a single Cheeto—she has the capacity to fly 2,640
miles (or 13,939,200 feet) a day. That's New York to Los Angeles. Her
wings necessitate a distance of three feet each to complete a single up-
and-down motion. That's six feet of movement per flap. As pigeons
are not anatomically designed for gliding on thermals and must flap
constantly in order to remain airborne, they propel themselves forward at approximately four feet per flap. That's six feet of wing movement per four feet of forward propulsion. In order to cover her day's
capacity of 2,640 miles, driven by her innate need to return home,
she must flap her wings 3,484,800 times—in a sleepless single day, on
a single Cheeto—her wings alone moving through space a distance of
20,908,800 feet. That's New York to Rome. Those are countless fish
threading the ocean far beneath her. That's her climbing and falling,
but not yet touching down. This self-flagellation costumed in instinct
propels her. This is flight as chastity and vision quest, faith and skep-
ticism. How can we greet such purity without thinking it aims to dupe
us, keep us ignorant? Such soft three-quarter-pound bodies, such
lima-bean hearts unbraiding their ventricles, pumping and pumping,
the world below her—great lake and soy field—reflecting dusty bursts
of some mystery light. She's not even hungry.

*

DRIVEN BY MALIGN CURIOSITY AND DREAMS OF SCIENTIFIC PROG-
ress, humans manipulate the bodies of pigeons with scalpel and scissors, ligature and syringe. We'll do anything to find out why and how
they "home," to strip the varnish from our ignorance. Given that a
pigeon can locate its loft even in overcast weather, we suspect that
the bird navigates via a covert diagram other than that offered by the
stars. Scientists refer to this mystery-map as an "inherited spatiotemporal vector-navigation program," or an inborn star map that interacts
with other inborn maps of the Earth's magnetic field, and an innate
"chronometer" that can "read" the sun's elevation and arc.

In 2005, in order to agitate these "inborn maps," ornithologist
Hans Wallraff and his team of German interns trapped pigeons in
a drum, deprived them of light, and rotated them at speeds of up to
100 revolutions per minute (for hours, sometimes days at a time) in
a variable magnetic field. When released, these birds were still able
to home perfectly, so the next step involved trapping them again and
severing the horizontal semicircular canals of their middle ears. Still,
mutilated, in some kind of baffling pain, carrying their fresh lesions,
these pigeons found their way home.

In the spirit of human determination, of undoing natural law, we've
pumped the birds with heavy anesthesia, put frosted contact lenses
into their eyes. We've shifted their internal clocks by locking them
into darkness chambers during daylight hours and subjecting them to
artificial light at night. We've forced them to carry ponderous magnets
on their feet and beneath their wings.

Never mind that, in many of our favorite mythologies, we've considered them holy. (In scientific nomenclature, there's no difference
between a pigeon and a dove.) Never mind that the Bible engages the
pigeon variously as the harbinger of spring and purity and peace, as
an object of perfection and beauty, glistening with gold, as a symbol
for our own wistfulness, the gentlest term of endearment, as an exhib-
itor of the temperament to which we should aspire, as a stand-in for

the Spirit of God descending; and exalts it for the softness of its eyes, simple displays of affection, comeliness of countenance, richness of plumage, and sweetness of voice. Never mind that Jesus overturned the tables and chairs of abusive dove salesmen, and drove the men out of the temple. Never mind that the ancient Greeks called pigeons *peristera* (the female form of the word) and named their prettiest islands after them. Never mind that, in Hebrew, the word *yonah*, dove, also refers to the holy warmth generated by an act of mating.

Never mind. In order to see if it would affect the birds' homing abilities, scientists have affixed wire coils to their necks, through which pumped electric current as they flew. With dirty needles, they punctured their air sacs, which contain what we believe to be important chemical sense organs. They stuffed their nasal cavities with wax. Severed the nerves that carry olfactory signals to their brains, and severed their trigeminal nerves so they could no longer detect fluctuations in magnetic fields.

All of these mangled, overloaded, electrocuted birds—though their speeds were subject to what ornithologist William Keeton dubbed a "disturbing variability"—eventually and twitchily found their way home.

For centuries, exasperated scientists the world over have discarded their convalescing subjects into fields and meadows, back alleys and bogs, to invariably become meals for lazy hawks.

After these experiments produced unclear results, some ornithologists began to get philosophical, questioning the difference between the ability to read a compass and to conceptualize a sense of "home," replete with all of its furtive narratives and comforts. They chalked up the pigeon's ability to home to a complex and mystifying network of "multifactorial . . . back-up systems." Some scientists threw up their hands and deduced that the answers they desired remained hidden in the shadows of quantum physics paradoxes, using phrases like "subtle connectivity," "interacting particles," and "strong holistic flavour."

Other discouraged scientists, unsatisfied with these vague "conclusions," began to seek answers to this very peculiar but inspiring pigeon behavior in subdisciplines of pseudoscience: parapsychology, ESP, morphic resonance, even principles of Newtonian alchemy.

"This philosophy [that codified alchemical formulas lurk between the lines of the Tanekh, or Hebrew Bible]," Newton wrote, "both speculative and active, is not only to be found in the volume of nature, but also in the sacred scriptures, as in Genesis, Job, Psalms, Isaiah and others. In the knowledge of this philosophy, God made Solomon the greatest philosopher in the world."

Newton believed that the First Temple in Jerusalem, which Solomon designed, contained in its architecture the answers to mathematical conundrums, among them how to calculate pi and the volume of a hemisphere. And he believed that the Song of Solomon contained secret messages in lines such as, "O my dove, that art in the clefts of the rock, let me see thy countenance, let me hear thy voice; for sweet is thy voice, and thy countenance is comely," which inspired him to meditate on the face of the pigeon and the pigeon's coos, which further inspired him to search for connections. He found, as a result, Archytas and the wooden bird, and, in turn, his third law.

But after the tenets of Newtonian alchemy failed to answer their questions about pigeon navigation, some desperate ornithologists began to seek unlikely overlaps between principles of neuroscience and heritability. If said ornithologists are to believe neuroscientist Marcus Pembrey, of University College London, who concluded that "Behaviour can be affected by events in previous generations which have been passed on through a form of genetic memory . . . phobias, anxiety and post-traumatic stress disorders . . . [even] sensitivity to [a] cherry blossom scent," then the pigeon knows of its ancestors' lives as Genghis Khan's messengers, as carriers of Tipu Sultan's poetry, silk plantation blueprints, and schematics for the advancement of rocket artillery.

The pigeon knows that it was once used to announce the winners of the Olympics, the beginnings and ends of wars; that Paul Reuter, founder of the Reuters press agency, compelled its progenitors to transport information about stock prices from one telegraph line terminus to another. That apothecaries depended on them for the delivery of medicine. That rival armies trained hawks to eviscerate the pigeons of their enemies, causing a communication breakdown. That we've given to them our voices, that we've made of their bodies the earliest and most organic of radio waves; that when we place our faith in the tenacity of the carrier pigeon, our lives and our loves and our heartaches and our deaths can float above us, and the most important parts of our self-narratives are on air.

These ornithologists seem to be stressing: Perhaps it's not God who has the answers to our seemingly unanswerable questions about ourselves—as Newton may have believed—but the loaded-up pigeons, some of whom, in a crisis of weight, will unexpectedly land and offer us a clue into the circulatory map of all the things we wish to hide from the rest of our species.

*

"I FEEL LIKE THERE'S A POINT WHERE SCIENTISTS GET BORED," WRITES commenter Digivince on the YouTube page "Pigeons in Space," "and just do things because they can." In the video, three bioastronautics scientists of the Aerospace Medical Division of the U.S. Air Force float in zero gravity with disturbing grins, alongside a bunch of bewildered pigeons. The scientists belong to the 6570th headquarters, purportedly responsible for toxicology research. In the "Weightless Bird" clip, in voiceover narration, a man's measured voice intones, "Pigeons normally keep their bodies in a horizontal axis while in flight. These zero-g birds have lost their feeling for what is up or down, and point in all directions, some even flying upside-down."

In nature, a pigeon will turn itself upside-down only when it's suffering from disease, particularly the paramyxovirus, which causes the afflicted bird to peck at but miss its seed, stagger, crash land, tremor about the eyes and head, have fainting spells, and suffer from painful torticollis (or "twisted neck") before its nervous system collapses. Experts who work in pigeon rescue joke that the only pigeon that stargazes is a sick pigeon.

When the video is slowed, one can see the floating scientists reach to pluck at the birds' feathers as they confusedly flap, covering, in spite of their exertion, to their surprise, no distance. They are saddled with the symptoms of disease, though they are well. This is not normal.

*

TO TRAIN A PIGEON, YOU MUST BLIND A PIGEON. KEEP IT IN A BOX so that its wings can't fully expand, confusing the pigeon as to the parameters of its own body. The pigeon believes its wings are shorter than they are. Some people have neglected their better natures in order to successfully breed a pigeon—like the Oriental frill, for instance—that has a beak so truncated, so misshapen according to the dictates of nature, that it can't even peck the earth for food. It must eat from a special cup, designed by the breeders who designed the bird itself.

To train a homing pigeon, you must build a dovecote. The better of these pigeon houses include architectural flourishes—mansard roofs and turrets, faux chimneys, and top-of-the-line chicken wire. Prove something to your neighbors. With the chicken wire, define a confined space within the dovecote and, for the pigeon's own good, tell yourself, lock it into this space for at least five weeks. Feed it, but don't overfeed it. Pray, before bed, that the pigeon does not damage its feathers on the wire. Your bedroom floor will be dirty with the tools of your training. Pick the seed from your knees.

At the end of the five weeks, take the bird into your hands. Feel its heart screaming against your fingers. Tell yourself this means that the bird is excited, and that it loves you. If something's heart beats so furiously into your hands, how can that represent anything but affection? Take the bird outside, remove the wire from the dovecote's small opening, then push the bird back inside. Its body should hardly fit through. It should be a struggle for both of you. In this struggle: communion, ownership, something of parenthood even. Love.

Repeat this removal and this shoving back in for the better part of a day. Eventually, the pigeon will realize that if it wants to be fed, it must push itself back through that opening without your guidance. Without your hands. It will do this: shuffle its body along the shaft, shedding its shit and its dander, bumping its head, until it learns how to contort its neck just so. After a couple of weeks, the pigeon will have mapped out the neighborhood—about a square mile of it. Now, you can take the bird even farther out. Try north, south, east, and west, so the pigeon can find its way back to the dovecote from all directions. Two miles this week, five miles next, then ten, then fifty . . . Have faith. Wonder whether faith is always leashed to some prior manipulation. Wonder which is the product of which.

Tell yourself, *my bird will come back*, and your bird will come back. Over above-ground swimming pools and in-ground swimming pools, and sprinklers, and garbage trucks, and dim after-hours bars filled with smugglers and insomniacs, your bird will come back. And this is home now.

*

THERE'S A PIGEON IN SPACE, BUT THERE'S ALSO A PIGEON IN THE shadows of a bar in the Namaqualand desert, where I watch it bathed in Wurlitzer light and, in panic, making constellations of the sawdust. A pandemonium of wings. The syrupy fluttering of the bird throat.

Again, Louisa and I can't sleep, so we've come here to drink soft drinks, pretend that they're hard. We remember the days when that sting of the alcohol on the uvula was a pleasant thing, the precursor to quick, shallow dreaming. We worry about our drive south tomorrow to Alexander Bay. We've heard that this isolated stretch of road is often patrolled by armed guards—the unofficial and freelance security force employed by the diamond conglomerates. We worry about encountering Mr. Lester amid the desolation.

Above the bar, the pigeon collides with a light fixture and the fixture sways as if in an interrogation room. Men laugh. Men sip and swallow and fight in at least three languages. Men exchange secret things in paper bags from Bismillah Superette and Take-Away. On the floorboards, blood or tar or tomato sauce. The pigeon eats a little cloud of stale, too-yellow popcorn. I wonder if Msizi is still awake on his mattress, or if he's sleeping peacefully. I wonder if he and Bartholomew are planning to smuggle tomorrow. Louisa sips her Appletiser soda, her face so blank it's not even bored. A man at the bar is showing off a diamond the size of a baby tooth, then thinks better of it and hides it first beneath his coaster, then in the inside pocket of his yellow windbreaker. He will not order another drink. No one will follow him out of the bar but the pigeon. I wonder if they came in together. He is lucky tonight.

I touch Louisa's left earlobe—my favorite one. The pigeon, as always, will find its way home, and I just know, sipping my lychee juice, I know that outside, many strange other-hemispheric stars are falling. I can feel it. Great chunks of fire screaming across the cosmos among our satellites, either on their way to terrestrial graves or else destined to tumble, dead, somewhere in the sort of universe we ache to raise birds, and hope, and wealth, and children, within. I wonder how anyone—how anything—can know something if they can't see it.

Bartholomew Variation #1

ONE TO FIVE DAYS PER WEEK, BARTHOLOMEW WAKES INTO THE SORT of circular white light that one might mistake for the sun if it weren't surrounded by all that darkness. Msizi's headlamp sweeps the pigeon's body like a searchlight as he quietly opens the coop door, the hinges of which he greases daily with sunflower oil to protect what he believes to be the bird's sensitive ears from the squeaking.

Bartholomew has the coop to himself. He's Msizi's last bird, the others having been confiscated by mine security in response to the directives of Mr. Lester, their heads stepped on or twisted off, their bodies ripped by knife or bullet or ballpoint pen or the quill of a previously executed bird—or so the rumors go.

The sky over Namaqualand turns milky, but the sun is not yet up. Inside, in the kitchen, Msizi's mother opens the cupboard, traces her finger through the dust on the second shelf from the top. Her shirt pulls up, and her spine presses from her skin like a stack of nickels. She assesses the plastic bottle of sunflower oil, and frowns. Msizi thinks she's prettiest when frowning. That doesn't mean he looks forward to disappointing her. She wants to yell at her son but says nothing, permits him his superstitions, his tenderness toward his final bird, her final chance at wealth, and a pilgrimage south toward some nicer area of the Cape, where houses have shingled roofs, windows that close. Some of them even have balconies. The kitchen light flickers, turns itself off before turning itself back on.

Beneath the orange streetlight in front of their house, the dead bat-eared fox, flattened there since last Friday, decomposes. The insects have taken its eyes, and the red dust has pooled in the sockets. Onto these dunes-in-miniature, the wind has drawn ripples. In the adjacent dead palm, the abandoned and dried nest of some long-gone bird now houses giant crystals of salt. Down the street, that pile of white cinderblock overgrown with red mosses (also dead) used to be a house. The flagpole at the corner sports the tatters of the old apartheid South African flag, and a pair of drying blue overalls.

Per his neurotic ritual, Msizi hugs the bird to his chest, and says, "Good morning," three times fast. Msizi replaces the bird in the coop and speaks his name before heading inside for breakfast. Msizi eats his Jungle Oats ("The energy champion!"), and the shadow of his spoon looks large on the inside wall of the dining room that is also his bedroom and his brother's bedroom. He coughs before swallowing the oats, larded with a little milk and medium-fat margarine. In this way, he nourishes himself for a day spent digging for diamonds at the local mine.

He coughs and swallows and coughs, as the sun turns Bartholomew's feathers orange. The bird refuses—given the photopic spectral prowess hiccupping in his genes—to close his eyes against the brightness. It's like he's trying to hoard the light for those hours spent packed into a metal lunchbox next to a halved peach chutney sandwich and a single-serving bag of Simba tomato sauce–flavored potato chips.

Bartholomew, like most other pigeons, is so adaptable, so good. He knows when to coo and when to be quiet.

Though mineworkers have to pass through the X-ray machine upon entering and leaving the mine, South Africa has made it illegal to overradiate a person; so the machines light up and whir in the same way whether or not they're conducting an actual X-ray. In this way, the mineworker never knows whether his innards, or the innards of his lunchbox, are being scanned or not—whether they've been mildly poisoned and mapped, or given a placebo.

Msizi finishes his breakfast, cups his hands over the bird's wings.

More than 1,300 kilometers away, in a boardroom of the South African Diamond Centre on Johannesburg's Fox Street, beneath the stuffed and mounted heads of kudu, springbok, blesbok, and sable, a man named Ngoako A. Ramatlhodi, Minister of Mineral Resources, signs into law amended regulations detailing the penalties for diamond industry infractions, including illicit smuggling and trade. Though the documents do not actually include the word *smuggling*—costuming the word in *heretos*, *herebys*, annexures, and subsections—they do reference increased imprisonment for an indeterminate length of time, increased fines of an indeterminate amount, the termination of mine employment, and expulsion from the mining town. Of course, they mention nothing of the actions of security guards, who sometimes take it upon themselves to bite off the heads of birds and break the fingers of boys.

Msizi again assesses his companion's dimensions perfectly, leaving just enough room for his body in the lunchbox, just enough for him to lie his head on the foil of the potato chip bag. As he closes and latches the lid, the bird's heart quickens.

Msizi kisses his mother, lets his brother sleep, before walking. His body stutters with each stone he steps on. He passes beneath the town's sole working streetlamp—the electricity illegally tapped into by the neighborhood's residents who embody what an anonymously written local newspaper op-ed dubbed "the malign ingenuity of the poor and the damned." For the eighth day in a row, Msizi passes that dead eyeless fox. It's starting to depress him.

Chapter 3

Beyond the Pits of Alexander Bay

IN THE SILTY DIAMOND PIT OUTSIDE ALEXANDER BAY, A TOWN AT the northwest corner of South Africa, on the southern bank of the Orange River, boys and men leash diamonds to pigeons. Msizi is among them. They know how not to be seen, how to invisibly hatch their plans. The pigeons are hiding in lunchboxes or amid baggy clothes, or in places more inscrutable. The pit mine is an irregular circle, maybe 400 yards across, where boys and men harvest their portions of what should be about 89,000 total annual carats. Maybe one will get lucky, as one did in 2004, and unearth a flawless diamond of perfect color and clarity that will sell for over 1.8 million U.S. dollars.

To be flawless of color, a diamond must have no color; only then can it be called chemically pure and structurally perfect. You must see through it. Its internal characteristics must be clear, naked; its ability to transmit and scatter light unimpeded by cracks or clouds. In this way, flawlessness allows the light to reach its desired destination after traversing the passageways in the air, a successfully transmitted message. A diamond takes light in, breaks it into pieces.

The miners, the diamonds, and the pigeons are caked in sludge. There are fewer of all of them than there used to be. Akin to over-fished coastlines, much of the earth here has been overmined, and once diamond conglomerates like De Beers (or the much smaller Alex-

kor) decide that it is no longer financially viable to continue their operations, they pull out and seek new territory that may harbor a higher
concentration of gems. Just about every town on South Africa's Diamond Coast has been, or is about to be, deemed "overmined."

Operations here, though waning, persist. The noxious groundwater
rises above the miners' knees. Gas-powered water pumps suck and gurgle, like a collection of asthmatic mutant water birds. The tributaries
do what they always do: they run away. Security gates groan and beep
in the distance. One poor pigeon hops in a dusty trench, three miles
inside the front gate, but can't take off. A novice smuggler—probably
one of the child miners—improperly saddled the bird, didn't consider
its anatomy. "The tape attaching the diamonds," a local police inspector will later declare, "was wrapped beneath the wings. It was blocking
the air bags that pump blood into the veins. The bird could not fly."

Or perhaps the perpetrator wasn't a novice smuggler at all, but, as
the police later suspected, someone, or *something*, "more mysterious."

"That bird was planted," the police inspector claims, but no one
knows why. "Was it a pigeon hater's subterfuge? Or a carefully planned
decoy? Or maybe a fearless smuggler's teasing?"

I am here in Alexander Bay, ten kilometers south of the Namibian
border, to speak to this police inspector (who asked not to be named).
When I ask him if he has heard of Mr. Lester, and if this is the sort of
offense that would warrant a call to him, the inspector stiffens, lowers
his voice, and says, "N-no. I-I don't think *that* would be necessary."

In a whisper, he tells me that no one he knows has ever seen the
real Mr. Lester, as he's rumored to have more body doubles than Jacob
Zuma. "He's invisible. He's like a spirit."

We are standing outside the station on a dusty street littered with
broken bicycle tires, driftwood, and at least four species of sun-dried
amphibians. The inspector has an angry razor burn at his neck and
cheeks, and it appears to redden. He clears his throat, shakes his head,
and wants to get back to the story he's rehearsed.

The offending pigeon, he tells me, rendered flightless and struggling to breathe, was saddled with six carats destined for the alleyways of Port Nolloth, 90 kilometers south of Alexander Bay—for the pockets of the street hustlers who lurk there. Eventually, after navigating a serpentine network of buyers, sellers, fences, and polishing houses, smuggled diamonds sometimes find their way back to the envelopes of the international suppliers working for De Beers's Central Selling Organization.

Law here dictates that all pigeons in and around Alexander Bay are to be shot on sight. The law was first implemented in April 1998 after a pigeon was found hopping through the center of town with diamonds cinched to its feet. The board of the local Alexkor mining corporation collaborated, over the course of a handful of meetings, in writing the law. The local police force, many members of which are in cahoots with Alexkor, immediately implemented it. Many pigeons have been shot here since 1998; the police inspector tells me that no one has maintained a count.

"But I can tell you this," he says. "When a pigeon is shot, it explodes."

If the pigeon is a smuggler, someone working for mine security is charged with wandering into the landscape to pick the dropped diamonds from the viscera.

"Boom," says the police inspector. "It's really something."

*

WHEN A PIGEON EXPLODES, ITS FEATHERS, ACCORDING TO AUTHOR and pigeon enthusiast Andrew D. Blechman, "sashay" to the ground—that is, by Merriam-Webster's definitive standards, the feathers move in "an ostentatious yet casual manner, typically with exaggerated movements of the hips and shoulders." Though an exploded pigeon may be classified as atypical by a dictionary's rubric (if not Alexander Bay's), the hips and shoulders, when mapped onto the feathers, would be—depending on the diagram—the downy barbs and the vane, or the afterfeather and the leading edge. In square-dancing, partners "sashay" by circling each other flirtatiously, taking sideways steps.

The word can be traced to the Old French *chassé*, or "chased," from the verb *chasser*, "to hunt." While there's nothing but wind chasing the feathers as they fall, this description seems nevertheless appropriate, etymologically speaking, though the movement of the feathers seems to evoke more of a cascading than a sashaying—the movement of running water, of rain webbing downward over a car's backseat window, of a cataract slowly overtaking an eye. They land silently in the dust, these skinny ruined shrouds with such soft bones at their centers. They rest there for a moment, before blowing away.

The movement of the feathers, bullet-ripped from a ruptured carcass, is important to us. In his book *Pigeons*, Blechman writes of the competitive pigeon shooting contests that were once a popular pastime worldwide—especially in the U.S. and Europe, and especially among the upper classes. Such contests were often held in resort locations, private ranches, and plantations; the purses were typically enormous, and ancillary gambling rings abounded. Live pigeon shooting was even one of the official events at the 1900 Paris Olympics.

Soon after the Paris Olympics, after activists successfully petitioned to ban competitive pigeon shoots, companies began manufacturing glass pigeons. After the early versions of the product netted meager sales, the more innovative manufacturers began stuffing the glass birds with real pigeon feathers, so the shooter could feel a post-kill satisfaction similar to the real thing, exhaling into his gunsmoke, watching the seared feathers sashay or cascade sadly, triumphantly, to the earth.

*

IN THE MIDDLE OF MY CONVERSATION WITH ALEXANDER BAY'S police inspector, another officer approaches us. He eyes me warily, and actually kicks a clod of dirt at me. He leans in, whispers something in the police inspector's ear. The police inspector's cheeks redden and his eyes grow rueful. There's a white crumb of something in his eyebrow. He holds his open palm up to my face and backs away, retreating inside. Like that, the conversation is over. I make my way through the dusty streets, occasionally stopping in at one of the few remaining businesses or squat municipal buildings, mustering bravado, introducing myself to anyone I encounter.

There's little to do in this area of the Kalahari Desert; Alexander Bay is dying, street by street. The long-closed tourist lodge has been stripped of its windows and wiring, tiles, and doors. The "bioscope" (cinema) recently closed, all the restaurants closed, the public swimming pool was drained and is now used as a garbage dump, a thorn bush miraculously growing in the deep end. In an adjacent lot, children kick a deflated soccer ball in the dust. They are industrious about their play. None are laughing.

When I pull open the cracked glass door to the closet-sized butcher shop, a single jingle bell, near the upper hinge, announces my presence. Koos Coetzee, Alexander Bay's butcher and president of the Alexander Bay Pigeon Club, who owns two hundred homing pigeons, says, "I have two shotguns and I will shoot back if they come to shoot my birds. It is not pigeons stealing diamonds. It is people." Hanging from a nail on the wall behind him is a handsaw. The meat in his display case is thinly cut, and graying.

Also graying, and sinking into the sand, is the scoured shack that now serves as the meeting space for Alexander Bay's town council. No bell here rings when I pull open its screen door and find the town's board chairman eating a banana, a stack of papers anchored to his desk beneath a snow globe within which is a small plastic hand extending its middle finger. When he sees me, he quickly turns the top piece of paper facedown, and fixes his hair. He gestures to a rusty metal foldout chair, and I sit. He has a diamond-shaped freckle on the tip of his nose. "If we can't afford to handle [the infrastructure] properly," he says, "we could have sewage running all over the mine . . . The problem is that nobody wants the town, not even the people themselves." After about five minutes, he says he has to get back to work and gestures to the door. In the bagless metal trash can beside his desk is a mound of banana peels in various stages of decay.

Along the coast, in a sandy parking lot that fronts no building, I find a local resident trying to remove a headlight from a derelict pickup truck. In the truck's backseat are piles of clothes, plastic bags, jugs of water, books. She wears a baby blue Garfield-the-cat T-shirt. Garfield defiantly lords over the bubble-letter phrase, "Big Fat Hairy Deal." "We have no water, no power, no petrol," she says, thumping a Bible against the truck's roof, "and people come in [from remote villages] and settle in the vacant buildings. We now have theft and drugs. Something needs to be done."

The area's surviving town councils, as mouthpieces for the mines, have hired bounty hunters to shoot the birds, and others whose sole role is to gather the carcasses of shot pigeons for the pyre. No cinema, no pool, no water, no power, no petrol, no birds.

"We are trying to go about it in a civilized fashion by asking pigeon owners to remove their birds," says Steve Thorpe, general manager of the mine's mineral division. "But the only practical matter is to shoot them."

"We have to do *something*," says vice mayor Neville van Wyk. He asserts that secret agents working for De Beers's Central Selling Organization are killing pigeons in an attempt to remove illegal diamonds from the market "so they can control it."

"But, listen," says the town clerk, "people have to make a living. We are living next to the sea, and we can't even make a living off the sea because the mine even owns the underwater mineral rights."

"I know it's an emotional issue," says a member (who asked not to be named) of mine security, in regard to the edict demanding the execution of the pigeons, "but we see no other way. Some people believe it is their birthright to own the diamonds under the ground here, so it is not seen as wrong to take a few home. There is a whole mind-set that has to be dealt with."

"I have loved pigeons since I was a boy," says Coetzee, the butcher. "It just tears me apart to think of them killing these birds."

"Shoot all pigeons on sight," cries the chairman of the mine's parliamentary committee. "The security of the product is paramount!"

When I mention the name of Mr. Lester to these folks, their responses are oddly similar; their voices quiet, they look around warily. Depending on whom I ask, Mr. Lester either does or does not really exist, is human or giant or spirit or half-man half-animal. He's the guy De Beers sends in to "disappear" the bigwigs of the diamond smuggling cartels—whether domestically or internationally—but he's also the guy rumored to control various illicit smuggling cartels of his own, all across the world. He's so smart he can read your thoughts, detect fluctuations in your body temperature to determine whether you're telling the truth or lying. Even De Beers corporate is afraid of him. No one, though, has ever seen him. No one wants to see him. In the salty air here, even the words *Mr. Lester*, the words I inked onto the back of that gas station receipt, are beginning to fade. I decide that I have to find this man, or entity, to see if he is real, to uncover the secrets he harbors, lest all evidence of him and the anxiety he inspires here completely disappear.

*

IN 1997, APPARENTLY AS A RESULT OF A MEMO ARCHITECTED BY ONE of Mr. Lester's underlings, local authorities in Alexander Bay conducted a sting using police-trained homing pigeons to entrap and arrest over one hundred people working for the Alexkor mine (called by the local newspapers "the centre of diamond laundering on the West Coast"), including the (now ex-) chief security officer. Those laboring in the mines apparently couldn't resist the attractive presence of these "snitch" pigeons. When the workers took possession of the pigeons as their own, the local member of mine security tells me, they often trained them only cursorily, overeager and in a rush to smuggle. "But the pigeons were too smart," he tells me, "and they remembered their original police training," which, he assures me, was much more rigorous and imprinting. The diamond-bearing birds often flew right into the hands of the authorities, and arrests were made.

"How did you know exactly who the offenders were, though?" I ask him.

He shrugs. "It doesn't really matter. It's this mind-set, you see? Everybody is guilty. Every one of them."

Rumor has it also that the Alexkor mine, on behalf of De Beers, unofficially regulated the importation into South Africa of conflict diamonds from Angola, which were controlled by Jonas Savimbi's rebel UNITA forces, the sale of which further inadvertently financed Angola's civil war.

"If you get too close to the truth," said one anonymous South African newspaper source, in an article I read earlier this morning, "you can get a bullet in the head."

According to local narrative, after the 1997 arrests, human body parts were found in the Orange River—fingers and ears, knobs of flesh later identified as tips of noses, knees, elbows—and the names of only seventy of those arrested were officially recorded.

"Some were necklaced," an elderly woman tells me in the checkout line of the Spar supermarket, her passion fruits and lychees rolling along the conveyor belt, bumping against her sheep's neck in cellophane. She's referencing a brutal form of punishment wherein truck tires filled with gasoline are stacked over a person's body and set aflame—the rubber fusing with the flesh. She shares this with me as we wait for our groceries to be weighed and scanned. Louisa is having a bad day, and is waiting for me back at our motel room. The old woman nods, holds onto her shopping cart for support. It seems she can't stop nodding. We're both buying painkillers.

Chapter 4

Port Nolloth and the Halfway Desert

DECORATING THE BEACH SAND OF PORT NOLLOTH ARE PIGEON bones. There's a rib with the barbs of a sun-bleached feather wrapped around it, angling into the ocean wind like the bristles of some post-apocalyptic toothbrush. There's a three-quarters decomposed head, beak open wide, as if gasping, or praying, or trying to put together some feeble incantation against death.

The bones are hard to look at, they're so white. The sun is hard too. At the end of the beach, behind a chain-link fence and scribbles of razor wire, forklifts hoist pallets wrapped in blue plastic, and back up beeping. Though accessible to the eye, this key marine-mining De Beers outpost retains something of the impregnable fortress. Perhaps the corporation felt that, in setting up shop in an impoverished coastal town, they didn't need to ratchet up the visible security to usual levels. Who, after all, is within earshot of Port Nolloth's whispered secrets?

I am here in Port Nolloth to snoop around the local De Beers outpost, which is responsible for deploying a fleet of ships to vacuum diamonds from the seabed. As ever, I don't know quite what I'm look-ing for, so Louisa and I kill time walking along the beach. Had we driven straight from Alexander Bay, Port Nolloth would have been a two-hour drive south on a rough road of sand and rock. Instead, we chose the longer, rougher scenic route through the town of Springbok, a gateway to a series of ghost villages that went defunct after the land surrounding them had been sufficiently mined and companies such as De Beers pulled out and redoubled their efforts in places like Alexander Bay, Port Nolloth, and Kleinzee, until they began to exhaust that land too.

To get to Port Nolloth from Springbok, we drove along Highway 7 until greenery gave way to burnt desert scrub. We passed tiny municipalities named Nababeep (a crumbling copper mining village) and Bulletrap (where Louisa counted three overturned donkey carts, and one overturned donkey). Later in the year, this landscape—the richest bulb flora arid region on the planet—will be blanketed, for two weeks' time, in orange and purple desert flowers, before returning to its apparent infertility. "Bloom hunters" will descend on the region hoping to spot and photograph as many of the 3,000 plant species as possible, and temporary "flower hotlines," replete with all the latest updates, will spring up. People will drive fast in order to outrun the dusk hours, when the flowers close up for the night. They will use phrases like "flower hour" and "petal to the metal." In the evenings, people will fill under-prepared cafés, sip chenin blanc, and compare pictures, speaking animatedly of kaleidoscopes and rain-daisies. But this is not that time of the year.

We drove in waning sunlight among the naked dunes. When we turned west on Route 382, no more municipalities, only the expanse of arid semi-desert—a landscape so forbidding that even *desert* didn't want to fully commit its name to it. I prayed for no engine trouble, no flat tires. Something screamed overhead, following the car, and it was no pigeon. We ate while driving from our plastic snack bag—cold boiled eggs and biltong, the beef strips having been hung and spun dry at a roadside slaughterhouse on industrial clothes cleaners' wheels. After we finished eating, I said, "I'm worried," and, without asking for clarification, Louisa took my hand, put it beneath her shirt against her belly. I drove one-handed, feeling with the other the parenthetical marks on Louisa's warm skin—like scars but not scars—reading them, as if foolishly expecting this action to inspire any kind of growth, a twist in our story, a fresh plot beyond consolation.

We drove like that in that "halfway" desert, the road threading the no-man's-land between the Namib Desert and the Richtersveld mountain desert, a land that the Port Nolloth tourist office assures me "offers a huge opportunity for those enjoying vast, unspoiled land-scapes." Soon, the ocean—a gray ribbon in the distance—presented itself like some meek sacrificial lamb. I took my hand back, clutched the wheel.

There seems to be no way out of Port Nolloth but the way you come in. There is no road south along the coast, and the public road north dead-ends at barricades and security guards who stand up from fold-out chairs, their guns clapping their hips like pterodactyls, prepared to ask confused travelers the nature of their business here. Beyond these guards, the road to Oranjemund, Namibia, is private, closed off to all except those who labor in, or direct, the trade. My heart is disturbed by the knowledge that the Khoi people once called this area "Where the Water Took the Old Man Away." In one brochure, I learn that by "Old Man," the Khoi were likely referring to God.

The Port Nolloth De Beers hub is as haphazard as an Indiana railyard, equipment parts that once belonged inside boats and tractors and trucks scattered willy-nilly and rusting in the sea air. Like many other rural villages on the continent, this place once saw the influx of intrepid diamond evaluators from De Beers's headquarters, who, having left the comfort of their air-conditioned London offices, jet-lagged and suffering from intestinal duress, navigated remote jungles and coastlines with attaché cases filled with cash. Here, as elsewhere, they were charged with negotiating with intricate rings of smugglers, thieves, and local middlemen, most of whom distrusted any official operating for the so-called legitimate cartel. Many of these De Beers officials disappeared in the process, their bodies unrecovered.

The corporation launched local campaigns against the smuggling rings, arguing that if more diamonds were "illicitly" smuggled than "duteously" exported by De Beers themselves, this would rob places like Port Nolloth of their due taxes and, as such, infrastructure would suffer—roads, schools, and hospitals would go to hell. De Beers began infiltrating local government offices and building their hubs, outcompeting the smugglers and, eventually, persecuting them. Next to Port Nolloth's broken jetty, a blue and white diamond boat lies beached, its flank run through with oxidized stalactites. Somewhere inside the ramshackle building—also blue and white—diamonds are being rinsed and sorted and packaged.

"We don't want to be part of a legacy of ghost towns," says Manne Dipico, deputy chairperson of De Beers. To that end, offshore, the De Beers ship *Peace in Africa* (which cost 1.1 billion South African rand and has a life expectancy of thirty years—only seven years less than that of the average diamond miner), penetrates the seabed with its big drill, sucking up the sediment with a dredge pump into the bowels of the boat, which double as an onboard sorting plant wherein some sixty-odd boys and men sort through the slurry for diamonds. De Beers hopes that the *Peace in Africa* will reap an average of 240,000 carats per year, until the ship dies.

On the ship's deck, a man with an automatic gun scours the sky. If he sees a pigeon, its body will soon plop into the ocean with hardly a splash, and its parts will be churned up by the ship's drill and pumped back into the sorting plant, where it will be distinguishable from the rest of the slurry only by the very discerning eye. Some of these boys and some of these men will be picking through the atomized viscera of the pigeons they trained to one day make them rich. If pigeons are spotted near the boat, these boys and men will be interrogated at the end of the shift. The less experienced will be fired. The more experienced will be retained, but not before undergoing a more unofficial kind of punishment. Severed human fingers, when tossed overboard, also hardly make a splash.

*

THE TOP THREE THINGS TO DO IN PORT NOLLOTH, ACCORDING TO the tourism office?

1. "Spend time on a solitary beach."
2. "How about some stargazing?"
3. "Do some birdwatching."

The Port Nolloth tourism office recognizes the De Beers outpost, which they've nicknamed, adorably, "Captain's Corner." The painted sign itself, with its white lettering superimposed onto a serpentine blue banner, looks as if it should be fronting some Caribbean shanty peddling five-buck oyster buckets and watery beer.

"The De Beers Captain's Corner," the tourism office advertises, "is behind high security fencing, and the solemn warning that appears on the board" [which reads: "Diamonds Are Not Forever: The Supply Is Expected To Run Out And An Alternative Source Of Income Will Be Needed For This Region"].

"As you can see," says Ann Allan, assistant curator of the Port Nolloth Museum, "it's not really an ideal tourist destination."

When I ask her if she's heard of Mr. Lester, she simply says, curtly and paradoxically, "Yes. Nope."

*

ANIMAL MEANS "HAVING BREATH," WHICH MEANS THERE'S NO SUCH thing as a dead animal. The carcass is something new. The pigeon bones on the beach look like shards of some hellish toy tea set.

There's something foreboding about the sea air here, as if our inevitable demise is out there riding the tide, and, once it breaks onto the shore, all that will remain of us is some hiccupping spark of DNA drowning in the tabula rasa.

Louisa and I walk the sand. "Ulna," she says, and at first I think we're doing this again—playing this game, making this silly list of potential baby names for a potential baby. Then, she says, "Femur."

Louisa—once a student of anatomy—knows bones more intimately than I do. She names them. Tour-guiding, she holds my hand with her left, points to the sand with her right, and lists, "hyoid, atlas, ilium, scapula, patella, pubis, phalanges . . ." I want to say something to her about love, about weight, about the things to which we assign value, about flight. I want there to be an easy overlap among all of these things. My throat catches. The sand cuts our feet.

"Thoracic vertebrae," Louisa says. We watch the mosquitoes suckle in vain from them.

In the mythologies of the Blackfoot tribe, the Scottish Highlands, and ancient Egypt, the pigeon is a shape-shifter which communes with the mosquito. At various intervals, each becomes the other, to better fly, or better hunt, or better suck the blood from men and horses. In these stories, the pigeon is cast as an intellectual—sometimes a dangerous one, sometimes one responsible for salvation. Scientists have proven, in fact, that pigeons are among the most intelligent of the birds, and have demonstrated their capacity to recognize all twenty-six letters of the English alphabet, to differentiate between two different human beings in a photograph, and to acknowledge their reflection as their own image, in what naturalists refer to as the mirror test. For some reason, in our myths, we have decided to couple intelligence with a thirst for blood. When fed human blood, it stands to mention, pigeons are said to go mad.

I wonder how long these mosquitoes journeyed to get here, if, like the mythological pigeon, they are body-hoppers, single spirits endlessly reincarnated over time, as the Old Norse and Old German religions believed, as the Druids of old Gaul believed, as did the twitchiest of the Welsh bards; reincarnated over and over again to carry messages between worlds, the land of the living and the land of the dead—the tin-can telephones of our ancestors and our descendants. According to Hindu myth, once the pigeon has carried all of its messages to all who need to receive them, it will die another death, shed its avian form, and be reborn as a rose.

The average mosquito weighs 2.5 milligrams, or 0.000088 ounces, or 1/137,000 of a pigeon. So, 137,000 mosquitoes, carefully swarming, shaped into a dove by the updrafts, can carry the weight of our messages. A single pigeon, carefully dissected into 137,000 equal-sized pieces, can be a swarm of lazing mosquitoes. Of course, when filled with our blood, the largest species of mosquito can weigh in at ten milligrams. At that moment, before digestion asserts itself, the mosquito is mostly us—our blood-borne secrets and genetic schematics coming undone in its foregut. This is not the same as being carried.

*

HERE, ON THE PORT NOLLOTH BEACH, THE AFTERNOON MIST ERASES the ocean from the far side of the world. I can hear the birds sending their distress calls, but I can't see them. The load-carrying pigeons are panicking in the blinding white, above the obscured homes and still-empty hands of the waiting mine wives and mine husbands who will never refer to themselves as smugglers. Some of the birds land here on the beach, and some press on through the mist, saddled with the task of traveling north along the coast to Alexander Bay, or south to Kleinzee.

I'm readying myself for my lunchtime meeting with Nico Green, a former head of security at the De Beers Kleinzee mine. From the beach, the entire town of Port Nolloth—including Vespetti's, the Italian restaurant where we're supposed to meet—is cloaked by this mist.

More than one resident has told me that this mist "freezes" the

Diamond Coast, that the townspeople are forced to stop what they're doing until it passes. I imagine so many bodies sleeping in so many cars pulled off to the sides of the mine-restricted roads, giving in to sleep, or massaging the rubber of the steering wheel; bodies of children frozen into the dustfields, clutching rugby balls the size of their entire torsos to their middles; lovemaking couples frozen into position; dogs' tails confused and hovering—a cold wet Pompeii, the civilized world rendered to an ashen clay moldable only by the sort of weather that shrouds, and the cries of the invisible birds coming undone within it.

Exactly 147 kilometers to the north, the mist deletes the world's largest desert lichen field—all twenty-six species—and the Alexkor miners on their way to work lose the road, stop their cars, and wander in it like ghosts. They sink into the spongy earth, their world having softened. As in the mines along the bank of the Orange River, the soil of their hearts feels alluvial, rife with stones both precious and feral, the metastable carbon allotropes (now responsible for their livings and their crumbling towns) having eons ago exploded from the center of the earth through kimberlitic pipes and been carried by wind and water all the way here to the South Atlantic coast. Blinded, they collide shoulder to shoulder with the earlier shift, with prospectors, option hunters, diamond divers, and diamond dredgers, some of them carrying lunch pails that conceal butter sandwiches and trained pigeons, and if they say anything to each other, it takes the form of apology.

Along the shore, children net crabs. Skeletal old conmen in knitted hats work the beach, offering to go get us live lobsters, if only we pay them the money upfront so they can afford the diesel to drive to their source. When I shake my head, the mist eddies, and the men try to seduce us with words like *best* and *still alive*.

Louisa and I walk into the murk. We hear birds and donkeys and sheep, a bleating lamb chasing its mother through the mist in an act repeated throughout time and species. If the mist hadn't blotted out the landscape, we'd see the hoofprints in the sand, ants crawling among the broken glass, dipping below the earth and coming out elsewhere—rich, flat pans where broken windmills gauge no wind, and dates dangle from the trees.

These trees—the date palms, also used to make brooms, rope, and medicine—were brought to Africa from Mesopotamia during the Islamic expansion, and their successful cultivation depended on an enslaved workforce responsible for digging, irrigating, and harvesting. Though the Islamic expansion primarily affected North Africa, West Africa, the Horn of Africa, and the Swahili Coast, a minority but significant population of Muslims found themselves in South Africa. When the Dutch began to colonize South Africa in 1652, establishing in the Cape a refreshment station for the Dutch East India Company's trade ships, they claimed that they were unable to successfully enslave the indigenous Khoisan population and began to "import" Muslim people (many of whom were prominent clerics) from elsewhere in Africa (but also India, Sri Lanka, Madagascar, and the Indonesian archipelago), saddling them with—among other labors—the task of date farming.

Though the Dutch claimed they were unable to enslave the Khoisan population, they were able to force them into indentured servitude. According to historian Ashley T. Brenner, the settlers "sharply discriminated between the two forms of labor. While the status of Khoisan indentured servants certainly resembled that of the enslaved . . . Khoisan were nevertheless thought of as separate from the enslaved population in a number of key ways. Contemporaries distinguished between the enslaved and Khoisan indentured servants based on their status under the law, the free or slave status they inherited from their mothers . . . and the levels of violence that could be perpetrated upon them."

The enslaved Muslims could legally be mutilated and murdered when the occupiers deemed it necessary, but the Khoisan—due to the strange fact that the Dutch deemed them "free," which made their lives worth *less* than the lives of the enslaved—saw an even greater frequency of violence perpetrated upon them. Khoisan men were indiscriminately slaughtered (their livestock subsequently stolen), the women and children captured and forced into indentured servitude on the farms. "This action," says Brenner, "was taken on the grounds that it would be wrong to murder women and children."

Between 1652 and 1807, when the British colonists abolished the transoceanic slave trade, approximately 65,000 enslaved people were "imported" by the Dutch into South Africa. During this time, subsequent generations born into slavery were of mixed parentage, due to liaisons between the white occupiers, the Khoisan, the enslaved Muslims, and the so-called Bantu peoples (a cursory label for about six hundred different ethnic groups, including South Africa's Zulu population; *Bantu* simply means humans). After the British imposed legal and racial limitations on the populace, this group of mixed-race offspring became known (and still today is known) as "Coloured."

The enslaved and indentured alike found solace from the brutality in keeping and training pigeons—to which they'd feed the dregs of the date harvest in acts of quiet defiance. This: the desperate passing on of any sweetness in the face of atrocity, dates being the sweetest of all fruits, with a sugar content that can reach 85 percent. In the clandestine eating of the dates, and the clandestine feeding of the pigeons, the laborers were able to increase their levels of serotonin and the levels of serotonin in their pet birds, that essential neurotransmitter called upon when we're in need of calming and glimpses, however brief, of happiness. The eating of the dates helped to make life more bearable, the pain less acute, sleep easier to find, the psychology of sweetness some thin defense in the face of the psychology of violence.

The sweetness did all it could to dilute the burdens, to fuel the muscles and bones, as the bodies of the date-farm laborers—like those of the diamond miners—were forced to carry heavy weights, conditioned to bear loads that their bodies initially could not abide; loads that, had they been airborne, would have dragged them to earth.

Some psychologists say that the literal carrying of weight can have a reciprocal effect on mental stress, and various social issues. Bearing a physical burden can change the way we think and act, about and unto ourselves and others—a notion known as embodied or grounded cognition.

When bearing weight, when carrying, when subject to the psychology of carriage, our priorities shift, and things that aren't typically important to us become important: immediate bodily (and thereby mental) relief, the putting down, the releasing, however premature, of the cargo—the confused, at-random landing, the anxious returning to the earth and to a version of our corporeal selves that we can once again deem homeostatic. Sometimes, in order to return home, to gel with our notions of ourselves, we have to put down our diamonds.

The laborers kept the date palms alive via flood irrigation, furrow and basin irrigation, and micro irrigation, the latter of which was soon abandoned as it was too dependent on wind and temperature, which influenced spray pattern and rate of evaporation. Soon, the micro irrigation method passed from the date trade to the mining industry, which found it perfect for efficiently irrigating mine dumps so that the wind would not carry the tailings away.

*

HERE, AMID THE DATE PALMS, LOUISA AND I EAT TWO HOMEMADE marshmallows, rolled in toasted coconut, that we bought from an entirely pink farm stall on the drive out here, just past Ventersdorp, the self-proclaimed "cradle of humankind" and self-proclaimed Prayer City. The mist makes shapes that aren't really there—fins of great albino fish, petrified. Beyond it, flashes of lightning, or the headlights of a car, or the reaching beams of an asthmatic diamond trawler. In this dampness, the town rusts, creeps ever closer to immobility.

Two anxious fishermen in one small boat return with their catch, exactly one eviscerated snoek, which they will salt and try to sell in the parking lot of the Spar supermarket. One of the men has a triangular open facial wound and smells of booze and piss. He's bleeding into his gray beard. They drag their dilapidated boat onto the sand amid other crushed hulls, cable tethers cured in the salt air, broken bells.

Up the beach, we come to a peach-painted corrugated iron shanty. Kicking at the driftwood littering the sand is the man who lives there, a forty-year veteran diamond diver named George "One Time" Moyses. One can't sneeze here without hitting someone who works—or has worked—in the trade, and Moyses, curious about our unfamiliar faces, is eager to strike up conversation.

"You're not from here!" he shouts to us as a greeting.

Diamond divers are often independent contractors for De Beers, but the boats from which they work are themselves separate independent contractors in an intricate system that sees the divers unofficially hopping from boat to boat after they've made deals with HR, giving them a cut of their haul. The divers believe that such practices are necessary in order to best navigate a system they deem "feudal," with all marine diamond rights in the area controlled by the De Beers, Trans Hex, and Alexkor corporations. Though profound mineral wealth exists in the seabed and could be extracted with independent divers' pneumatic jackhammers, the corporations' desire to release diamonds ever so slowly onto the world market elicits an economic stranglehold that keeps these coastal communities in poverty. Many local divers believe that if the corporations allow their diamond concessions to be underused or to lie dormant, then it's the moral imperative of the divers to go in and get them, in order to feed themselves and their families—in order to set a precedent that will allow some of the spoils back into what they now see as their exploited community.

"If I don't get diamonds, I don't get money," Moyses tells us, dragging half of his cigarette in one pull. He tells us that in 1981, De Beers paid diamond divers the equivalent of a nickel per carat. "But I was shrewd," he says. "De Beers forced all the divers to carry picture IDs, and I was the only guy in town back then with a camera. I made more money taking ID photos than I did on diamonds."

Moyses kicks at the driftwood. His gray hair is long and his gray beard is long and his long yellow linen pants are rolled up to his knees and reggae music blasts from inside his shanty. He rests his arm on a great white shark he carved to scale out of foam rubber. He nuzzles the shoulderblades of a marmalade cat whose patchy fur smells of dead fish and salt. From his pants pocket he pulls a folded-up piece of paper—stashed there as if for my benefit. When unfolded, he shows me a black-and-white photo of six topless young women. Moyses points with his pinky to his own handwritten caption: "The Diver's Women (1980–82)." "During the early 80s, most of us divers resided in little matchbook houses in Diver's Row, Port Nolloth. There were jackpots on jackpots. Lots of diamonds and money around. The stukkies [girls] would then come up from Cape Town and entertain the divers."

"Fuck if those days aren't long done," Moyses laments, staring at his bony toes and refolding the paper. Louisa snorts. Moyses will not make eye contact with her. "The sea is still a treasure trove," he says, "but we're not allowed to get it. And they [De Beers] are the shady characters. They [deal with] the CIA, or warlords, [do] a straight exchange of armaments for diamonds . . . And you can't even trust [De Beers's] own records and statistical data. They're 60 percent accurate, at best."

"Does the name Mr. Lester mean anything to you?" I ask. Louisa squeezes my forearm, as if to say, *Don't . . .*

"Ha!" Moyses says. "You know more than you let on! Who are you anyway? No, he's not a man at all, but many men—like a whole secret government organization. The entire agency."

"So he's just, what? A composite character?" I ask.

"Yeah. Like Jesus," Moyses says and giggles nervously. "And they keep secrets even from themselves, from one [corporate] subdivision to another."

In fact, when the crews of six Port Nolloth diamond-dredging boats were recently suspected of defying the corporation, the boats were surreptitiously attacked in the night, the seawater inlets slashed, which resulted in their sinking. Port Nolloth was already suffering from an unemployment rate of nearly 70 percent, and this attack put another forty crewmen and divers out of work. "Sabotaging boats in this community," according to an article in the local newspaper, "is a crime akin to murder." The local rumor mill suspected that members of the police force's Diamond Squad who were on the corporate payroll carried out the assault. When accused, one detective, snarky with the immunity with which De Beers supplied him, replied, "Don't look at me. It wasn't our members. If we had done it, all the boats [not just six] would have been sunk and they never would have raised them." The crewmen and divers could do nothing but declare bankruptcy, make soft threats about blockading the harbor and the town. "These waters are being raped," said one. "The diamonds sucked out of our backyard fly over Port Nolloth and end up being sold in Antwerp. Port Nolloth will end up a ghost town. I think [the corporations] want this town to die so they can mine the gravel under our feet."

In order to avoid being labeled as smugglers, and to preserve what they dub "a once vibrant and unique diamond diving heritage," a collective of diamond divers, skippers, and boat crews have organized, calling themselves the Equitable Access Campaign. "[The corporations] just sit back and collect 'rent' from the small guys without adding any value," says Gavin Craythorne, the group's technical advisor. "There is zero risk for the concession holder. We carry everything. This feudal system could have worked in the past . . . before climate change, when the resource was more abundant. But today, there is no place for [this]." In spite of the Equitable Access Campaign's lobbying, the group's chairman, Joseph Klaase, a sweet-faced man with a fatherly mustache, finally had to admit defeat. "Despite our best efforts to engage with De Beers," he says, "we were unsuccessful and discovered to our dismay, in the press, that [decisions had already] been made," and the corporation's PR machine attached such a stigma to the group that they were portrayed as just another consortium of smugglers.

"Good luck finding out whatever it is you want to find out," Moyses says as he retreats inside.

"I'm not quite sure what that is," I admit to him.

"Well, then everything's an answer," he says. "That's kinda like cheating."

He pulls his door closed, and we continue on. The dumpster, rusted orange, up the beach is marked with the sign "Asbestos Only," and the mist lifts and, from above, the birds can once again recognize the illusory trails that lead out of Port Nolloth into the desert. These paths look like snakes, like rivers, and if we followed them, they would lead us into certain loss, the sort of oblivion that both Plato and Euclid so desired to make real and immortal, to make pure, if only geometrically, in the face of the finite. Maybe the animals can navigate these paths—the jackals and the hares. Maybe not. Maybe these are the dead ends that only the birds, and the mathematicians, can recognize.

*

LOUISA TELLS ME ABOUT THE ARTICLE SHE READ LAST NIGHT IN BED, unable to sleep. According to the Astronomical Society of the Pacific, "Astronomers today believe that a large fraction of the atoms in our bodies were once inside stars that became supernovae, and that they were 'launched' into the universe when these stars exploded. Furthermore, we believe the explosions of supernovae have flooded the Galaxy with high-energy radiation that . . . drives the evolution of life on Earth." We look up, and wonder what we've inherited into our bodies from above. We look up, and can't make a single constellation here gel.

Somewhere up there are the *Voyager* Golden Records, that series of blips and sounds, language and song, meant to greet the extraterrestrials with a cross-section of Earth's best media, at least as we define it. The cooing of pigeons made the final cut, as did the sound of the kiss of a mother and child. Footsteps, heartbeat, laughter, the wind, the rain, the surf, and the mudpots. Diagrams of conception, fertilized ovum, a fetus, birth, a nursing mother, continental drift. Eventually, the Golden Records and the vessels that carry them will be rendered to smithereens and, if we've learned anything from the behavior of prior space dusts, said particles will find their way into our bloodstreams in a new sort of informational pregnancy. Bach and Berry, not to mention heartbeat and rain, will be returned to us, inside of our new alien breed.

Now, we listen to the ocean evict its tentacular seaweed—the rank bullwhip kelp, creephorn, dead man's bootlaces. Attached to each variety, and responsible for the rankness, are mussels dead or dying. I think about how babies born to people much younger than we have already grown into adolescents, and are here now, mining diamonds, and raising pigeons to smuggle them. I think of Msizi's hands, and I stare at my own.

When Louisa returns to the motel room to rest, I make my way to Vespetti's, the ramshackle Italian joint on Port Nolloth's Beach Street, for my meeting with Nico Green. The place is kept running by Oom Koos (a.k.a. Oom Polony), a be-aproned old man with an enceinte belly and a lazy eye, who resembles Captain Kangaroo on meth, and who doubles as Port Nolloth's part-time butcher because "who else is going to cut the meat?" Though lunch requires no pre-planning, it's the sort of place you must call ahead—by noon—if you want to eat dinner there that night. If Oom Koos is to be cooking, it's perceived in town as a real event, which they announce all day on the radio. There are no menus, and the waitress can neither read nor write, so I'm asked to write my order on a scrap of the magenta paper placemat for her to take to Oom in the kitchen.

At the bar, large men fill their amber ashtrays and sip their brandies-and-Coke, checking out their distorted faces in the pyramid of empty Jägermeister bottles that serves as ersatz sculpture. The bartender, a raspy-voiced woman with a broken tooth and baby blue hoodie, sits on a stool next to an old rotary phone and blows her nose into half a cocktail napkin. The stone fireplace is more shellac than stone and shines like some rheumy eye. Its mantel supports three tarnished prize cups, testaments to the golf contests that were once held here, when there were still things here that could be won.

Nico Green, the former security guard at the Kleinzee mine, is over forty minutes late for our lunch appointment. I scratch the soggy crumbs of the amber breading that once interred a lovely piece of hake. When he finally arrives, he orders no food, only a brandy-and-Coke, and he does this before even sitting down. He is about six and a half feet tall, and his legs are stretched and babyish. He wears a skin-tight neoprene rugby shirt, has a flattop haircut, Coke-bottle glasses, blue-striped tube socks pulled all the way up to the demilune of his knee, and little navy shorts. Rooster-chested and scrotal, he struts to my table, snatches up my hand like a kingfisher a guppy, and plops himself onto the chair across from me.

The first thing he does not do: apologize for his lateness. The second thing he does not do: let the tiny pink and white crab spider crawling on the windowsill live. "Nico," he says by way of introduction as he wipes the spider guts from his thumb with the paper napkin.

With very little prompting, he begins to tell me how every single public official of Port Nolloth was arrested for diamond smuggling. Following mayor Nick Kotze's arrest, one sheepish local informer, asking to remain anonymous, told the papers, "Kotze [whose local nickname is J. R. Ewing] behaves like a movie character. He owns half the town. We are not scared of who Kotze is, but of what he can do." Nico tells me how sometimes the mayors' parents, wives, children, and siblings were arrested as well, for running their own rackets on the side.

"Until they're caught," he says, "they live in the lap of luxury. Big pink gangster houses ... We once found all these diamonds mixed with stolen ammunition in shoeboxes under the mayor's bed. He had this big syndicate going. Thirty-three people from Port Nolloth alone. The owner of the hotel. The family who ran the [now-shuttered] fish-and-chips restaurant. Several were women! When I was working for De Beers, if I see a pigeon, it's my sworn duty to execute it. If I don't, I'm encouraging bad behavior.

"Still, smugglers find a way," Nico continues, whether it's shoving a tobacco bag filled with diamonds and lubed with beeswax up their asses; or slitting open their forearms and stuffing the diamonds inside the wound, whereupon, due to fear of AIDS, the security guard would often rush the bleeding worker to the hospital unsearched, whereupon a doctor or nurse, who was in on the scam, would either retrieve the stones from the gash, or—in some cases—sew them into the arm; or using something called the Human Torpedo, which Nico refuses to expound upon. "Still," he says, "they use the reliable pigeons.

"But we learned a few things since previous operations. [A few years back] the Prosecuting Authority sent in an undercover agent who ended up having a steamy affair with a woman diamond smuggler in Port Nolloth. This time, when we sent in undercover guys, we sent in married men [laughs]. Handwriting experts. Nobody but the top commanders knew the whole story. We had our roles. We had to gain their trust, and we did. I worked constantly. You couldn't make plans to go away for the weekend. We worked during the night. If it's a positive case, though, there's nothing better. It's like a game—to outsmart them. It's the best. Best of all, illegal diggers know they're doing wrong, and they know who I am. They know me by name. It's long hard work. These investigations can go on for months. If people start driving nice cars, they're investigated. I had to go after good friends. Even if it was a friend, I don't get emotional, because that's your downfall. It's not easy, but I don't get emotional. We swooped in simultaneously on all the targets in all the areas. Seven hundred uncut diamonds confiscated, plus two luxury BMW 4x4s. It was part of this top-secret affair we called Operation Solitaire. Look, I can only tell you so much," he says. "Even though I no longer work for De Beers, I signed a confidentiality agreement and take this very seriously . . ."

He speaks of local businesses used as fronts—auto parts shops, seafood stands. He speaks of diamond deals gone wrong, of bodies found in the desert, shot through the head. I ask him about Mr. Lester's involvement in all of this. He eyes me as if I know something I should not. He shakes his head. He tells me that Mr. Lester knows everything, that he "pulls the strings," that he's responsible for "this James Bond–style security," that he's "the executioner who controls all the other executioners," that he's sometimes responsible for disciplining the "less effective executioners." He does not ask me how I've heard of Mr. Lester, because he clearly wants to stop talking about him, saying his name aloud. He grows impatient at my follow-up questions. He does not respond when I ask him what he means by "executioner," and he refuses to tell me if he's ever seen or met Mr. Lester. He does not tell me a lot of things, actually.

He does not tell me that those arrested as part of Operation Solitaire were hooded as if hostages and paraded at gunpoint along Port Nolloth's beachfront main street as a local newspaper photographer snapped pictures and residents booed and cheered, and threw fruit and cans and wadded paper and seashells and dried starfish at the captives, as armored vehicles idled in the background and police helicopters roared overhead. (One newspaper article stated, "Port Nolloth looked like an opium smoker's den after the police raid, smothered in fog. Little figures disappearing in the coastal milk, slipping off to the Coloured shanties on the outskirts as an angry rooster crowed.") Nico intones a quiet treatise on pigeons coffined into lunchboxes, taken into the mine. He speaks of diamond-bearing pigeons landing in cricket fields, disrupting the games. He tells me that there are desperate people who trade their successfully smuggled gems to tourists for alcohol. He lowers his eyes and says nothing when I ask him about the physical punishments exacted on the laborers for such infractions. He sips from his empty glass that once held brandy and Coke, but now holds nothing, not even an ice cube. Still, he sips from it.

"If you talk to people in Namaqualand," Nico says, "they say God put the diamonds in the ground, that there's no such thing as an illicit diamond, and that we've taken away their birthright, but it doesn't work that way. Adam and Eve said you can't murder people, and that's that. We say you can't take uncut diamonds. So that's the way it works. My wife still works for De Beers, and I told her, if you step over the line, I will take you out," and I wonder exactly what my face does here (I can't imagine it smiling) because Nico follows this with, "No. Really."

Nico is a white man, and he does not tell me that, even though mine security was considered one of the few racially integrated occupations during South Africa's apartheid years, the black security officials would have to patrol the mine on foot while the white officials made their rounds in the comfort of white pickup trucks. On the lookout for potential smugglers and their pigeons, the guards scouted the dig sites, the compounds, the married quarters and single quarters, staff quarters and Coloured quarters, the tennis courts, the hospital, the church, the mess halls (wherein the chefs were able to purchase "offal—not cleaned" at half the price of "offal—cleaned"), the tailings heaps, the paint store, workshops and offices, carpenter shop and general store, trenches, reservoirs, conveyors and pulsators, tracks nicknamed "the gravity loop," "the crescent," and "the return," the cocopans full and the cocopans emptied, the rusting windlasses and the aerial tramways, the horse-drawn whims and the decomposing horses, the power station (which, with its ramps, conveyor belts, and scaffolding resembled a waterslide park in hell), the laundry, the septic tanks, the stables, the hay hot with piss beneath the horses.

In an extension of a tradition started circa 1893 by diamond baron and De Beers founder Cecil John Rhodes, these security officials, regardless of race, were given off-the-books commissions for catching smugglers, which resulted in many a fabricated charge, which itself resulted in the beating or maiming of the falsely accused. Rhodes hired mercenaries to slaughter the Matabele people who lived along the South African–Zimbabwean border, clearing the land for his mining endeavors. Rhodes renamed this land, Rhodesia, after, of course, himself. Each mercenary was given a reward determined by his number of kills, beginning with two claims and nine square miles of personal property. Once the mines were established, some of these mercenaries stayed on as mine security. The bodies and body parts of those suspected of smuggling were often tossed into the bends of the Limpopo River, which runs along the 140-mile-long border. Today, those who attempt to flee Zimbabwe for a chance at a better life in South Africa must cross this crocodile- and hippopotamus-infested river, at which point, should they be lucky enough to make it across alive, they are often met by mercenaries belonging to the Guma-Guma, a xenophobic militia armed with machetes, who rob and rape the refugees before butchering them. The bodies and body parts of the émigrés are often found tucked into the same river bends. "If I have to die," said forty-year-old refugee Sipho Mujuru (one of the few who survived crocodile, hippo, and human, losing only one shoe in the process), "I might as well die in South Africa."

Nico and I stand to leave. Oom Koos steps bespattered with grease from the kitchen and waves goodbye to us with tongs. His socks are short and yellow. His body moves like a Lawn 'n' Leaf bag infiltrated by chipmunks. Outside the restaurant, Nico makes a call on his cell phone, arranges for some of his friends to pick me up and take me on a "shoot" of some of the pigeons that have been rounded up by De Beers's "unofficial" militias.

"They'll pick you up here just now—in thirty or forty minutes," he says. "You'll love this."

As he pulls out of the lot, he reaches his arm out the window and, with one of the goofiest grins I've ever seen, gives me a cartoonish thumbs-up. His two bumper stickers read, "No Fish In Lambert's Bay Today" and "Only Dogs And Isuzu Bakkies Get Stuck."

*

AFTER MY LUNCH WITH NICO, AND BEFORE MY DATE WITH THE pigeon shooters, I walk Port Nolloth's shoreline again. At the end of the beach, anchored into the sand, stands a crooked white crucifix, cobbled together of picket-fence posts. The sand is loose, shallow, picked clean of its diamonds. The cross is marking something, but it can't possibly be a body. I'm unnerved, and try to calm myself by invoking happier times. I think of how, in 2001, Louisa told me, after our first kiss—the one that was to lead to marriage—that she kept mopane silkworms as pets when she was a girl growing up on the outskirts of Johannesburg. How she fed them beet greens so they would spin red, her favorite color. How she could never feed them enough beet greens. How the red would spin out, leave their systems. How they are not worms forever. How they morph. I think about how red is no longer Louisa's favorite color.

At about the same time the Islamic expansion brought date palms to South Africa, Muslim warriors attempted to launch sericulture there, exploiting the preponderance of native silkworms. They descended on many indigenous Nama villages, including !Gami‡nun, or (loosely translated) "Celestial Constellation," which, according to one local legend, the Nama decided to settle because of a rotund stone they discovered there, split exactly in half. This stone—this split sphere—served as an idol of sorts, evidence of the gods' visitation to earth in the form of doves dragging a ribbon of stars in their mouths, which they smuggled into our universe from one more holy. In the shadow of this stone, the Nama raised their oxen, built huts from whalebone and sedge, and sewed cloaks of penguin skin. For water, they constructed collection pods for dew and fog and the mist. When they were forced from their land by wave after wave of invaders who claimed the Namas' communal water sources and pastures as their own, legend has it that, upon crossing the Orange River, the dispossessed were infected with a homesickness so profound that they had to turn back for one last glimpse of their homeland, and were (like Orpheus and Lot's wife) subsequently punished, turned into the tall, thorny, northward-facing plants we today call *halfmens*, or "half-person."

While the Nama engaged in sericulture and silk-weaving, the cochineal—a sessile parasitic insect—was introduced into South Africa to feed on invasive cacti. From this insect, the weavers extracted the brilliant red dye carmine. According to *A History of the Materia Medica*, carmine was used "externally, ground with Vinegar, for Wounds, especially those in nervous Parts. It is also in great Esteem among the Midwives as a Cordial, and Strengthener for lying-in-Women, and as a Preventer of Abortion."

"The Pigeons," says the *Materia Medica*, "are very fond of the [cochineal], but they prove hurtful to them; they throw them into a distempered State of Body, in which they void a great Quantity of thin Stools of a Blood red; they also sometimes kill their young ones by feeding them with [it] . . . We know very well that things may be fatal to Birds . . . and yet harmless in Regard to us." Sericulture in South Africa eventually petered out, reportedly due to a silkworm plague—a cosmic revenge, perhaps, for the damage done to those holy doves in the name of lovely red thread, while all those worms, believed to be extinct, anticipated their revival, faithful moths waiting in the dark for some light to turn on.

Bartholomew Variation #2

LIKE SO MANY PIGEONS, BARTHOLOMEW IS BROUGHT INTO THE light, transferred from the lunchbox into the loose folds of Msizi's overalls. The bird's eyes adjust quickly, recognize this expanse of muck as the pit mine. From under his tongue, with his good pinky, Msizi picks out the rough diamonds he earlier dug out from the sludge. He packs them into the four little bags he's fashioned and binds one to each of the bird's slim feet and one beneath each wing, with ligatures sewn of gemsbok hide. He looks around. The other diggers keep their heads down, their backs bent. If they've seen what he's done, they're pretending not to notice. They may be hatching similar plans. It's never good to call attention to oneself here, for any reason, to fall under the scrutiny of the guards.

Msizi's head eclipses the sun, and Bartholomew coos softly to him. The child opens his hands and the bird lifts off. Msizi bends to the earth again, resumes his digging. He cannot afford to watch Bartholomew fly, though he would love to.

From the sky, the mine looks like a terrible network, cogs and gears made of boys and men. Even the gun-toting guards become mere pulleys from this vantage. Somewhere, faraway and faceless, Mr. Lester pulls their strings. Again—such fortune!—they haven't seen the bird, fixed as they are on the intricate expanse at their feet, the sucking and whirring of this labyrinthine hive.

Bartholomew flies over columns of hand-dug gravel that line the edges of the pit, and earth-bridges that connect bank to bank. This is coliseum in hell, big business. Beyond the mine, fields of green and orange lichen whirl into the hills—hypnotic patterns of it, a fertile galaxy amid the beige blankness.

Bartholomew flies above the wall of overburden—the spoiled waste rock, soil, and entire ecosystem, really, that lies above the mine—all 33 million cubic meters of it. At its base, one team of workers exhumes piles of soil from beneath dead lichen, shovels it into rickety wooden troughs lined with mesh sieves. Sometimes, the handles break from their shovels in the effort, and they're made to continue digging with the blade alone, the edge of it cutting their hands. Msizi has spoken of this. Sometimes, if he has the energy, he tells the bird about his day. His mother and brother never want to hear about it. They're interested only in the diamonds.

Below, the sifting crew sifts. The overburden towers above them. The muscles in their forearms jump. Another team takes this sifted rubble and passes it through smaller drum-head-sized sieves, separating the pebbles and, ideally, diamonds, from the oatmeal. Some are shirtless and some wear wet shirts. Some keep their blood inside them, and some bleed.

The men with the giant guns patrol the property, the mine's lateral and medial recti, walking the overburden. They orbit, the guns cradled in their arms. The bird holds his sounds within. His body sloshes as he flies hard beyond the mine's borders, still whole and unshot and full of romance and dyspepsia, if not quite home free.

Chapter 5

Riding with the Faceless

THE OPEN-TOPPED WHITE LAND ROVER PULLS UP IN FRONT OF VES-petti's, driven by a friend of a friend of Nico's, and this seems like a new dream starting, the truck stripped of its shell, filled with four blond white men with identical crew cuts, barrel chests, and boyishly fat faces, all in their mid-thirties. They nod, and I climb in the back, and these men, perhaps because they refuse to be named, quickly lose their individual features, personalities. I remember them as if identical pillars fronting some official building—a post office or a courthouse. As if pancakes, they are faceless, and their voices sound the same—monotone and kazoo-ish.

One of them says something about a pair of marked terns who landed on the outskirts of Port Nolloth a few years back. The bands around their feet were marked *Museum of Zoology: Helsinki, Finland.* Apparently, they had flown off course and were trying to find their way back to their flock, rejoin the great migration. A local amateur bird enthusiast (who was suspect in the area due to his contextually subversive enthusiasms) planned to copy the reference numbers from the bands and send them to the museum, so they could further trace the nuances of the migration, but the birds, after having been discov-ered, were dead by nightfall. It was later rumored that De Beers officials, believing them to be potential friends to smugglers, put a bounty on their black-banded heads.

The men laugh and touch one another in that slappy way. They are dressed in yellow overalls, their hands on steering wheels or brandy bottles or the butts of leg-long guns. I sit on the flatbed's metal bench between two of the overalled men, and I don't like the way their hips peck at mine. It's still afternoon and they're drunk, driving too fast on these forbidden roads, and we're cocooned in the dust and I'm surprised at how cold I feel. They drink from the bottle and pass it to me in lieu of introducing themselves, and I sip, and their saliva on the bottleneck tastes vile and bubblegummy. They are playing with their guns, taking things apart and fitting things together, filling chambers and blowing things clean. Their knuckles are tomato-red. The driver flattens a patch of dead gladioli and I watch a tortoise lumber over the orange sand toward some new cover.

The men shout to one another—in English, for my benefit—their voices metallically *Kavalierbariton* and staticky, struggling to assert themselves over the truck's engine and the wind, pressed as if through the gaskets and dustcaps of an airport loudspeaker, determined but muffled, imparting some urgent information I can't quite make out but upon which the status of my flight depends. I try to wake up, but it seems that I am awake, and the fabric of this desert and this Land Rover threading us through it seems metataxonomic.

Broken oyster shells shoulder the road. A tall man in blue overalls walks into the desert, carrying a wriggling white puppy by its foreleg. The driver shouts something to him that sounds mean, taunting. The tall man doesn't turn, keeps walking toward the old Angler's Club, its roof caved in, now a shelter for those who have nowhere else to sleep, their bodies carefully angled on the floor amid rusting kitchen supplies and treble hooks, too-green taxidermied fish mounted on the walls above them, the dust piling up in their aghast mouths. The wind is too loud to tell whether the puppy is making a sound or not.

The road dips and crests, and at red apogees, the ocean reveals itself like an eyelid in the distance before disappearing again. A seagull stands amid a field of rotten seaweed and mussel shells, hangs its head, coughs like a person.

We pass a silver trailer desiccating between two dunes. Here, some-one once tried to cultivate a row of palm trees, but they have failed, pathetic and scrubby, their overgrown fronds having turned gray and drooped all the way to the sand, taken into the wind like the beards of petrified wizards. A flock of flamingos flies away. One of the men points to a mosquito-shaped helicopter in the distance, says something about how rich poachers rent them to flush herds of gemsbok from Namibia over the border into South Africa so they can shoot them here, where it's easier to pay off the authorities.

I'm not sure how these men fit together with the beach toward which we're driving, and the distant Orange River estuary and its seventy-five species of water birds that one small town council is try-ing and failing to conserve; I'm not sure what the flagless flagpole at the end of the beach parking lot can tell me about the shards of plastic bags caught on the barbed wire fence, themselves whipping like the emaciated flags of the doomed. I'm not sure how the *me* on the back of this Land Rover amid these anonymous human canaries gels with the *me* that is partner to Louisa; how the picture of Louisa in my head (napping beneath the turquoise blanket of yet another desert motel bed) gels with the real her—her real body in that real room with the real pain inside of her.

The driver parks the truck and the men leap out with their guns, one of them kind enough to offer me a chapped hand. Single file, we walk off onto the beach, the sun reflecting from the ocean turning everything graphite and gauzy, each thing rendered to its silhouette. The beach is huge—the ocean seems unreachable—some Venusian pan striated, some pink-flooded caldera.

Though not officially sanctioned by De Beers, small anti-pigeon militias, like the one I'm with, still thrive here, kidnapping people's pets right from their coops on nighttime stealth runs, rounding up lost birds, baiting those misguided enough to roost in the eaves of defunct buildings or build their nests in the crevices of the shipwrecks, and bringing them here, to this spot on the beach hidden in the labyrinth of dunes. These purloined birds are kept in stacked cages. These men are bored. What with nearly every recreational outlet in the small towns along the Diamond Coast having been shuttered, this is what they do, in part, for fun.

In one cage, I convince myself I spot eggs. They seem less white than other eggs, dismal and matte, just another component in this flock of inverses: the pigeon's eggs and the sun, the sun and the ocean as a downed sun gone splat.

Illicit pigeon shoots still take place throughout Europe and the Americas, and at these, sanitary issues are paramount; concerns over the safe disposal of the corpses demand a cleanup crew armed with trash bags and pickup trucks bound for the landfill. Here, there is no such need. This shoot takes place in the land of disposal, this beach long practiced at hastening decomposition and blanketing the remains. In many shoots, there are separate rings, so the marksmen can compete simultaneously; there is a trap operator (oftentimes a boy, the son of one of the shooters) who, from a safe distance, pulls a rope attached to the cage doors, opening them concurrently at the call of "Pull!"; there is a forefield strewn with spent shells, scraps of feather, splinters of beak and blobs of organ, waiting for sunset and the arrival of the cleanup crew.

Here, things are not so organized. When one of the men opens the cages, the birds look confused, but not frantic. They bob their heads, muster their bearings, and the ocean crashes, and the seaweed stinks. They do not fly away, so used to trusting us, and I know that it is in vain that I root for their safe escape. The men sound as I'd imagine the bedchamber of an orphanage sounding—full of breaths. They put on their shooting hats. Light cigarettes. Call birds as if corner pockets. One of the guys brags about having once shot a rare Eastern bronze-naped pigeon—member of a threatened and protected species, possessor of the most golden hindcollar, amethyst nape, and dusky breast—which was clearly the pet of a fancier and not a diamond smuggler. One of the guys passes me a bottle of Castle beer. Lone strands of beachgrass angle away from the ocean.

The shooting begins, and it's softer than I expected, dampened by dune and ocean. Over the pops, the men posture and cheer. They keep saying *something-something-American, something-something-American*, and are clearly performing for what they believe is my benefit. I don't know. Maybe it is. Most of the birds are dead, and some are twitching, their beaks wrestling with the air, but no sound is coming out. I wait impatiently for the men to plant their gun butts and bottles in the sand, walk over to them, and wring their necks. They do, and rinse the blood from their hands in the seafoam.

From the back of the truck, they take jars of beetroot salad from paper bags, and we eat our snack with our fingers, the tips purpling. One of the men talks about keeping a CB radio on his nightstand, by which pigeon spotters communicate their reports. He speaks of working in the conveyor belt business.

Two dying pigeons, slumped against a dune, turn to each other like lovers on a mattress, and, I swear to God, they make eye contact—their waning ciliary muscles resembling those of reptiles, their four color receptors going crazy, confusing, in the face of imminent death, the ultraviolet spectrum with polarized light, the coming mist with the magnetic fields—and open their beaks to proclaim, I'd like to think, their final expressions of love.

I listen to these men overuse and misapply the word *love* ("I'd love another brandy," etc.), as we all do in order to simultaneously demystify its spell and convince ourselves that we're under it. *Love, love, love,* the men say, as they make a beach fire with brush. They bring a pot of seawater to steam and plunge the bird carcasses into it, scalding them, which loosens the attachment of feather to skin. I drink more brandy, and they invite me to help with the plucking. The feathers come easily loose. One of the men stains his jumpsuit as he relieves the pigeons of their heads and feet, makes his scalene incisions along their naked torsos, cleans them of their insides.

As we skewer their bodies onto bamboo spears and roast them like marshmallows, the mist thickens, and every so often I see a disembodied yellow arm reach through it, the hand filthy with pigeon blood and beach grit, offering me another swig of brandy, which I accept again and again, because it feels good to say, "Yes." Time and temperature compress. I feel drunk and hungover at the same time. Hot and cold.

I'm desperate to stylize this whole scene, even as I'm part of it, turn it into some unholy and displaced landscape by Canaletto, that sad, lonely Venetian painter who would set up his easel along the canals in the mid-1700s and work his brushes against the canvas, ignored by passersby. He was ignored by friends and lovers too, spent his life in solitude. Though he was a master at rendering the sky (he favored the most expensive Prussian blue—the first modern synthetic pigment, dependent on ultraviolet rays for what Marie Curie might have called its seemingly "spontaneous luminosity"), he ornamented his skies with Venice's famed pigeons in only three early paintings (of a lifetime's total of 585), and then, inexplicably, refused to render them ever again. Here, on this wreck of a beach, it seems, all of those birds missing from those 582 skies have been returned—across century and continent—lifeless as splotches of dyed acrylic and insoluble ferric ferrocyanide. *This is only a painting*, I tell myself, as if one of Canaletto's *capricci*, a fantasy cityscape stretching itself toward believability.

The men are standing at the border of something, the point at which good dream turns bad. They flavor the meat with shakes of barbecue spice. We eat without plates, and burn our fingers. In eating these pigeons, and in thinking that they are delicious, I can't help but feel a little blasphemous. Maybe I'm eating a retired smuggler. Maybe, as I teethe on the sail-thin meat that once connected rib to rib, my tongue buzzing with paprika and anti-caking agent, someone's still waiting for it to come home.

In ancient Egypt, pigeon excrement was a valuable commodity, responsible for a then-untold agricultural windfall due to the high nitrogen content in the resulting fertilizer. We're eating rarefied food, pigeon meat being reserved, for centuries in Old England, for the plates of the aristocracy. For hundreds of years, all pigeon feces within English borders, by legal decree, was claimed as property of the Crown—a portion of it devoted to increasing the abundance of agricultural output, a portion of it used to fabricate saltpeter, an ingredient essential to the production of gunpowder, which was responsible for England's swift and successful colonizing of much of the world. Without the shit of the birds we're busy eating, history would be different, South Africa would be different, as would the mining industry, the schematics of this beach that we're standing on, the character and number of the shipwrecks in that ocean over there, and the cargo and crew that went down with them. Would the British have been such atrociously effective imperialists, I want to ask these men, without it?

Instead, I say nothing, and the men piss the heat out of the embers. Full, and a little nauseous, we pile into the truck and rove along the beach, collapsing the sand shelves, the ebb tidal deltas, the sheets and the shoals. A couple of them are taking bags of dead pigeons back to their families for supper.

Inexplicably, someone has strung a length of barbed wire fence across a portion of the beach, hemming something in or keeping something out. The man in the passenger seat hops out to inspect it. Running along the top of the fence is a long string of pink yarn, hundreds of feet long, and the passenger, curious, begins to pull it from the barbs toward him. We wait for either the yarn to break, or its terminus, which is hidden in the distance, screened in mist. This yarn-pulling, arm after arm, an endless tug-of-war, the pink string spooling into the sand at his feet, seems to take forever. I'm eager to get back to Louisa, but also eager to see what's at the end of the line.

Finally, after about ten minutes of careful pulling, the passenger comes up with his catch, a crooked crucifix of plastic translucent pipe and hose, cinched with the fingers of a rubber glove and adorned in the crooks of the crossbars—the pits where the stipes meets the patibulum—with deliberately waxed and curled barbs of feathers. Surely, we've disturbed some sacred site. Desecrated some omen or idol.

The silence of the men is unnerving. When they break their silence, they argue about whether or not to take this weird sculpture with us. In a lapse of judgment, I ask if I can photograph the thing, and they look at one another with faces I will not remember. The driver says, "I wouldn't. I wouldn't do that."

The passenger claims to have a "Coloured friend" who may know what this thing is. Reluctantly, the men succumb to their inquiring minds, and we bring the thing onboard. We recede into an introspective solemnity as we drive into the mist, looking for the street that will get us out of here.

When we find it, the makeshift centerline is comprised of dead proteas, having been squashed, it seems, beneath ostrich feet. Still, in the low evening light, the sad bees try for fertilization, the mist settling in their fur, their long tongues reaching into the flowers' tubes and finding nothing but road dust. At the shoulder, worker ants pour into a mussel shell. Should they fail to find food there, they will eat one another. To lighten the mood, to restore the sense of festivity that attended the pigeon shoot, the passenger passes around a wallet-sized picture of his two Pomeranians. When the picture is returned to him after having made the rounds, he kisses it before replacing it in his pocket. The driver keeps his eyes peeled for the female ghosts who are said to hitchhike this road, pointing downward at their bare feet, causing fatal accidents for whoever picks them up. Even they avoid us today.

We drive through a pan filled with cairns of dried horseshit, but no horses—monuments to some dead ranch, the people and animals who once trotted and rode there. Another confounding clue for the aliens to rove among, and decode.

We come to a shack of rusted sheet metal and burlap. The place is lit with purloined electricity, a complex jumble of spliced wires beneath the sand. A single, too-white bulb flickers inside. A man in blue reflective overalls sits in the dust out front, antagonizing an anthill with a pikestaff of petrified wood. It looks like the sort of rod that once urged water from rock. The ants are so huge, I can see them from the back of the Land Rover, the sand alive with black static. We stop the truck and this man stands, waves to the passenger. The ants attack his reflective pant cuffs and he pays them no mind. He's wearing brown rubber gumboots. The passenger swings the piece of yarn, the pipe and rubber glove sculpture arcing toward this man like a lure. When it lands between his feet, he seizes up, and his hands, as if electrified, pop open, his fingers splayed like the feathers of an anhinga. His staff falls to the sand and, in a matter of seconds, it disappears beneath the swarm of ants. He stares at the thing between his feet, and the passenger asks him something in Afrikaans, but the man does not answer.

The men shift uncomfortably in the Land Rover, whisper among themselves, and a few of them utter the word *Tokoloshe*, the name of the evil dwarf-like water sprite of Zulu mythology, an invoked harbinger of bad luck: financial ruin, lost love, illness, blindness, pain, and death. As the Tokoloshe is said to rape and bite off the toes of sleeping schoolchildren before jumping up and down on their chests, finally exhausting them to death, hordes of South Africans raise their bedframes up on bricks or stacks of wood, in order to prevent the diminutive spirit from reaching the mattress. Louisa, too, did this as a child.

The passenger stands in the truck, impotently holding the pink yarn. The driver takes a puff from an asthma inhaler. As if defibrillated, the man in the blue overalls turns from the thing we cast between his boots and sprints away into the desert. The passenger, literally, and with a utility knife, cuts the line. The man runs until we can't see him anymore, his path cartoonishly traced by a wyvern of accursed dust. I wonder if he'll ever return home. The faceless men force their laughter, try to convince me that this is no big deal. There are bits of feather stuck to the toes of our shoes. Amoebas of sand on the vamps and welts, outsoles and tongues, pasted to drops of bird blood. Through the doorway of the shack, something is cooking on a hotplate. Whatever it is, it is boiling over.

Chapter 6

Driving to Kleinzee amid Shipwrecks and Snakes

THE MEN IN THE YELLOW JUMPSUITS DROP ME BACK OFF IN PORT Nolloth. We have sobered up, and our goodbyes bear little enthusiasm. When I find Louisa at the motel, she is sitting on the bench outside reception, beneath the blue glow of the insect zapper, tossing cheese cracker crumbs to the pigeons. I try to tell her about the rest of my day. She says something to me about being careful, or taking care, and I consider the gulf between the acts of being and taking. She says little else. She empties the cellophane of the cheese crackers, and we go inside.

That night, I dream mundane dreams. In them, Louisa and I sit up in this very motel bed in the desert, our hands out in front of us, fingers splayed. Our hands, waiting for the rest of our bodies to catch up. Our hands are the empty nests, the eggless zeros, reddening only because our hearts are beating with so many old sadnesses. We are ever circling our losses, trying to find the way into them, so we can find the way out. Always getting over, always recovering. We need salve. Medicine and diamonds. We need to convince ourselves that we are strong enough to carry the weight of a pigeon—their soft 9.3- to 13.4-ounce bodies. They will come to us as we've trained them to do. They will have popcorn skins in their throats. Ketchup in their feathers. We've trained them well, and they slither in the air above us, recalling their serpentine ancestors, counting the seconds until they can land.

The next morning, we wake late, check out, get into the rental car and drive. The dirt road from Port Nolloth to Kleinzee is flanked by red sand on the ocean side, beige grassland on the other. Skeletal electric stations power places far from here, or no place at all, with their soft echoes and hiccups. Along the road's edge, ditches protect rusty pipelines. A sign meant to educate God-knows-who about the Nama people rusts toward illegibility, tilts in the dust toward some idea of the ocean, the sole remaining readable sections proclaiming, "*They were desert dwellers; Reform will come in the form of communal land tenure and land redistribution through the surface use of mining land and ownership of small mining operations; They poisoned the tips of their arrows with the latex of Euphorbias; Today some Nama men work on the diamond mines as contract labourers; Their dwellings today may be covered in sacking, cloth, or plastic...*"

Signs reading "Mining Area" and "African Star Minerals," lone barrels, and abandoned whitewashed mining camps decorate the waste, all oxidizing amid tangles of forgotten razor wire, the things it was meant to protect no longer valuable, or usable. Offshore, bathymetric, echo-sounding side-scan sonar blasts reverberate from the ancient bays submerged beneath the sea, and the boats, concealed in fog, send their probes downward to poke among these gullies for diamonds. If they're found, the stones will be sucked up by remote-controlled crawler robots, through slurry pipes and sorting screens, and hermetically sealed inside "fortune cans." Deep below the surface, the tiny foraminifera fossils help map the way, guide the drills and the men who compel them.

Once we get to Kleinzee, I intend to find Johann MacDonald, the elusive and (according to senior environmental manager Adele Wickens, my contact at the De Beers mine in Oranjemund, Namibia) "very cautious, very wary" mine manager of De Beers's Namaqualand Mine. Weeks ago, I submitted fifteen copies of my passport to his office for the requisite background check on anyone who wants to come within a certain radius of the mine.

Kleinzee is one of those towns along South Africa's Diamond Coast that has been deemed "overmined." MacDonald is now responsible for slowly laying off the workforce and shutting down the tremendous mine (and, to some degree, by extension, the entire town of Kleinzee). Once he is finished, the smaller Trans Hex company will take over and, with a bare-bones workforce, mine the estimated three million carats (an amount that De Beers feels is not worth their time, money, and effort) still left in the Kleinzee area, and attempt to rehabilitate the desert after the decades of environmental pillaging (something about which MacDonald, a former geologist, is rumored to be passionate).

Also rumored (according to Wickens): Johann MacDonald has been known lately to take the occasional civilian onto the once pathologically secure and often violently restricted mine property, in order to share his knowledge, his burden. Wickens assures me that this is rumor only, and such a "tour" is "highly unlikely," as certain higher-ups within the De Beers conglomerate, if they knew of such "tours," such breaches of security, would not be pleased. I imagine Mr. Lester swooping into town like the mist, and "disappearing" Johann Mac-Donald. I want to find him before this happens.

I struggle to hold onto the steering wheel. My hands tingle. Isolated rock monoliths press from the sand like molars. Hawks circle. Weavers build their tumorous nests onto the defunct telephone poles. Whistling rats take the few remaining plant seeds from the mine dump sites into their burrows, and fertilize them with their droppings. The sand is beautiful, because it too has rusted, in the end stages of decay. We pass a crooked sign reading:

NAMAQUALAND MINES DIVISION
WARNING
PRIVATE ROAD OF DE BEERS
CONSOLIDATED MINES

FOR DE BEERS VEHICLES ONLY
NO UNAUTHORISED ENTRY
TRESPASSERS WILL BE PROSECUTED

On the other side of the sign, a skinny-legged emu threads through a flock of wild ostriches, head bowed to the sand, searching for food. I lean out the window and speak to the giant bird, and, to my surprise, it nods its head and stamps its three-toed foot listlessly into the sand.

On this private road bisecting Die Sperrgebiet—the Forbidden Territory—is a white bygone church that once serviced the miners, doorless, the panes of its windows having long ago been punched out, its steeple having collapsed inward with the rest of the roof. Abandoned houses surround crumbling hospitals and schools, hyenas and jackals build dens amid the old desks and operating tables. The sand overtakes the old social clubs where dress codes once demanded that women wear long dresses and carry parasols, the men long pants and jackets with fat lapels. An upturned bathtub turns orange in the air, sheltering lizards and their insect meals. The wind briefly unearths an old pair of gumboots, and a hairbrush with a mother-of-pearl handle, before a new wind exacts the reburying. A set of three stairs rises out of the sand and crests at more sand. Something yelps out in the dunes. Louisa draws something with her index finger on the glove box. It is not a heart.

*

LAST NIGHT IN BED, TRYING TO UNWIND, I THUMBED THROUGH MY book on Cherokee legends, one of many I've packed that feature other stories in which pigeons and diamonds intersect. Now, driving to Kleinzee, one of these legends seems to manifest itself through the windshield. The wind draws sidewinding shapes onto the sand that recall the passage of the great mythical snake Uktena, the mere sight of which was sufficiently toxic to kill a human being. The serpent's body was decorated with scales made of fire, horns of ice, and a diamond crescent at its forehead like a tiara, which emitted such a magnetic radiance that a human could not help but run toward the snake's light, rather than attempt an escape. Even if one *dreamt* of the snake, this signified the demise of the dreamer's entire family. Uktena had the circumference of a tree trunk, and it bore along its length luminous rings of many colors. The diamond crescent, known to the Cherokee as Ulunsuti, or "Transparent," would bring untold luck, and the ability to work wonders, to anyone brave enough to capture it. To attain the crescent, one would have to get close enough to Uktena to shoot the giant snake in the seventh ring down from its head, the ring that contained its heart. Countless attempts to attain it were met with swift and brilliant death.

In order to prove his worth as a Shawnee medicine man, and in order to end his torture as a prisoner of war by the Cherokee, Aganunitsi, or "Groundhog's Mother," was compelled to quest for the Ulunsuti diamond. "I will bring you the Ulunsuti, or die trying, or meet you back here in three moons to sing my death song," Aganunitsi said.

He was gifted by his captors with one ear of corn for his journey. Lesser snakes, an obese lizard, a frog the size of a bear, two turtles representing the angry sun and forgiving moon, and a confetti of leeches whirling like a dust storm, each, in turn, served as his guides. Eventually, he came to a mountain shaped like a diamond. His medicine pouch grew hot against his ribs, and burnt the flesh there. This burn was the talisman he needed to protect him from assured death. He rounded a bend in the trail and came upon Uktena who, as luck would have it, was in a deep sleep. Aganunitsi retreated downslope until he came to level soil. There, he dug a circular trench, surrounded it with pinecones, and lit the kindling aflame.

Again, he ascended to the sleeping snake, aimed his arrow, and shot it in its seventh ring. The beast woke and chased Aganunitsi down the mountain, the Ulunsuti bursting with fire. Uktena, dying, spewed a mist of venom over the slope, which Aganunitsi escaped by leaping into the center of his circular trench. Only a single drop of venom leapt over the wall of flame and struck Aganunitsi between the eyes. The snake finally succumbed, its body impaled on a grove of trees.

The medicine man exhaled, ate his corn, and summoned the birds of the forest who, for seven days, feasted on the great serpent's corpse, the doves competing with the ravens for the meat. One of the ravens tried to make off with the Ulunsuti, but was foiled by a dove who alerted the medicine man with its cooing. Aganunitsi wrapped the diamond in a deerskin purse, and returned to the Cherokee, where he became a famed worker of wonders.

The Ulunsuti grew within it an insatiable hunger, which took the form of a bloodred streak running through its center. In order for his magic to work, Aganunitsi had to feed the ravenous diamond the blood of doves, and so had to commit the sin of slaughtering the very birds who had helped grant the medicine man his powers in the first place. Should Aganunitsi fail to feed the diamond, the gem would burst into flame, fly into the air, descend to the human settlements, and slit the throat of a child, slaking its thirst on the blood. The diamond demanded that even the conjuror who used its powers must forever live in fear of it. As the years passed, on the site where the blood of Uktena filled Aganunitsi's trench, a doughnut-shaped lake formed, and the water was vermilion, and women would line its banks, waiting—sometimes for days and nights—for the chance to dye the cane splits of their baskets this impossibly beautiful red.

*

I RELATE THIS STORY TO LOUISA AS WE DRIVE. HER HEAD RESTS against the passenger-side window. I can hear the glass vibrating against her temple. "Those poor doves," she says.

The road to Kleinzee skirts the ocean, which entombs old shipwrecks. Over the years, many diamond rigs have run aground into this desert. In 1985, the 1,400-ton *Poseidon* (80 tons of which were diamond recovery equipment) crushed itself against the rocks 400 meters offshore from here, and began to tip into the sea. The ship's captain, A. Baptista, issued panicked calls for help over the radio with a bloody mouth as the hull ruptured and ruptured. The engine room and fuel tanks filled with seawater, and the starving, injured crew of twenty-six were eventually hauled away to the same hospital by Consolidated Mine–owned helicopters, their diamonds left behind. The sign once necklaced over its flank— "This Vessel Is Operated By Dawn Diamond Co. Ltd. And Is Subject To Diamond Security Regulations. Admittance Aboard Is Strictly Prohibited. Personnel To Report To Duty Officer Or Watchman"—washed ashore to rust in the quicksand. The famed tug the *Causeway Salvor* was deployed from Cape Town to pull the boat free, but failed, and today the shell of the looted *Poseidon* still slumps off the Kleinzee shore, as yet unable even to disintegrate to the point of a merciful sinking.

Thirty kilometers south and nearly forty years prior, in April 1947, the much smaller 285-ton *Border* ran aground onto an Elandsklip farm, having been blinded by fog. Her cargo of explosives was salvaged and carried ashore and over the dunes by a team of donkeys, their hides wet up to their withers. Nine donkeys perished in the effort. The explosives were later used in the Namaqualand mines, one of which killed a diamond digger and maimed four others. No record exists as to whether or not they successfully unearthed diamonds that day.

Down the shore, plants named half-man and Medusa's head spoon with the wreck of the SS *Piratiny*, the 5,000-ton Brazilian steamship bound for Cape Town that fell victim to a Diamond Coast storm in 1943 (or, as a conflicting local legend has it, was torpedoed by a U-boat), with its benign cargo of shoes, scrolls of clothing fabric, and tinned sardines. The wind broke the ship in two against the rocks, and the crew, broken-boned but alive, was searched by the vigilant diamond police who had been patrolling the coastline and who suspected that even such a violent accident may have been subterfuge, a ploy to come ashore and pluck diamonds from the restricted beach. The diamond police shook the crew's arms and legs into further breakage before arranging transport to a doctor in Hondeklip Bay.

Six weeks later, another storm—as predicted by the anxiety of the jackal buzzards—atomized the remains of the *Piratiny*, and the weeks following saw a windfall of shoes and fabric and sardines washing up onto the shore, a godsend to the poor communities of Namaqualand. Still today, beachcombers braving the dwarf adders can find the wayward leather shoe, sun-bleached and orphaned among the seaweed and mussel shells, and the local children—all hauntingly dressed in the same white fabric—still play in these hand-me-down clothes sewn from the *Piratiny*'s cargo. The tinned sardines were so plentiful that some of them still rest beneath the cobwebs of the local cellars, waiting to one day be unlidded.

Wrecks beget wrecks: wrecks named *Volo* and *Sagittarius*, *Phoenix* and *Shalom*, *Aloe* and *Athena*, *Pigeon* and *Diamond*—grounded, grounded, sank, lost, fire, failure, blown out to sea; terror attack, explosion, sank in a gale, sunk by the Germans, sunk by the British, struck a mine and sank . . .

There's still so much here that's buried, lurking on the other side of the wavy dark. Off the coast, between Port Nolloth and Kleinzee, ship parts litter the seabed, parts that once belonged to the vessels chartered by the East India Company that bore cargoes of gold ducats, silver bars, and copper duits destined for various European soldiers of fortune. These ships once traveled along the South African coast toward the island of Mauritius, on their way to India; docked at the Harbor of the Tortoises, where enslaved locals cut down nearly all of the heartwood and ebony trees, the wood slated for export. The Dutch forced the locals to cut even faster when the enslaved began to flee into the thick forests, effectively eradicating their hiding places. The landscape of the island was thinned for trade, and to make a more effective prison.

(This deforestation of Mauritius, along with the infestation of feral pigs, rats, monkeys, and insects that hitched rides on the trade ships, as well as the Dutch appetite for the "exotic," eventually resulted in the extinction of the indigenous dodo bird, cousin to the pigeon. Scientists speculate that a flock of migratory African pigeons got lost and tired and landed in desperation on Mauritius, where, over the years, they adapted to the habitat and, in what Alan Cooper, zoologist at Oxford University, calls "extreme evolution," became dodos. Had the dodo not been decimated by the Dutch, ornithologists wonder, how many different species of pigeon would have been spawned into the world?)

Also off the Diamond Coast: wrecks of East India Company trade ships that once carried the tea that led to the Boston Tea Party and the American Revolution; that carried to North America guns and enslaved people, and carried away furs. Many of these East India Company guns were eventually passed down among generations, and so these guns traveled from the Atlantic coast inland to places like the unincorporated community of Sargents in Pike County, Ohio. Sargents was a community founded as a safe zone for the previously enslaved, and was therefore an important station on the Underground Railroad. There, in 1900, one such gun landed in the hands of a fourteen-year-old boy named Press Clay Southworth, who, heart fluttering at the unnerving beauty of the strange bird eating from his family farm's corn stock, solicited his mother's permission to shoot the bird so that he could examine it more closely. His mother's granting of said permission resulted in the single shot that killed the last passenger pigeon—so named for its once mammoth migrations, once the most populous bird on the planet—ever to be spotted in the wild. A Pike County taxidermist sewed black shoe buttons into its eyes. In Ohio, still today, are eight villages named for the passenger pigeon, and eighteen villages known to house passenger pigeon skins and bones.

Bartholomew Variation #3

THE MOON IS BRIGHT AND FULL EVEN IN ALL OF THIS DAYLIGHT. ON earth, women in colorful headscarves stare at their feet, waiting for rides to or from the mine. They congregate around a sign that reads "Watch Out for Owls," itself decorated with owl shit. At its base, a beetle and a butterfly make a home of the same empty Old Brown Sherry bottle. The harmony won't last.

A pigeon's tiny shadow passes over an overturned and crushed carriage, still leashed to the skeleton of the donkey that once pulled it. A broken-necked meerkat bleeds out next to a tuft of Eragrostis lovegrass.

Bartholomew flies hard and heavy for Msizi. Over the rusty and decomposing machine parts no longer employed in the mining industry, having been heaved out into the back alleys of the desert—sieves and pans, cyclone sorters and washing drums. Over a flattened and sun-bleached diamond diving suit, lying face down in the sand, the rubber of it having once withstood the sharp noses of curious basking sharks. Next to the diving suit is an oxidized nozzle, once used to suck diamonds from the ocean floor, but also, secondarily, to ward off a shark attack by jamming the nozzle into the fish's mouth and vacuuming out its entrails.

Pigeons fly because they can't do anything else, shackled to the spasms of genetic code. The experiences of their forebears—Darwin's pigeons, the heroic Cher Ami, the sad Martha; their memories of ocean voyages, world wars, and pathetic zoos—are impacted within their hollow bones.

In Bartholomew's little bags, the rough diamonds shimmy and collide, and the bird can feel these vibrations in his ribcage, his furcula and coracoid. As most pigeons do when loaded with cargo, Bartholomew tries intermittently to scratch at these little bags with his alulas, the little bird-thumbs inherited from the dinosaurs that some vulgar ornithologist nicknamed "bastard wings."

The bird flies over old mining atrocities interred in sand. Like the skinny diamond digger who, in 1906, unearthed a 20-carat stone. He held it aloft and cried to his wife—also a digger—*"Vrouw, ek het hom!"* (Wife, I have it!), before being clubbed over the head by a spade-wielding security guard who wanted the stone for himself. The wife ran away into the desert, her hat falling off. She hid for hours beneath a downturned scotch cart with her child before the heat overtook them.

Below is the site on which once stood a meager sorters' camp, where hundreds of fingers once threaded through stockpiles of gravel. One of these sorters had as a pet a tame zebra foal, and one night, drunk on brandy, one of the camp's residents thought it would be funny to throw a vial of acid (traditionally used to "clean" the diamonds) into the zebra's eyes. The animal suffered in silence, even as it went blind, and it was the silence that proved so horrific to the drunk men that they rushed to cut the animal's throat, not so much to quash its misery as their own. Still buried in the sand are bits of the unfortunate foal's backbone, smoothed shards of the glass jars that once held the sorters' brandy.

Bartholomew zigzags in the air.

Sometimes, Msizi's lips bleed when he purses them to whistle at Bartholomew. Msizi likes jazz and often listens to the record his father left behind when he abandoned the family before Msizi was born. The Jazz Epistles' *Verse 1* album. He listens to it before bed, lying on his back on his mattress on the floor, the single yellow lamp bathing the space in a light that Msizi imagines would be right at home in the jazz halls of 1950s' Johannesburg. Someplace in that city today, it's rumored, his father lives. Somewhere in that city, his father has no idea that Msizi wasn't born "a little slow"—as his mother puts it—like his brother was. But Msizi has never seen that city, and its imagined bigness both frightens and exhilarates him. The only picture he has of his father is a blurry one, the man's face muddied. His brother, knotted into his blankets across the room, always eventually throws a pillow at Msizi, and at the plastic Capri turntable, and yells at him about noise and about sleep. So, Msizi stands up, his body cracking, and he goes out to the coop.

He hums his favorite tunes, highlighting Kippie "Morolong" Moeketsi's ornate sax solos, songs called "Gafsa" and "Vary-Oo-Vum" and "Dollar's Moods," the latter named for the volatile temper of the band's piano player, Abdullah Ibrahim, a.k.a. Dollar Brand. After the 1960 Sharpeville massacre, during which South African police opened fire on black protestors demonstrating against apartheid policies (specifically the pass laws, which required black citizens to carry an internal passport whenever they ventured out of their "homelands" or "designated areas"), killing sixty-nine people, the apartheid government doubled down on its viciousness and ratcheted up repressive edicts in order to discourage future protests. As part of this doubling-down, jazz was banned—the music could no longer be performed either in public or in private, could no longer be broadcast on the radio or sold to fans. The lives of the musicians were threatened, and the Jazz Epistles broke up, many of its members going into exile in Europe or the U.S. Only Moeketsi, Msizi's favorite, stayed in South Africa, though he was unable to perform, and so succumbed to alcohol abuse and died, young and penniless.

Msizi often hums to Bartholomew with his eyes closed, his chest sunken, his belly heaving, his ropy arms swinging, his armpits spicy, the moon in his hair. He hums, and blows into his thumb, makes a saxophone of his body, his lame pinky hanging as if some vestigial part of the instrument. Msizi has to get up early, but still, he makes music for his bird until his lungs can no longer take it, and he spits his blood onto the coop floor.

Before going inside, returning to his mattress and his brother's low snoring, Msizi will gather up the feathers Bartholomew has shed and scatter them over his pillow. He has been taught to believe that if he sleeps on pigeon feathers, his illness will eventually be cured, and he will never die. This local superstition has many variations. While some believe that the act of lying on pigeon feathers will keep death at bay, others believe that the sick person will remain sick, languishing in ever-escalating pain and torment without end. In an early version of assisted suicide, old merciful nurses used to pull the pigeon-feather pillows out from beneath the heads of the anguished, so they could more easily and peacefully die. But Msizi has not heard these versions of the story.

He lies on his pillow, and reads a book about whales. In the morning, he will have the imprint of feathers in his cheek. He will run his fingertips over it as he prepares for work and will like the way it feels, like the way it reminds him of a fossil. It will make him feel very old, part of some longer, larger story. If he had his way, Msizi would learn to play an instrument, speak a foreign language. "French," he would say, though he would be unsure as to exactly why he would make that choice. He would like to dig for something more important than diamonds: fossils, dinosaur bones, mummies, ancient cities. If he had more free time, he would be good at badminton. If he went to school, he would be good at math.

Chapter 7

New Rush and Kimberley

The De Beers Origin Story

I'VE PLACED NUMEROUS PHONE CALLS TO JOHANN MACDONALD'S secretary, Trinety, who tells me he's busy, and she never knows when he's going to be in the office. She keeps telling me to try back at a later time, and soon she stops answering my calls. I decide to drive straight into town to try to track him down myself. Louisa, too, decides to break the rules; she checks into a ramshackle roadside motel alone to find sleep during what's left of the day. She's getting tired of this. I realize that I should be a better partner, but I feel somehow chained to the anxiety that compels me onward. When I drop her at the motel, I take care to avoid melodrama. I keep the word *reckoning* to myself.

The road into Kleinzee town proper once bore only the commutes of the laborers, the company men, and their families. Barbed wire fences separate the road from the desert, which is lined here with knee-high green windscreens, each of which stretches for over a kilometer—another of De Beers's feeble attempts at restoration, wars against erosion. The effect is that of a desert swollen with a lattice of infected veins, its system having gone varicose and septic.

No one walks the road into Kleinzee. This forsaken outpost in the middle of a goliath nowhere belches its diamonds dully, inches ever closer to its status as ghost town. And yet there remains enough for the residual inhabitants to fetishize and protect, an ingrained wariness of outsiders, a dependency on the bizarre sealed-off bubble it has become, since the town's entrance is blocked by a boom gate and an alarm that flashes red and wails as soon as any vehicle approaches.

Crows line the barbed wire behind the rotating red beacon and its siren. They don't move a muscle, accustomed to the wailing. "Drive Safely," says the yellow diamond-shaped sign depicting a black stencil of a mining truck, "Death Is Permanent." The guard, in military boots, khaki uniform, khaki hat fronted with a Thorburn Security Solutions patch, and aviator sunglasses, descends the six steps from his tower, wordlessly hands me a clipboard and pen. The machine gun wobbles against his hip, the muzzle tracing dimples in the dust. The clipboard immobilizes exactly one piece of paper printed with columns in which I must record the date, my personal details, passport number, and reason for my visit. For the latter, I write, *bird-watching*. The last documented entry, the last record of a visitor to Kleinzee, is from sixteen months ago. I pass the clipboard and pen to him and he walks around the car and one-arms the boom gate upward for me to pass.

Inside the gates, what was once a De Beers stronghold seems to be sinking into the earth. Desperate hangers-on here are buying up the old diggers' quarters on the cheap, taking down the barbed wire, trying to convert them into tourist cottages; some are taking jobs as cashiers and stockers in the remaining convenience store, peddling Grandpa's Headache Powders and tinned viennas in brine to the other hangers-on; the only available uncanned food being sacks of squashed white bread, freezer-burned chicken necks, and rotten halves of iceberg lettuce in cellophane.

Kleinzee is still wheezing along, in spite of the initiative supported by Rob Blake, De Beers's project manager for town proclamation and local economic development, that "when mining ceases, all remaining structures, including houses, are classified as mining disturbances. By law, mining towns should be bulldozed, buried and planted over." One may wonder as to the accuracy of his title, the slippery, audience-dependent natures of *proclaiming* and *developing*. One may wonder how rumor dovetails with tragedy.

The De Beers name, printed on everything from old water tanks to the defunct hospital wall, to the rusted delivery gate of the defunct supermarket, is frayed and peeling, being stripped away. The complicated legacy of De Beers founder Cecil John Rhodes and his co-magnate, and sometimes rival, sometimes lover, Barney Barnato, is being sandblasted here until it shines.

Rhodes, seventeen years old, anemic and otherwise sickly, came to South Africa from England with his brother to farm cotton using slave labor in KwaZulu–Natal in 1870. When the cotton venture failed, he traveled, one year later, to the diamond fields of Kimberley, where, with the financial backing of a British multinational investment banking company (with whom he had familial connections), he soon succeeded in buying up all of the smaller diamond mining operations. With the backing of the bank, Rhodes was alone in being able to afford steam pumps to eradicate the water from flooded claims, which—given that they were presumed ruined—he had bought for a song. By this point, he was only eighteen. In public, he often wore white cricket flannels.

Young Rhodes organized what had been a ragtag jumble of tent communities and nomad diggers who had bought a site called New Rush from local farmers Johannes and Diedrich De Beer. Before selling their land, the De Beer brothers had been raising karakul sheep, the still-fetal lambs of which—prized for their downy pelts—were routinely forced from their mothers. (In years to come this practice would spawn a series of attendant articles with titles such as "Hamid Karzai's Famous Hat Made from Aborted Lamb Fetuses," and "The Secret They Don't Want You to Know.")

Rhodes soon exchanged his cricket flannels for suits of at least three pieces, and began carrying a diamond-studded watch on a length of gold chain, which stood out against the dusty overalls, drooped hats, and broken lutes of those who inhabited the diggers' camps. Rhodes, nurturing his greed aboveground, did not have to memorize their code of signals—a series of intricate and subterranean knocks, rope tugs, and bell rings with meanings ranging from *explosives may be loaded* to *accident to persons, stop all hoists* (colloquially known as "cages") *immediately*, to *help me, need more air.*

Greed, while bearing etymologies that range from "voracious hunger" (Middle English), to "death by starvation" (Albanian), to "passionate gladness" (Dutch), also derives from the ancient Greek word for "never fading." In the face of it, as always, the people toiling in the diamond industry told themselves stories. Many of the early laborers in New Rush, in fact, under the spell of a South African legend, endured these harsh conditions in silence, as they believed that they were doing divine work. In that legend, once upon a time, long ago, a great sorrow settled like a mist over South Africa. As that sorrow crescendoed, a kindly bird-spirit—its pity aroused—descended from the heavens, a fat basket of diamonds draped over one blue-gray wing. The spirit scattered diamonds into the Vaal River, flying from Delport's Hope to Barkly West, Forlorn Hope to Gong Gong, scattering and scattering. Once the spirit arrived at the place now called Kimberley, it was flying so fast that it impaled itself on a barb of a great camel thorn tree, and became entangled in the branches. Legend dictates that the great camel thorn is struck by lightning more than any other tree. In panic, the bird-spirit thrashed itself to pieces while trying to escape. Its basket was upset, and the remaining diamonds fell to the earth, arousing us with their glittering. The great camel thorn still stands, its seeds roasted and ground as a substitute for coffee beans, and its succulent leaves remain a favorite food of giraffes, who, in a mutation that especially excited Darwin, bear specially adapted tongues in order to cope with the thorns.

Once word got out that South African soil had begun disgorging these now-famed diamonds, enabling the greasy lifestyles of those like Rhodes, and enabling South Africa to depend on something other than agriculture to fuel its economy, the karakul farmers went into exile deep in the Karoo and the Kalahari, and European gem houses began sending emissaries to amass any still-available kimberlite claims as quickly as possible. Digging rules were legislated and amended, perpetuating such edicts as "No one shall be allowed to throw any ground, dirt, or filth on any other than his own claim," "Any person depositing night soil within the camp other than in the public latrines or private conveniences, shall be liable to a penalty not exceeding Five Pounds Sterling," "It is strictly forbidden for any person to purchase a diamond or diamonds from any servant (black or white), without a certificate from such servant's master or mistress," "No servant shall have drink unless he has a written permission from his master," "No license to dig shall be granted to a Native," and "The spot or locality for burial of carcasses and other filth shall be selected and pointed out by a Committee."

Barney Barnato, who falsified his name (he was born Barnet Isaacs) and his birthday (he claimed to share a birthday with Rhodes—July 5, 1853—but he was in fact born on February 21, 1851), initially came to New Rush to further his cigar business. He came of age motherless, as a child beggar and hustler, stealing theater passes and scalping them on the street corners of London. As teenagers, he and his older brother Harry would perform song-and-dance numbers at local music halls in matching sailor suits crafted from the fabric remnants that their father sold. Harry, the older brother, took top billing, and Barney (then Barnet) was always added as an afterthought onto the program as " . . . and Barnet too," a phrase that led to his adopted last name. When he arrived in South Africa during the diamond rush, having traveled in steerage, he had no money to pay for the coach to Kimberley, so he walked there. It took him over three months, and during that walk—through the deserts and the flatlands, the savannas and passes—he hatched his plans. On his journey, he saw animals die, and people die, the ants heaping their tailings over the corpses, the welts on his calves pulsing with insect venom.

In New Rush, due to his unique breed of charisma born of desperation, Barnato's cigar business was an unlikely success, and he used the proceeds to buy up a large number of claims, hire the most efficient diggers, and open a popular boxing club. Barnato himself was a keen boxer, and in many photos he appears swollen and slouching, puffy in the cheeks and bruised around the eyes—an odd mélange of resignation and readiness. In the course of ten years, Barnato's portion of the Kimberley mine equaled Rhodes's portion of the De Beers mine. By the mid-1880s, streamlined corporate operations had replaced much of the wild-eyed excitement that had attended the settlement and its discoveries.

The miners slated for the underground work—mostly native Africans—would line up single-file by 5 a.m., and trundle down the shafts. Underground, with shovels, one team heaped the pulverized kimberlitic ore (which they colloquially called "blue ground") into the cocopans—the trolleys that ran along the narrow-gauge sunken railways. Another team of men chipped away at the rock with pickaxes. These men were charged with squeezing themselves into crevices so tight that they had to chip mere millimeters from their bodies. As such, toward the end of the shift, ghostly parades of human-shaped depressions were left in the rock, hard outlines of the men who once labored there.

Around the tunnels' curves, in the insufferable heat, another team, saddled with long-fuse dynamite, was busy blasting the chamber walls in order to liberate more ore, which would await the shoveling. Sometimes, no explosives were needed, as the chambers of ore were prone to collapsing under their own weight. Because no one had previously designed an underground mine, the first attempts, born of a rudimentary hastiness birthed in greed, begat collapse after collapse. In a process of trial and error, after so many perpendicular shafts (vertical shafts from which horizontal passages were hewn) collapsed, the company decided to try inclined shafts—not necessarily because this design was any safer, but because it was cheaper.

Soon, designers began experimenting with a "gallery" method, cutting a series of arcades into the ore and leaving a few pillars of ore for support, until the underground mine evoked the ambiance of a pitch-dark honeycomb. With each new attempt, a team of fresh recruits would be deployed to remove the corpses of the previous crew who had drowned in rock, crushed in a deluge of diamond ore. Once finished with that, the recruits would be commanded to pick up their shovels. Hopefully, this time, the burrows would hold. If so, and once that particular level of earth had been deemed by the company to be "successfully mined," the laborers sank deeper into the earth.

Those who survived their shifts emerged only to be invasively searched by security guards who were empowered by the new "stripping clause" of the Rhodes-endorsed Diamond Act of 1882. The act decreed that the laborers were to be presumed guilty of diamond smuggling until proven innocent. Two separate search houses—one for the black workers, one for the white workers—were erected at each mine, and the workers were forced to pass through them upon both entering and leaving the property. "Unless this evil is crushed," said one mining manager at the time, justifying the clause, "the mining industry will be swept away altogether." For enacting and enforcing said clause, Rhodes has been commended by contemporary De Beers magnates with the words, "the madness and mayhem of Kimberley would have remained just that were it not for the ambition, enterprise and vision of individuals like Cecil Rhodes." The strip-searched men, in countless photographs, almost uniformly exhibited the symptoms of proptosis, their eyes bulging, swollen and wild, ruined by the dark.

By 1888, back up on the earth's surface, Chairman Rhodes seduced Barnato into a partnership by bestowing onto him the title of Life Governor, and making him the largest shareholder in what would be known as De Beers Consolidated Mines Ltd. In a matter of months, they monopolized the world diamond market, controlling the release of the gems, which they claimed to be their moral obligation, as "should the fields be thrown open to everyone, the market could be flooded with diamonds, rendering them worthless . . . [We must] take measures to prevent such a disaster." In this way, De Beers fabricated a narrative of preciousness, permanence, and rarity, in order to invent and fictionally justify obscene prices. When De Beers says, today, of Namaqualand, "There cannot be any doubt that [the early Khoisan people] must have picked up some shiny stones and that their children played with the stones without realising their value," they are of course under the spell of their own narrative, themselves not realizing that if or when these children were playing with these stones, they were, indeed, very much worthless.

I wonder what spells Barnato cast over himself; if he, having finally graduated from street hustler to tycoon, mused on his days on the stage alongside his brother, entertaining crowds with energetic renditions of "I Know a Pair of Hazel Eyes," "The Pig Song," and (heartbreaking for all involved) "Rock Me to Sleep, Mother."

*

IT'S UNNERVING, THE DEGREE TO WHICH KIMBERLEY'S MOTHERS AND fathers aim to preserve the atmosphere that once hung over New Rush, having restored it today to the point of an oppressive bucolia, adorned with vintage mirrors and signage and richly stained wood. In suffocating the old horrors of this place in the name of attracting tourists, Kimberley's councilfolk have opted to beat us over the head with quaintness; have opted to erect a marble headstone "in loving memory [of those] who died while working as labourers at the Kimberley 'Big Hole' Mine," underscoring the tribute with such platitudes as, "In death there is life, in bondage there is freedom, our grandchildren will honour you." The only grandchildren I saw there were too busy honoring their blue raspberry snow-cones purchased at the Big Hole Coffee and Dried Fruit Shop.

Present-day Kimberley (now asking in its brochure the very good question, "What better place to hold your corporate function than the Big Hole?"), in wanting to evoke a fictive past, reads like an objection to the lives actually lived here. The dead have been raised only to be costumed in the sort of chintz one can confuse with romance. Tourists long to occupy the center of what was once a historical repugnance, and, should the archival girdle be sufficiently cinched, mistake it for delicious and dramatic, if not authentic. In this way, Kimberley is a tart, rouged beyond shabbiness and vacancy. While tourists scramble for rooms and rump steaks at the Shooting Box (Cecil John Rhodes's old hunting lodge), ancient and forgotten Khoisan petroglyphs give in to erosion.

The derelict mining village of nearby Blyvooruitzicht ("Happy Prospect" in Dutch) is far more representative of what happens when the industry exhausts the land (and the people) and moves on. There, as the mining company no longer has an interest in paying for the village's utilities, the local government has cut the water supply. Resident Dolly Burnet—an octogenarian who cares for her quadriplegic son—speaks of a municipal water truck that visits the outskirts once a week. She speaks of hours-long lines as locals queue up to fill as many plastic buckets and containers as they can manage for the kilometers-long walk home. She speaks of old men and old women who tire while waiting, and come prepared with threadbare blankets and pillows. Those at the back of the line are often out of luck, as the supply runs out, which has spawned an underground market, run by folks who used to be hairdressers and construction workers, teachers and students. Burnet speaks of hitchhiking through the mine dumps to her daughter-in-law's place to trade what little money she has left, or the doilies she's taken to knitting, for water. "Water is the most precious thing to me," she says, "Nothing else matters. It's like gold, diamonds . . . When I came here [fifty-six years ago], we had free water, free houses, free electricity. The mine did everything for us. Now, there's nothing."

"They [live in] mining villages that don't fall under the jurisdiction of the municipality," says Chris Spies, municipal spokesperson. "We're not supposed to deliver services there."

Recently, in the night, portions of the village's old water pipeline were stolen for scrap, and the municipality considers it a fool's errand to attempt replacement and restoration. "Even if we did, there's too much crime in the area now, and the water would be poisoned," Spies says. In the abandoned mineshafts, bands of illegal miners colloquially known as the Zama Zamas search for anything of value, all manner of weapons strapped to their hips, their faces cloaked in ski masks.

"To me," Burnet says, "the future looks bleak." She picks at the tire of her son's wheelchair, before stepping outside into the street. Uranium dust hangs in the air. "There is no future," she says, surveying the neighborhood houses. Inside them, in the living rooms and kitchens, bedrooms and bathrooms, nothing with which to wash, to flush the toilets. Nothing to boil. On the stoops, heaps of empty containers.

Traversing the cute, dusty streets of Kimberley, on the other hand, I see a non-threatening bygone electric railway car, and the luxury Pullman coach once used by the De Beers directors as they traveled back and forth between South Africa and Rhodesia. There's a sign discussing how a little local boy, Erasmus Jacobs, found on the bank of the Orange River in 1866 what soon became known as the Eureka Diamond, a 21.25-carat stone that Jacobs used as a toy in a game of knucklebones and planned to gift to his little sister (who liked pretty rocks), before the local adults claimed it, spread the word. There's the sign titled "The Star of South Africa," referencing the 85-carat white diamond plucked by a semi-nomadic shepherd boy in March 1869 from the Orange River, who sold it for five hundred sheep, ten oxen, and an anorexic horse to a local farmer who eventually peddled it to a government official. By the end of 1869, the Star was a fixture of the South African parliament, where Sir Richard Southey, Cape Town's colonial secretary, bellowed, "Gentlemen! This is the rock on which the future of South Africa will be built!" There are, too, the now-defunct two thousand streetlamps that were once lit with thirty-two candles each.

All the old businesses are here, stripped, of course, of proprietors and customers and actual things to sell beyond glimpses of their shiny restored voids; their walls curiously hung with sepia photographs of old mining hells—the stepped pits and men with whips, and men with gaunt faces and dirty beards and broken glasses, and caved-in hats; close-ups of bent forks and barbed wire and dangerous ladders and empty dishes; buckets, bandannas, wheels, and diamonds; mangy dogs, sick cats, dead birds, progress.

There's R. Dixon's old music shop, where he professed the spiritual benefits of banjo-, violin-, and mandolin-playing. There's G. Verheyen's old shop, advertising his services as Signwriter and all-around High-Class Decorator, and the calligraphically etched windows of E. J. Lee: Practical Gun and Cycle Maker, and I. R. Trieber: Diamond Mounter and Seller; the Occidental Saloon with its balconied second-floor apartments, and the voluptuous awning of the Goodchild and Roth-schild Auction Mart. There's William Shilling's Soda Water and Lemonade Factory, fine purveyor of herb beer and ginger beer, and there's Mr. J. Perilly's Famous Hand-Blended Cigarettes. There's the coffin workshop filled with so many tiny coffins (no longer able to compete with Bakgat Caskets or Makumba Funeral—the active coffin workshops in contemporary working Kimberley). There's Wernher and Beit and Company, the *Licensed* Diamond Buyers, named after the famed art collector and impulsive political schemer, respectively. There's the Victorian cast-iron bandstand upon which no band plays. And, oh: there's the site of the old Kimberley Baths, where folks of Rhodes's and Barnato's status could choose among the varieties—Turkish, Russian, Swedish Hot & Cold, Shower, Massage, Electrical, the Gents' Entrance off Old Main Street, the Ladies' Entrance off the Diamond Market. All of these clapboards, restored and shellacked, sit atop the ravished dust that once held the stones the ancient Romans believed were splinters of fallen stars, and the ancient Greeks, tears of the gods.

What we don't see are the miners' "closed" compounds—the tents and other rudimentary shelters set up within a corrugated iron enclosure, itself roofless but covered with wire netting in the way of a chicken coop in order to prevent the laborers from fleeing with company diamonds, from having contact with illicit traders. Historians have described these caged settlements-within-settlement, trapped within the iron perimeter (the first of which was introduced in Kimberley in 1885), as resembling everything from concentration camps to beehives. The corporations defended such living conditions, stating that "allowing labourers [to be] free to roam around town encouraged IDB [illicit diamond buying]. In a final bid to eliminate IDB, labourers must be confined to the compounds throughout their contracts. They only leave to go to work, otherwise all their needs are supplied within the enclosures by their employers," who themselves lived close by, in real houses made of wood, with their bidets and hand-cranked dough-rollers.

There are no regal plaques etched with stories of malarial camp fever, lack of sanitation and clean water, medical tents blown upward at the mercy of the weather, shortages of doctors and nurses and medicine, a total absence of beds, and other lacks endemic to the diamond field camps. We see no testaments to the all-important compound canteens and soup stalls, the most popular of which was run by an old Zulu man known only as Roast Beef, an ex-miner turned stew chef (reportedly using his mother's recipes) after his leg was blown off in an accident that saw over four thousand laborers trapped in the underground walls. We don't see what the more poetic and dystopian of the brochures refers to as "A vast heaving crater. A world of dust, drought, dysentery, and flies, disease and despair, where some dug up a fortune, and others dug their graves."

In order to further demonstrate their loftiness here, and to deprive those who lived in this "vast heaving crater" of even the most meager of distractions, Rhodes and Barnato once kidnapped as many of the diggers' pet pigeons as they could. With these abducted birds, they staged "gentlemen's" shoots with visiting magnates on the muddy streets around the corner from Barnato's boxing club (the restored heartwood floor of which still bears the silver crescents of many coin edges pressed between the slats, and, in one corner, an amoebic spread of white threads that appear to be the barbs of a 130-year-old pigeon feather, coffined in shellac). Rhodes and Barnato believed they'd live, if only in the corporate argot—like the diamonds themselves—forever. Of course, these men were neither diamonds nor jargon bannered across countless pamphlets, and they too died, begetting controversial statues of their likenesses which inspired protests, the hurling of buckets filled with excrement both human and animal, and, according to the *Guardian*, a lot of "soul searching in South Africa."

In 1897, Barney Barnato may have been doing some soul searching himself. Now a very rich man—clad, as was typical, in his brown suit, bow tie, diamond lapel brooch, diamond cufflinks, and small oval blued steel spectacles—he boarded a ship from South Africa back home to England. Though the ship did not wreck, it did make a wreck of Barney Barnato, who, in an action variously interpreted as freak accident or suicide, fell (or leapt) overboard near the island of Madeira, his body filling with seawater as he sank to the floor of the Atlantic. Part of his corpse was recovered and buried in London, and the remainder is still preserved in the coral forests and seabed silt that lurks beneath so many old stub-routes of trade, and the shipbound men of dwindling conscience who pinned their stories to them.

*

THE WIND RUSHES INTO AND OUT OF THE BIG HOLE. BECAUSE THE pit is so cavernous, the wind makes no sound. One kilometer away, behind the front desk of the Protea Diamond Lodge, Kimberley's fanciest hotel, the framed sepia photograph of Rhodes and Barnato, stirred by the ceiling fan, rattles lightly against the wall.

Chapter 8

Beyond the Boom Gate, Touring the Erasure

IT'S 7 A.M., AND EVERYTHING WITHIN THE KLEINZEE BOOM GATES officially belongs to the Oppenheimers, which now includes me and the car I'm renting. In 1902, the year of Cecil John Rhodes's death, the London diamond brokerage firm Dunkelsbuhler and Company sent their hotshot twenty-two-year-old diamond buyer, Ernest Oppenheimer, to South Africa. At first, Oppenheimer worked for the firm as an independent dealer, but soon after his arrival, he settled in Kimberley and began to study De Beers's business principles. Seducing the locals with his financial prowess and oratorical charisma, Oppenheimer, in 1912—a mere ten years after his arrival in South Africa—was elected mayor of Kimberley. He used his position to further foster powerful political and economic connections, and leveraged them to take control of the De Beers empire as chairman in 1929. He thereafter consolidated the company's global monopoly of the diamond trade. When Ernest died in 1957, he passed control of De Beers to his son, Harry, who in turn passed control to his son, Nicky, who in turn passed control to his son, Jonathan.

Driving through this place—occupied essentially by four generations' worth of white male Oppenheimers—I'm wondering if the penchant for perpetuating atrocity is a heritable trait. I'm wondering if soul-searching is—the sort that kept Darwin awake and nauseous on the *Beagle*, as he too considered the pigeon. Today, I am to meet with Johann MacDonald, the man who still bears the title of De Beers Mine Manager.

In 1938, as Kleinzee was being developed, the mine manager declared this of the workers: "They are unsophisticated as regards to organized sport and know very few or no games; they are uneducated so have little desire for intellectual entertainment. Any recreational device . . . should fit in with their natural background as far as possible, that is, to be understandable by them and appeal as a recreational device." Soon, the workers' tastes expanded; their desires evolved, and the recreational "devices" with them. Swimming pools and playing fields were measured and fabricated, though drawing boundary lines on the fields "was impractical because of the sand." De Beers furnished boxing gloves, "but there is no demand for them," the men preferring to box bare-knuckle.

Now, these defunct clubs—the yacht club, fishing club, diving club, clubs for enthusiasts of rugby, darts, snooker, and squash, cricket and dancing, ping-pong and cinema, radio and wrestling, hunting and shooting, tenniquoits and *jukskei* (tossing horseshoes at an ox yoke)— are slowly becoming piles of rubble, rock cairns stacked at their doorless thresholds, mourning heydays.

The riding club bears no trace of the Appaloosas who once were boarded in the twenty stables. Though I see no cars, there is a gas station, or its leavings, in the middle of the sand, the pumps hooded in black polyester bags that flap thickly when the wind blows. Once, babies were born here. Once, people carried Christmas trees through doorways, and had barbecues in the town center, where residents heaped porcelain plates with steaming portions of oxtail, and drank beer and drank wine, not to drown out, but to celebrate.

Beginning slowly in 2007, and accelerating in 2009, De Beers downscaled their interests in Kleinzee, sending the residents in a forced exodus into other parts of South Africa, onto the couches of

distant family members and friends, and into other possible occupations. De Beers did little to help these residents find housing or alternative work.

Now, for those who remain, survivalist proposals hang over the
town: to turn the pit mines into hazardous waste dumps, to turn
the migrant worker dorm into a prison. The three schools—primary,
secondary, high—are cavernous and echoing shells, though rumor
has it that some of the town's few remaining children take private
swimming lessons from a former diamond diver in the high school's
Olympic-sized pool, which is no longer heated or lighted (when the
town was thriving, electricity, water, and housing were provided free
to the residents), the water jaundiced with decomposing pinkstink
dung moss.

Chimes made of bleached fish jawbones hang from the porch eaves
of Kleinzee's abandoned houses—each of which is low and square and
painted white. The wind piles the dust against their walls. No one sits
on their stoops, and the only people I see are rail-thin and clad in the
same brown gumboots, the same palatinate blue overalls X'ed over the
backs with yellow reflective tape, walking not into homes, but down
the middle of roads that end at further boom gates, and beyond them,
incalculable measures of diamondiferous red sand, and dead birds
decomposing in the dunes-cum-tumuli. Empty flagstaffs, declaring no
specific loyalty, jut from the dust. When the wind comes, the sparse
spiral grass—thick, ribbony ringlets whose penchant for strangling out
the local flowers belies its own wild beauty—rattles like something poisonous about to strike.

I am on edge here within the gates, somehow unbound and impris-
oned, euphoric and morose. I can hear the blood whirring in my ears,
imagine the hearts of Kleinzee's hidden residents beating in their bodies. So many dry rivers and their expired arms. The silence seems to be
ticking, waiting to go off, and because of this, something inside me—
also now property of De Beers—leaps with a cold fear each time a bird

so much as whistles as it passes over. And each time a bird passes over, there's a chance that a diamond will slip loose and drop, once again, to earth. I hold my breath and think of Louisa, likely still sleeping, and the words *trying again* seem less like an incantation and more like a canary's cry into some dumb bottomless dark.

*

THE DIAMONDS HERE REPRESENT THE MOST EXPLOSIVE (AND exploded) of our origins, the seeds of some ruined nostalgia—the compacted carbon, rendered to crystalline shrapnel, that is responsible for all life on Earth, having, like a good, strong cancer, the ability to metastasize. They are the prettiest version of our lifeblood, so much better-looking than coal and graphite and peat, and certainly methane clathrate (which one can't easily ring around a finger), and in a town like Kleinzee, they impacted themselves after having traveled the great distances we associate with romance—upward and westward. Having formed as the Earth itself formed, nestled, carrot-shaped, in the mantle, the rare volcanic kimberlitic pipes incubated diamonds in deep-origin magma sources and provided their passage to the surface as the volcanoes—as is written into their code—erupted.

The low ring of ejecta—the things thrown skyward by the volcanic eruptions—twined briefly with other prehistoric flying things that were in the middle of their evolutions—the germinal insects and birds—before falling to the banks of rivers with a westerly flow, rivers such as the Orange and the Vaal. This ejecta, partly comprised of diamonds, meandered downstream toward what became the Diamond Coast—the Atlantic of Kleinzee and Port Nolloth—where the ocean did what it always does: tried its damnedest to reject the land that was forcing its way inside, belch it out in the form of beaches, and even further—back into the rivers that carried the sediment in the first place. There, the diamonds roosted in the mud, and waited for humans to evolve to the point of conceiving the alluvial mine. In the process, the "crud" (what those in the trade call worthless, or non-gem-quality diamonds) was pulverized, leaving only the choice stones.

And the evolving organisms did what they did—they roved among diamonds and built their nests and lairs and hives, and killed each other over sex and food, and humans gave them names like fruit chafers and whip scorpions, baboon spiders and ticks, beetles named after rhinos, after jewels, after shit. Ostriches occasionally swallowed diamonds, and so laid the deformed eggs which would be collected and displayed on the bottom shelf of the case in the Kleinzee museum, the sort of exhibit that visitors bypass on their way to look at the pictures of the recovered diamonds that ruined the eggs in the first place.

As kimberlitic pipes were named after the town of Kimberley, South Africa, and as the town of Kimberley was named for John Wodehouse, Britain's First Earl of Kimberley, only in 1873, this represents a reversal of naming—the older thing named for the newer thing. Kimberlitic pipes clearly existed before human beings settled the site of Kimberley, and the site of Kimberley was settled by native cultures long before the Brits dispersed them, saddled them with demimonde attributes, before indenturing them, and named the place after one of their lords—before revising the teleology of this place. In a reversal of naming of this sort, barbarity often attends, and giant holes are blasted into land that once supported many homes. The purposes of things become confused, or, somewhat differently, we recast the purposes of things. Landscapes become estranged from the features with which we pock them, and from the concrete rectangles we name *foundations*, atop which we anchor our various nerve centers, affixed with fluorescent lighting and typewriters, and furniture made of the species of good, strong wood that once allowed the dodos to live and be well.

Here, in this compression of landscapes, time also seems to compress, and it's tough to distinguish between the ancient and the contemporary, old stories and new ones. As it's the beige monolith looming like a headstone on a bluff at the edge of town, the mine headquarters—the location of Johann MacDonald's office—is, by comparison, not hard to distinguish.

The parking lot, littered with shards of sun-dried eggshells, runs uphill to the building and the structure appears askew, bearing the angle of some giant utility knife tip surfacing for air from its plastic holster. The surrounding caldera of mine dumps conceals old land collapses, and, as the wind sweeps over, the primordial bumps-and-grinds with the post-apocalyptic, each indistinguishable from the other. A sign at the parking lot's border bears two red arrows, each pointing toward exactly nothing, in opposing directions. At least there's a choice. Old wires no longer carry electricity, sag to the scalped tops of the dead star lilies that once had the strength to crack through this ruined asphalt. Along these wires, not even the ants make passage. The languishing carports reserve spaces for the fired and the dead—"Mining Engineer," this sign says, "Mine Garage Foreman," says another, "Dragline Overseer," "Snr. Perimeter Walker," "Safety Mngr"—all having been ferried across the river that now flows only in the imagination, or deep beneath the excavated sand.

Still, in the distance, the ocean asserts itself. Its foam breaks soundlessly and serrated on the coast. The clouds look snotty. From the antennas on the mine office roof, a faint crackling, an upward sending of signals. In panic, I rush up the five steps inside.

I see MacDonald's office before I see MacDonald, having been directed down a narrow hallway lit with flickering fluorescents by a secretary sitting behind a dirty thermoplastic window and her arthritic finger. The place has the feel of a temporary satellite headquarters in a trailer, while the real thing is being constructed. But this is the real thing.

The office, for the time being, is unmanned, but it is fully decorated, littered with accoutrements that seem to argue with one another—the coat tree hung with reflective chartreuse safety vests, the desk cluttered with papers, a stained De Beers coffee mug, a multibuttoned office phone with a red message blinker, toy tractors and dump trucks, a blue and yellow box of Choice Brand condoms, distributed, via Johann MacDonald, by the South Africa Department of Health to the remaining mine workers; a laminated instructional titled *Diamond Route Standards* ("All communication about the Diamond Route highlights the link between De Beers, Oppenheimers, diamonds and conservation; All proposed research projects are appropriately evaluated using the De Beers Family of Companies Research Guidelines and approved by the Diamond Route Research Committee; All sites promote and market other Diamond Route sites"); the notecards printed "We use lower hazard alternatives to high risk hazardous substances when possible; We manage effluents, wastes, emissions and hazardous substances to prevent pollution wherever possible; We aspire to normal levels of discharges to sea, including sewage." Tacked to the bulletin board behind MacDonald's desk are little greeting cards printed with De Beers's "Statements of Values" (Pull Together, Build Trust, Show We Care, Shape the Future, and Be Passionate, the latter bearing the emblem of a Valentine's Day heart).

Johann MacDonald enters his office behind me. He is big and beleaguered, orange-haired, with skin easily given to reddening and rash. His stubble resembles beach sand. Aurally, he is the sound of clothing coming together and apart—the swish of his yellow and turquoise De Beers windbreaker, a voice that sounds like it's unzipping something heavy, meant for winter.

When he inhales, there's a soft, guttural clicking at the back of his throat. He wears generously cut khaki pants. He exhibits the infectious anxiety of an overworked exile. He slams a clipboard on his desk, and a toy crane rolls off the edge. He fumbles for it in a half-hearted way, resigned to let it clatter to the floor.

In sight and sound alone, I like him almost immediately. He utters the phlegmatic command, "Sit," without so much as pulling out a desk chair, and I comply, and quickly feel oppressed not so much by the office decorations but by all the beige and pale green paint; the room is reminiscent of a 1970s' guidance counselor's office, and I feel about to be pressured to declare what I want to do with my life.

"So, pigeons and diamond smuggling?" he says. "I guess you heard, then, about the recent cave-in. That's what everyone's heard." Behind him, on the wall, are a poster of a Great Dane staring down a Chihuahua, and a printout of the Oscar Wilde misquote, "My tastes are simple. I am simply satisfied with the best." MacDonald's head is perfectly centered between the two. He speaks of how a ring of smugglers illegally tunneled into a nearby diamond pit excavation, having, in the middle of the night, cut holes into the security fences and dug channels many meters below the surface, just above the pothole, or bottom of the pit. "It's an open cast mine," MacDonald says. "*Open* because there's no ceiling, and *cast* because of the leftover sand that's cast out." These pits resemble pyramids in reverse, as if excavation sites for upside-down stepped necropoli—the actual structure which once took up positive space having been hauled away, so only its grave remains. "And these tunnels are so narrow, only children can fit, and in there," MacDonald says, "is a hell you can't imagine."

Due to the lack of air, teams of hired children fill the tiny culvert, forming a constantly rotating Möbius strip; those digging for diamonds at the terminus of the tunnel dig until they can no longer breathe, whereupon they circle back toward the entry point, gulp for air like whales, and then reenter in turn. MacDonald picks up a pamphlet from his desk and hands it to me. It is filled with De Beers marketing prosaicisms, including an image of smiling black children captioned "ABCDEBEERS: We dig deep to support our young gems."

"These syndicates are huge," says MacDonald. "Chinese mafia, Italian mafia, American mafia," and here he raises his eyebrows and points at my chest with his pinky, as if I'm somehow guilty of the American mafia's trespasses onto De Beers territory. "The KGB once paid their operatives in diamonds. God's honest truth. What they're not getting directly from mine employees who still get in with pigeons in their lunch-bins, they get out with child slave labor—kids of poor families who have no choice. And do these kids get paid? Sometimes they're given food, clean water, but usually they work for *tik* [crystal meth], so they become dependent on these syndicates. God, you have to be drugged to endure the hell you find in these tunnels. They can't be more than 60 centimeters around. I have photographs"—he rises in his chair as if about to produce them, before falling again—"which I can't show to you. Security reasons." This particular tunnel collapse killed two of the would-be smugglers. "And this is why De Beers has to prevent this thing. It's not just that they own the mineral rights. It's that there's this. Smuggling is wrong. These diamonds are not responsibly harvested. Right here in Kleinzee, a few years back, there was a collapse that killed ten. De Beers claims an environmental responsibility."

As part of this "environmental responsibility," pigeons here, too, he tells me, are seen as suspicious and shot on sight. They're not part of the corporate ideal of the mine as a closed system—a pure zone, invulnerable to bacteria. In order to maintain this invulnerability, workers are not only subjected to the random administration of concentrated liquid suppositories (reportedly stored in blue bottles labeled "State Secret"), but also X-rayed when they enter and again when they leave. "The X-rays are random," MacDonald says, fingering the bed of a toy dump truck. "Legally, it's a human rights violation to overdose someone on radiation, so these X-rays have to be spaced out. Sometimes they're getting a real X-ray, but more often they're getting a placebo. They never know which they're getting. And the diggers risk it sometimes," MacDonald says, even though, he tells me, that there are thorough pat-downs as well, "and sometimes they make it." Laborers sometimes modify their clothing with lead-lined pockets and boot soles, train pigeons to fly over the Orange River from South Africa to Namibia and back, between the mines of Alexander Bay and Oranjemund and safe houses lining the border—to the hands of wives and mothers and sons and grandsons.

Anyone keeping pigeons is monitored by De Beers operatives, oftentimes 24/7, with hidden laser cameras and night-vision binoculars. If someone is caught with a diamond, MacDonald keeps repeating, "it is not only a crime against De Beers, but also a crime against the state," and they are "punished" by mine security, hauled away within hours. The offender's spouse and children are evicted from the town, too, thrown out into the gullet of the desert. Photographs at the Kleinzee museum show suspected smugglers and their families being held in barbed wire enclosures by the mine's perimeter guards. The suspects stare beyond the wire, emaciated and afraid, into the photographer's lens. The guards' faces are hidden in the shadows cast by their hat brims, and their hands hover at their sides, ready. The image isn't unlike those taken of the Second World War concentration camps—the ones my grandparents showed me when I turned thirteen, because, according to tradition, I was now man enough to behold the faces of my dead relatives.

"Even if you possess an unpolished diamond," MacDonald says, "it's a crime against the state. Even for one second. Which means that if you were to pick up a pebble on the beach, and that pebble turns out to be a diamond—whether you knew it or not—that counts as possession." If a De Beers operative were to catch me with it in my hand—and the beaches of Kleinzee and Port Nolloth are covertly patrolled by men with guns—I would be detained, fined, and carted off to prison.

"Mm-hmm," MacDonald says, and gestures with his chin to a strange—and, I fear, self-congratulatory—installation on his office wall: the upside-down nameplates that once fronted the desks of all the people he had to fire: "Mine Secretary," "Cashier," "Environmental Manager," "Exploration Manager," "Driver Instructor," "Safety Officer," "Chief Safety Officer."

"Diamond divers especially," MacDonald continues, "are a slippery bunch. You know that 30 percent of the diamonds are lost to smuggling." MacDonald speaks of how the artisans and engineers responsible for designing and implementing new and more efficient mining equipment also form teams to unofficially design crossbows and catapults—some hand-held, some industrial-sized—in order to shoot hollowed-out steel bolts, packed with diamonds, into the desert. These teams calculate the trajectory of the bolt, and pinpoint the small area of desert where it has landed. Later, they or their co-conspiratorial friends and family will comb the sand for the bolts. "And the wood pallets that carry cargo and machine parts are rarely X-rayed, so folks drill holes into them, line the holes with lead just in case, pack the holes with diamonds, and seal them off," MacDonald says. "And with the underground mines, it's worse." Smugglers are lowered by rope over two kilometers into the earth, where they live in darkness for years, MacDonald assures me, supplies being lowered in the dead of night by co-conspirators, and when they are finally found ("They're always found," MacDonald says) and brought up to the surface, they have to be brought up blindfolded.

MacDonald tells me that in his entire time with De Beers, he's held a diamond only once. "You can see why people get the fever," he says, though when I ask him what became of that diamond, he tells me that's an off-limits topic, and turns on his defusers. "No, no, really, it was just an ugly rock, I'm telling you, nothing became of it. Honestly, okay . . . well . . . okay . . . I put the diamond back exactly where I found it, and . . . well . . . I know exactly where it is . . . But, anyway, they grow them big here. In 1974, [there was one amounting to] 175 carats, found right here in Kleinzee. How are you going to smuggle that, but with a pigeon, or inside the crop of an ostrich?

"Look, you really need to talk to Lester," MacDonald tells me. "He used to direct mine security for De Beers, and not just throughout South Africa. Overseas, as well. He's big. Actually, he's due into Kleinzee late tonight, on an assessment call. To see how things are doing here. He always stays out at Die Houthoop—a guesthouse in the middle of the desert. He'll know about you."

"Mister . . . Mister Lester?" I stammer.

MacDonald smiles. "Yes," he says. "He'll know about you."

"How?"

"It's Lester," MacDonald says, as if I've asked a stupid question.

"He's real?"

"Flesh and blood," MacDonald says.

I ask MacDonald to write down the name of the guesthouse, and he pencils *Die Houthoop* onto the back of another of my gas station receipts. I look at the receipt before folding it into my pocket. Though I know it translates as *the,* I remain unnerved that the first word of the guesthouse's name is *Die.*

"C'mon," he says, and motions for me to rise, and follow him. Pinned over his office door, as if an exit sign, is a glossy photo of a meerkat captioned "Everyone calm the fuck down." MacDonald leads me into a low-ceilinged conference room. On the walls are several diagrams depicting, based on the downwardly zigzagging lines, some schematic for decline; and three antique maps of Namaqualand farms. On the dry-erase board is the directive, written in blue script, "SELL ALL PROPERTIES."

MacDonald allows me to witness a safety meeting comprised of eleven employees who down coffee and eat yesterday's doughnuts (all the chocolate ones are gone). The room feels like a gambling den secreted behind a bar. He introduces me as a writer from the U.S. ("I'm always wary of writers"), before speaking on hydraulic safety and a recent incident of "failure," whereupon an unidentified worker lost an unidentified limb, but, based on the solemnity of the coffee-sipping and doughnut-chewing, everyone in the room but me can identify both the worker and the lost limb. When MacDonald lapses into Afrikaans, his secretary, Trinety, retrieves a lambskin drum from the room's corner, and each employee ceremonially slaps out a clumsy riff as a way of adjourning the meeting.

I try to pay attention to all of this, to record the details. I look at MacDonald and, though I don't know the man from Adam, I try to convince myself that he wouldn't send me into certain danger, that my disappearance would look bad for the company. But, of course, that isn't really true, and I don't know . . . I don't know.

Suddenly, MacDonald is standing right over me. I can feel his breath on my face. I can smell it. Yellow mustard, mostly. Such proximity silences me.

He never touches me, much less looks into my eyes, as he leads me where few non-De Beers affiliates have been led, along cramped pale green hallways lined with doors with blacked-out windows and no nameplates on the outside. Exposed piping, a seemingly pumped-in humidity, and low ceiling evoke the boiler rooms of nightmare grade schools. When we reach the first stage of security, I must blow into a Breathalyzer held by a guard with prodigious pectorals and shaking hands. He wears a dull blue uniform, crisply ironed. In his belt holster, a handgun, a two-way radio, and what appears to be a glow-in-the-dark rectal probe. Behind him, a sign reads "You Are To Place All Loose Items On The Tray," and, in the corresponding picture, a blue tray holds such benign and inexplicable things as a beaded bracelet, a blue plastic fork, a bottle of magenta nail polish, a battery, a coin, an apple, an orange. I have none of these, but I have my wallet, and the wad of tissues often carried by the allergic, which often raises the suspicion of non-allergic security guards who are driven, as is this one, to go through every tissue, as if flipping the pages of the Book of Revelation. Satisfied with the state of my snot-rags, the guard hands me a yellow security vest. MacDonald meanwhile checks his company mailbox, a tiny locked cabinet amid a wall of others, each with a blond wood finish, evoking a 1950s' bowling alley locker room. At the second stage of security, the tops of my shoes are combed by a rotating shoe brush, and I must drag the soles along a serrated grate. The same guard waits for me to finish so he can give me the pat-down during which he finds my pen and paper.

"I told you it's a closed system," MacDonald says, as the fluorescents flicker like doom. "Just know that what goes in, stays in. It never comes out. No pens, no glasses, nothing. Even this [gesturing to my pen], up until a couple of months ago was taboo. Up until a couple a months ago, De Beers was still mining here full-force. There's no way you would've gotten in here, let alone with a pen. *De Beers* people couldn't bring pens in here."

We proceed to four separate X-ray chambers, each barred by a locked door. Each chamber is a right-angled womb-for-adults, unfortunately green and about three feet square. An unseen security guard buzzes open each subsequent door only when the last one is closed. In these chambers, MacDonald warns me, "You can't see out. If the doors open and a big blue guard is standing there, it's trouble. It's over. Testing the system is grounds for dismissal. Of course, that's terribly vague, but the value of the product demands it," and I want to ask if *it* refers to *vagueness*, but a big blue guard ushers me through door number one.

MacDonald is not exempt from any of this, and when we come out on the other side, the sun has become perfectly white, reflecting off the old mine hostels and razor wire. The multiple wire fences are spaced so as to prevent the diggers from throwing a diamond beyond all of them. Behind the hostels, a once-menacing guard tower sinks into the sand, shortening inch by inch as the days pass. When a digger died on the job, his body was to be buried right here on the mine site, as De Beers believed that the corpse would be used to smuggle diamonds. He simply disappeared, his family notified—oftentimes many days later—by postcard, if at all.

MacDonald ushers me into the passenger seat of the white Toyota De Beers company pickup, and we take off into the waste within the waste, a blank spot on the map, an erasure. All 32,000 hectares, erased.

Officially, MacDonald tells me, this mined expanse doesn't exist; it's private, cloaked, off anything resembling the grid, and indeed the miles upon miles of it are absent of visible life—an eternal breadth of undulating rubble of various shades and grains.

"Welcome to nowhere," he says. "There are no birds. We're driving through the heart of destruction. It's totally closed. There's no agriculture here. No game, no farming. Even the birds avoid it. There are no birds. There's no agriculture! It's lockdown! There's nothing here!" his voice growing high-pitched and panicky-excited in a *What have I done?* sort of way.

The place defies prefixes—every single *other, extra, pre,* or *post* I try to heap upon it: otherworldly, extraplanetary, prehistoric, post-apocalyptic. So of this Earth, and so not; the mine honors the look of the Earth, as if a synthetic model of the planet wedged into this corner of the planet itself; something ancient cast in new polymer, which itself has degraded to the point that it seems like the oldest thing in sight—older than the actual mountains, which are still capable of growing their new scrub. The mine property feels biospheric, so insular with its false trenches and false mountains. The mist settles in the crotches of the barrens before steaming upward, as if this whole thing were still cooking, in-progress, waiting to cool and settle. Strange how, not long ago, so many people milled about these endless anthills looking for the shiny crumbs that stand in for our professions of love; 2,500 full-time employees, carried from home to mine and back by private, 24/7 hourly bus routes.

"No birds," MacDonald says again, but I don't believe him, as I distinctly see tiny dark things whirling in the thermals above us—the thermals even De Beers can't block out—watching the earth for patterns, listening out for its borborygmal supersonics, looking for home. When I blink, they are gone, and I wonder if our brains, as some salve against loneliness, out of instinct to ornament all of that empty space when beholding a blank sky, conspire to put birds there.

I squint against the sun, which seems to have dropped onto the scene from another solar system; everything here is so unlike the other stuff on Earth it usually brightens. I feel something hungry is stalking us. I want Louisa's hand, and cool spirals of methylene blue ultrasound gel on bellies, and monitors that register puny heartbeats in clicks instead of beeps. A healthy pregnancy, finally, in no-man's-land.

We drive. The company truck is fitted with a speed governor that beeps each time MacDonald exceeds 80 kilometers per hour, about which he complains, pounding on the steering wheel. The roads are sand, compacted until they've become dirt, and rutted with ridges that resemble the spines of some Paleozoic mudfish about to be unearthed into our present, about to become part of our story.

I'm a horrible interviewer, easily distracted by things like the clouds and memories I can't pinpoint as either good or bad, which made me an equally terrible athlete as a child, when I preferred to pick dandelions and watch the passing birds in right field than catch pop flies. I never know what I'm looking for, what sorts of answers I should try to elicit, so I let MacDonald talk. He points out the window, references the rows of green windbreaks anchored at the foot of dump slopes and pit rims, has an argument with himself; like me, he's trying to work something out.

"Look at all this effort at restoration!" he says. "The nets are fiendishly expensive. I'm spending 300,000 rand a month to keep Kleinzee going now. You see these dumps with the holes next to them? I've moved 30 million cubic meters of soil since 2011. We round it off, re-create a natural-style surface with the dozers. You don't hear people talking about De Beers doing this, rehabilitating the environment. It's an ongoing cleanup of the mess we made. I don't like De Beers because diamonds are a silly product. De Beers knows you can't sell a diamond on the secondary market, because it's forever. You're selling his love. No! It's a cold bloody stone! Sell it for hard cash! De Beers does a lot of bad, but also some good. The Oppenheimer family was friends of

Mandela and the ANC and tried to smooth things out before 1994, to embrace the change. Look: apartheid is our national shame. Some at De Beers did not take change lightly . . ."

I think of the Oppenheimer family inhabiting their estates and urban sanctuaries, roving the grounds among their man-made forests, Japanese gardens, and tennis courts. When forging business deals with other companies, the Oppenheimers required the chief executives of those companies to send out official memos to their own employees thanking De Beers for their willingness to work with them, and pledging, "We understand that diamonds are different, special, and not a commodity." MacDonald raises a hand from the wheel as if to silence my thoughts.

"But I like De Beers because of the rehabilitation," he continues. "It's all about the phytoremediation, you know?" and I don't. "I'm a geologist, okay? I never said, 'Hey, you know what? I want to close mines.' The opportunity presented itself and, well, I'm good at it. They call me the Executioner."

I suddenly remember Nico Green's use of this word back at Vespetti's in Port Nolloth. "You?" I say. MacDonald nods.

I ask him if he can tell me more about Mr. Lester, and his role in all of this, executionary or otherwise. "No, I really can't," MacDonald says. "And besides, *I* don't even know the extent of it. I've met him, sure, when he's been here on prior assessments, but I've heard he's a real chameleon. I'm not even 100 percent on whether he's really South African or not. I'm pretty sure he is. Some people think he's KGB or CIA, or without any real allegiance. A mercenary, or king of the mercenaries, or the guy who hires the mercenaries. But I just know him as the former director of all security, everywhere, for De Beers."

"But if he's a former director, why does he still come here to assess the goings-on?" I ask.

"Not 100 percent on that," MacDonald says. "I just know what I know. He's the only guy De Beers trusts to do certain specialized things. Like I said, if you want to know these things, you need to speak with him directly. Go to Die Houthoop. Tonight."

"Okay, but someone I've spoken to referred to Lester as the Executioner who lords over other executioners," I say. "And your nickname is the Executioner?"

"Who spoke to you?" MacDonald asks, a meanness creeping into his voice.

Uh-oh. I feel as if I've slipped up here. "I . . . I didn't get his name," I say.

"What did he look like?" MacDonald says.

"I . . . I . . . Look, I . . ."

MacDonald snorts, and shakes his head. "Fuck it," he says. "It's not like it matters anymore. Not like it used to, even last year. Even a few *months* ago. You don't want to tell me, don't tell me. Who gives a shit now, right? I can pretty much guess anyway."

I hold back a cough.

"So, yes, to answer your question. They call me the Executioner," he says. "Sometimes, I'm the Hangman. But it's all in good fun."

I nod, and I let out my cough, and I know that I've gotten away with something here. I know that I'm lucky. Still, I wonder how all of this will end. I'm trapped here with this man, and nobody but Louisa knows where I am, and she's all alone, and have I now endangered her?

"Don't worry so much," MacDonald says when he notices the look on my face, the assured paleness of it, my reluctance to open my mouth again. "It's all in good fun," he repeats.

I wonder about the nature of fun here, on this blank spot on the atlas, where we are now officially disappeared according to the rest of the world and its radar. I wonder exactly what Nicky and Jonathan Oppenheimer meant when together, as father and son, they sent a memo to their employees on August 16, 2012, overstating, "We have spent decades exalting anniversaries and unbreakable bonds. We are good at it. It is in our DNA! We love De Beers. My father loved De

Beers as did his father before him. Through it all, the diamond has always been our guide."

In spite of their rhetorical sunniness, the Oppenheimers—along with the remainder of the De Beers executives (when taken together, they are known as the Syndicate)—were banned from conducting first-hand business in the U.S. from 1948 to 2004 due to their insistence on price-fixing, a violation of antitrust laws. Still, they were able to peddle their diamonds in the U.S. via loopholes and "indirect methods"— a network of separate contracted entities and retail conglomerates. Before entering the U.S., every De Beers diamond passed through a "sight" (one of a series of clandestine international diamond-dealing houses), and it was that "sight" that often directly sold to U.S.-based luxury retailers.

Until 2004, when De Beers agreed to plead guilty to criminal price-fixing and pay a multimillion-dollar fine, the Oppenheimers and their cohorts were, in fact, treated as an organized crime group in the U.S., which legally prevented any more than three De Beers executives from even *being* on U.S. soil, for any reason, simultaneously. I wonder if Nicky and Jonathan considered this treatment a badge of honor, a testament to what Cecil John Rhodes once called "so much power." I wonder if they even laughed a little on the inside when they wrote, "You reinforce our brand through the way you think and act every day. As you have heard both of us say many times before, the men and women of De Beers [whom in other memos they dubbed "the magic people" and "the best kind of people on earth"] have a responsibility to live up to diamonds. The diamond's place in modern—and future— cultures, and the promise it holds for every person who possesses one, acts as an invisible force, pushing us inevitably and irrevocably toward the right side of history." I wonder which of their secretaries took dic-tation for this memo. I wonder if she rolled her eyes when they decided to sign it, "Forever."

MacDonald and I pass through an area sans windbreaks, and when

I finally find my voice again, I ask him why there isn't any attempted restoration going on here.

"Look," he says, "we want to rehabilitate the environment, but not at the expense of the surrounding economic area. This is still to be mined for diamonds once Trans Hex comes in. They're the managing group—big operations in Angola. There's still an estimated 4.5 million carats here that they know of. It's just not economically viable for De Beers to take them out right now." He tells me the forthcoming miners, like the miners before them, will brace themselves on one level or another in the pits and, as the diamonds collect in gullies, sweep the bedrock of the sixty-some meters of sand atop it. "It looks like an old slave-type setup," MacDonald says. "They literally sweep the bedrock with brooms and dustpans. The sweepers are known as the Lashing Gang."

The oftentimes all-black Lashing Gang (a group of about one thousand, sweeping in teams of twenty) is responsible for clearing out, or "cleaning," about 130,000 square meters of bedrock every month. In earlier days, each member of the Lashing Gang had in his overalls pouches a stack of brown envelopes preprinted with charts, into which he would pack his diamond pickups, recording the details on the outside. His hands were gloved, as are the diggers' hands still today, as are those of the sorters. According to security measures, a worker must never directly touch a diamond, and devices are invented to prevent them from doing so.

Sorters insert their hands into white gloves which are attached to sorting boxes, sealed off with Plexiglas. The ore is funneled into the case through a pipe at its rear, and the sorter pushes the dross through a chute that passes it outside the box, and drops the diamonds into an attached secure container. In this way, neither the sorters' hands nor their breath reach the stones. The device resembles an old arcade prize dispenser.

"So," MacDonald says, "they can't lift a glove up and scoop [a diamond] into their mouths. Unauthorized contact equals loss." In the old days, the Lashing Gang had on mine property their own tea room, where they sealed their envelopes with pliers, turned them in to their superiors and received, as a bonus, a small sum and a cup of tea. The meager cash bonus was based on De Beers's calculated overhead, which they determined to be about four rand (or forty cents U.S.) per meter swept. On average, the Lashing Gang had to sweep sixteen square meters in order to unearth one diamond, so De Beers calculated their expense at about $6.40 U.S. per gem, the mean size of which was 0.9 carats, which, today, has a market value of anywhere from $4,000 to $27,000. The Lashing Gang members received as a bonus less than 1 percent of $6.40 per diamond found—about five cents; less than 0.00019 percent of the market rate.

This was back in the day (circa the 1940s to the 1960s) when mine security carried sharp assegai spears with which they sometimes maimed or killed those suspected of smuggling. "Mine workers were commonly sacked," says *Glitter and Greed* author Janine Farrell-Robert, "whenever 'on balance of probability' the mine management decides they might have stolen diamonds." Management often ruthlessly interrogated workers after they bought new clothes, or hats or boots or a car, intimidating them into resigning, or calling in security and their assegais.

"The Lashing Gang are still known for using pigeons," MacDonald says. "They want more than that small bonus. I just bought a bunch of those old envelopes at auction. Out of sentimentality, I guess."

The mine dumps slough and recede, depend on one another for support. The bedrock beneath them conceals just enough water to hatch the mosquitoes favored by some insectivorous species of pigeons—the ones who eat the curvaceous ectoparasites who have recently fed on our blood—as we train them to shoulder our baggage, convince them that our home is their home. They are accidentally vampiric, and full of sanguine love.

But even this airspace is as barren as the macadam, which conceals the mass graves of people and pigeons—marked only by our drive to heap more dirt upon them, parabola after parabola, memorializing not the dead, but the diamonds that killed them. MacDonald parks the truck, and we stand windblown and isolated at the vertices, our clothes percussive, our bodies soft beneath sleeves and collars and cuffs, atop so many corpses and the volcanic pipes that support them, and our vantage point is horrifying and privileged and, out here, seemingly ultimate.

There, on the upslope, the same windscreens that De Beers uses to lord over the wind form a kind of chalk outline around the holy burial site where the remains of a Khoi man were recently found by diggers searching for diamonds. The man's skull rests among the foreleg bones of jackals, snake vertebrae, fish vertebrae, springbok teeth, lizard mandibles, crayfish swimmerets, the badly burnt carapaces of two angulate tortoises, the wing bones of birds, the petrified stomach contents of the inert and the extinct, the relics and refuse of human consumption, sacramental and throwaway. The remains' knees are bent to his chest, his arms and hands reaching toward his skull to cover either his ears or eyes. The position is not quite fetal. This skeleton clearly couldn't bear to look at something.

Select members of the Kleinzee Museum Committee (who were not allowed on mine property) were consulted from a distance regarding the logistics of the excavation. They named the corpse Alfred. Initial reports on the excavation read, "The first find was the remains of a tortoise skeleton and shell. Not far beneath this, an anklebone was exposed. Clearing the sand with great caution, the complete skeleton was revealed." Following said revelation, the De Beers–approved excavation team took out their tape measures. The bones were buried among diamonds, 70 centimeters deep, in what the reports dub "typical Khoisan manner lying on its left side in a contracted position, with the head pointing east and facing south." The man was thirty years old when he died. In his mouth were the adapted "peg teeth"—single-rooted, straight-sided teeth whose function remains an evolutionary riddle to us. One of the excavators tried to smuggle out a rib bone for analysis and dating. A mine security guard confiscated it, and it was likely returned to the burial site. The excavator, without the aid of further analysis, believed the bones to be between two hundred and five hundred years old.

"So this is like some sacred burial ground?" I ask, and MacDonald stares at me as if I've watched too many movies, which I have.

"There are burial grounds all over the place," MacDonald says. "If you travel from here to Cape Town, you'll probably drive over some kind of burial site every twenty meters . . ."

Something changes in MacDonald's demeanor after we stop the truck again for a communal pee. "Pick nothing up," he instructs, and I want to tell him that, yes, I *get it*. The sleeves of MacDonald's windbreaker roar. His shoulders drop, and, after issuing this directive, he seems lighter, willing to confide or confess. Maybe it has to do with emptying his bladder.

"My wife loves pigeons," he says. "She feeds them all the time." He points to the silhouette of a giant line drag—an elephantine crane, both decrepit and a technological marvel—the pickup truck about the size of one of its lug nuts. "That's to move the overburden," he says, "which is the word used to refer to any portion of the Earth that lies atop the diamonds"—the crust, the stuff we walk on and build our homes on, and raise pigeons and children on, and eat turkey and salad on, and get sick on and die on. The overburden. "Isn't it beautiful? That baby can excavate 75 to 125 tons of earth in one scoop. So big and it takes only three guys to operate it—the driver, the oiler, the spotter."

"What's the spotter do?"

MacDonald looks at me and shakes it off, zips up.

"Yeah," he says, "a real gorilla. A real gorilla in the mist."

He watches me take my notes on a bunch of torn scrap paper and old receipts and asks, "Why don't you get a proper notebook?"

I have no doubt that if we were the last two people on Earth—and it appears that we are—I would have been eaten by now. He puts his hands on his hips, surveys this place. "I think I love it out here," he says. "Sometimes I stay longer than I'm supposed to. You're a writer. I bring books out here. Out here, I learned Gaelic to cope with the stress. There are only 60,000 people in the world who speak it. I've seen so many people come and go because of AIDS . . ." I can tell he's working something out, repeating things he's said before in bars and in bed, but trying to pinpoint some larger shadow-story that will help put all of his time living in and on an erasure into context. "Before that, I was eating pills. I was on every medication known to man." He squats and his knees crack. He scoops up a fistful of sand and tosses it into the wind.

"Fuck!" he says. "This attempt to replant is a complete failure! The big challenge is to get things to grow. Some of these dumps have been reshaped and replanted for ten years, twenty years, and still nothing grows." Though De Beers wants to restore this land, the indigenous population wants to devote it to farming, and are busy fighting—likely in vain—MacDonald's efforts. The De Beers environmental division perpetuates the rhetoric that the land they disturbed has been so thoroughly ravaged that it has reverted to what they call "a pure state, pure Namaqualand territory." De Beers believes that the desert here has ultimately suffered not from mining, but from the grazing of farm animals. They don't want anyone else making money off it in the name of "restoration" and company policy back-patting. So, the corporation wants to block the indigenous people from farming here, wants Trans Hex to have their way with a small portion of it, and wants the rest as their private garden, their little spot to play with their bulldozers, compost cocktails, cardboard "grow" circles, shovels, and pails.

The mist draws lassos over the ruin. It settles over these 32,000 hectares that will never be a private garden; over the larger-than-life line drag left to rot in the middle of the nothing. To what degree is this sort of restoration a disturbance of the disturbance?

This is another story of self-importance. Restoration is a fallacy here, as is conservation. To what do they want to restore it, and is it theirs to restore, as if there's no consequence to this marauding? Conservation psychologist Richard Osbaldiston stresses, "One of the strongest predictors of conservation behavior is the situation or context . . . [O]nly a small percentage actually observes conservation behavior; rather, most of them are based on self-report measures . . . [and] people regulate their own behaviors by changes in their cognitions, emotions, or perceptions . . . All of this fuzziness . . . is important to acknowledge." This land resists both restoration and fertility, at least as we define it, cognitively, emotionally. The extinct passenger pigeon knows: nothing goes back, or stays put as it is—not even our lovely attempts to make such impossible things so, with squat green screens pressed into sand-stripped-of-sand, against the wind.

"The reasons that the passenger pigeon was unable to recover from the period of overexploitation are not fully known," says endangered species scholar Craig Kasnoff. Even our best grief evolves in spite of what we know or don't know, want or don't want. Strange how hurt diffuses, but maintains its intensity, settles malign, as if some offspring-of-lightning fog. It becomes harder to find the way out of it, and it becomes a part of us, fills us out. Strange how we grow into it like the laughable turtleneck that we're bemused finally fits. Our inability to recover becomes fuzzier, which is important to acknowledge, perhaps, in this way: I think of Arlo, our fourth miscarriage, his ashes scattered into the mud of the Mississippi River, dead as Barney Barnato, and the sort of sadness that drops over us, another curtain of dust doing the disappearing of the happy people we once were, and the stupidity of restoration, how that desire is simply not up to the task. How the water carries the diamonds and the earth and Arlo, away. How consolation in the face of the barren is ever an insufficient, incomplete tool. We have both the heart, and the theorems, to tell us this.

"I rehabilitated a flamingo once," MacDonald says, staring into the negated hectares. "Amputated its injured wing, carried it out to a flock of flamingos, and it was good for a couple days until the jackal got it. I did as much human intervention as I could, and then the jackal came in."

Even if this stab at rehabilitation did work, even if Johann Mac-Donald and his puffy, flamingo-surgeon hands could make of this havoc something verdantly botanical, even if the jackal didn't call foul, wouldn't that also be insufficient? Atrocious, even? Wouldn't it be a case of environmental restoration as a concealment of decades' worth of gleeful corporate atrocity? Given that atrocity is often birthed of passion, and should De Beers's senior environmental managers and spokesfolks be successful, the real atrocities perpetuated since the days of the East India Company, Cecil John Rhodes, and Barney Barnato will be redacted by, and overgrown with, scrubby plants that will struggle a little harder than the rest of their species to flower.

"You know what the best thing about a diamond is?" MacDonald says. "You can't break it. You can't break a diamond. Gem-quality diamonds are indestructible."

I nod. Anything that escapes destruction so completely seems the product of absurdity. Perhaps it's De Beers's gender narrative that seduces us into believing that diamonds are not absurd—that to be a man, one must woo a woman with a proper diamond, and to be a woman, one must want to be wooed in such a fashion—but surely there's more to it than that: a desire to possess something so ancient and so hard, fixed, a portion of the Earth's history—however cut and polished—in which we did not yet participate. A stage of fire, lava. A claiming of ownership of things that survived a stage which we could not, making them measurable in carats, and wedged motionless into a strong setting; a claiming of ownership of the thing we call our home before we inhabited it, as it lay in wait for us, when the insects were as big as pigeons and the pigeons, crows, and the crows, cows. Such subterranean stories our wedded ring fingers silently keep! So much more than the story we thrust upon it of kimberlitic pipes and rivers, oceans, mines, mine closures, the blood, the collapses, the dumps, the failed restorations, MacDonald, Louisa, and me.

In a 2012 farewell memo to their employees, after selling most of their shares to a sister company ready to bleed Southern and West Africa—aptly named the Anglo American Group—Nicky and Jonathan Oppenheimer actually wrote, "Moving forward, we will be out of the diamond business, but we will be keeping our eye on you."

"The mines are exhausted," MacDonald says, then tells me that, before he became a mine closer and moved to Kleinzee, he wooed the woman who was to become his wife not with a diamond, but with a pet duck. His wife and two daughters have since separated from him, moved to Cape Town, waiting, month after month, for him to get another job. "I never pursued my dream of becoming an artisanal brewer of beer," he says.

"I'm a terrible manager," he says, and walks uphill, away from the truck. I follow him until I reach a spot on the dump slope soft as quicksand. I sink to my shins. The windbreaker is taut over his back. He's looking for something. He bends down, examines the dirt, picks something up, and runs down the hill to me. I like the way his body bounces, slides down the sand as if in slow motion, clumsy running crossbred with clumsy skiing. He shows it to me, holds it to my face. It's no larger than a pinhead. It's radioactive blue. "A seed," he says.

*

ON THE WAY OUT OF THE MINE, THE PAT-DOWN IS MORE THOROUGH, the shoe scraping more scrutinized. The guard confiscates my pen, but, at MacDonald's urging, lets me keep my notes. Once outside, I feel as if I have surfaced from a depth, and take in air in gulps. I watch the wind animate the sparse plants. The shock of life. It's so good to see bees again. They build their nests in the twisted sculptures of rusted chassis and bumpers, engine parts and tailpipes of all the old cars that entered the mine but were not allowed to leave, as they had so many crevices perfect for smuggling diamonds. The bees make a life for themselves here beneath the sign that reads:

NO ENTRY
UNAUTHORISED ENTRY PROHIBITED
IN ACCORDANCE WITH REGULATION 3–1–1
OF THE MINERALS ACT 50 OF 1991
ENTRY BEYOND THIS POINT IS STRICTLY FORBIDDEN

There are two more lines of text on the sign, which have been sun-bleached into illegibility.

Bartholomew Variation #4

WERE THIS NOT TWENTY-FIRST-CENTURY SOUTH AFRICA, BUT ancient Rome, the oracular priests known as the Augurs would be craning their necks, watching the sky for bird behavior. To them, the divining of the future depended on whether the pigeons were flocking together or flying alone, uttering their coos or keeping quiet. They would have seen Msizi's bird, the sky otherwise as vacant as an urn awaiting its ashes, and they would have prophesied of doom.

But Bartholomew can't take on the superstitions of others, especially those of the underlings of long-dead emperors. He has enough to carry. Many things are preparing to die in this desert, and he flies over them as if immune, but he is not immune. The air above the desert is still the desert.

Back at the mine, Msizi is covered in sludge up to his thighs, elbows. He feels mummified, plaster-cast. The earth burbles at his feet like farina. Men shout at other men, beat other men. Two diggers sing a song that begins with the words "Mayibute Afrika," before they are silenced by the boot heels of mine security. Msizi imagines himself the only boy in a city of vampires, and indeed the mine resembles such an intricate city, webbed with aerial ropeways, stout ladders joining the stepped catacombs and blind alleys, pyramids, plateaus, arroyos of mud. He prays he will not be hurt today, will not slip and fall, be beaten back to his feet by some vampire whose eyes are hidden beneath the visor of a guard's cap.

Msizi wonders where his bird is. He gives thanks for miracles already come to pass—that he and his lunchbox received only a dummy scan from the X-ray machine today; that no one noticed as Bartholomew wriggled fully loaded from his cupped hands. The sun is strong, and Msizi gives thanks for its brightness, for the way in which it blinds the guards who scan the sky.

Shirtless men pass by carrying blue stretchers. Sometimes, on these stretchers, mounds of diamondiferous gravel; sometimes a man's broken body. One can only dig into the earth so deep before the earth decides to collapse.

The dust whirls red and white below the bird as he passes over the unearthly Klipbakke, the sun-bleached rock bowls, huge amphitheaters gouged into the scrub.

Some time ago, when Msizi first began to train him, Bartholomew injured his left leg. Msizi held him and sang to him; Bartholomew squirmed, then calmed, as Msizi wrapped his leg in newspaper, fashioned a cast from a lengthwise-cut drinking straw, and secured it with Scotch tape. The bird needed a lot of sleep to recover.

Bartholomew can't endure these expeditions for much longer. Still, something in his genetic makeup compels him to keep flapping. He's likely dizzy, and could go for sugar water and seed. Though he is losing his bearings, he still senses, via the world's magnetic humming, that "home," with its familiar light and smells, and sounds of scratchy jazz records, is still far away, likely, this time, beyond reach.

Chapter 9

Pilgrims and the Mountain of Light

A Link Between Myth and Human History

SURELY, IF THERE EXISTS THE MAGIC OF THE PIGEONS, AND THE almost mythological quality of Bartholomew's resolve, there exists also evidence of Krishna's immodest diamond—the famed Koh-i-Noor, the *Mountain of Light*—smuggled into our human world by one of the Hindu god's servants. It was given its temporal name in 1738 by Nadir Shah, born Nadir Kuli, and nicknamed "Slave to the Wonderful." Nadir was an eighteen-year-old shepherd when he and his mother were abducted by raiding Uzbegs and sold into slavery. His mother was worked to death within four years, after which Nadir escaped into the desert, and eventually talked his way into the service of a local governor. With his quick wit and survivalist instincts born of bondage, Nadir dethroned the ruler of Persia in 1732 and subsequently defeated the Afghans and Turks, kept the Russians out of the Caspian provinces, and cast his attention toward the declining Mughal Empire, the ruler of which, Mohammed Shah, was an oversexed drunk famed for his fatty bacchanals which often ended badly—with someone dead, injured, or in tears.

In 1738, after defeating Mohammed's army in less than two hours at the battle of Karnal, Nadir was invited to the conquered shah's palace for a final orgy. Mohammed had to give up his treasures to

131

Nadir, including the famed, soon-to-be-named Koh-i-Noor, which he did not give up willingly. At the orgy's intermezzo, post-coital, one of Mohammed's harem whispered into Nadir's ear that the defeated shah had hidden the diamond in the folds of his turban. At the feast that followed, while gorging on pigeon breasts in rose petal sauce, and pigeon legs poached in their own fat and topped with pistachios and pomegranate, Nadir suggested that he and Mohammed exchange turbans in a gesture of mutual respect and lifelong fraternal ties, if not exactly friendship. Mohammed—flustered, overfull, and spent of *qi*—reluctantly agreed, and spent the remainder of the supper neurotically wiping his mouth with a thick napkin of golden silk.

When the party ended, Nadir returned to his quarters, and, on his bed's shantung sheets, unraveled Mohammed's turban. When the diamond came tumbling out, he was so alarmed by its beauty that he cried out, "Koh-i-Noor!" ("Mountain of Light"), while the city outside the palace walls rioted. Mohammed died soon afterward, of "grief," locking himself in his apartment and undertaking a vow of silence and hunger strike. In counsel with the Koh-i-Noor, Nadir began ordering the slaughter of all those who opposed him, building towers from their skulls. His guards feared that he would soon execute even them, and so they attacked Nadir in his sleep, stabbing him through the heart with their swords. Empowered by his beloved Mountain of Light, Nadir was able to disembowel two of his assassins before succumbing himself. That loose-lipped member of the harem lived a long and supple life, without fully recovering from her youthful exhaustions.

The diamond, according to legend, was worth the equivalent of all the world's wealth amassed in seven days' time, and would bless its possessor with the ability to rule the world, but bear also the curse of non-monetary misfortune. The Koh-i-Noor first slipped into our world from the realm of the gods in the late fifteenth century, and soon thereafter fell into the earthly hands of Babur, the first Mughal ruler of India, and a descendant of Genghis Khan on his mother's side. A vicious warrior and twitchy poet, Babur, in 1526, was solicited by Daulat Khan, the ruler of Punjab, to help him defeat his despotic nephew, Ibrahim Lodi, the murderous Sultan of Delhi. Babur hypnotized Lodi's squad of 150 war elephants with his battlefield verse, compelling one of the beasts to gore Lodi through the heart. Through the perforation in the sultan's dying body, his soul crept out, along with a flock of doves. The doves flew back to the realm of the gods and perched on Krishna's shoulders, filling the space vacated by the stolen diamond, which had been sent for safekeeping by Vikramaditya, one of Lodi's (now slain) right-hand men, to the fort of Agra.

Babur sent his son, Humayun, to the fort in order to seize the dead sultan's jewels, but the Koh-i-Noor, after a thorough ransacking, was not found. The servants of the treasury were questioned and tortured by Humayun's foot-soldiers; their bodies slicked in black honey and covered with bees and ants, who had a lovely insectile conversation among themselves about inheriting the world, which the servants perceived only as a chorus of stings and bites, the anxiety of venom and anaphylaxis. Finally, one servant, whose forearm had been slashed open, pointed in the direction of the late sultan's palace. As his reward, Humayun commanded his men to close the servant's wound with a stitching made of the ants' mandibles. As the ants bit the poor man's wound closed, the foot-soldiers decapitated the once admirably eusocial insects, until the servant's arm stopped bleeding, decorated with a jagged bolt of ant heads. As he wept, and recovered in shame, the heads shimmied.

When Humayun arrived at the palace, he found Lodi's mother sobbing in the courtyard. She moved as if lost in some faraway dream, her arms shaking as she lifted the gold box to Humayun's sternum, presenting the Koh-i-Noor to its new owner. She said nothing—made no proclamations of love or hate, offered no words of warning, as she fell against Humayun's chest, weeping. Soon after bringing the diamond to his father as commanded, Humayun fell ill. Babur struck a deal with the Koh-i-Noor, and walked prayerfully around his son's sickbed with the diamond raised above his head; when he vacated the room, servants and concubines laughed and kissed as they anointed Humayun's body with oils and petals, and, secretly, made a xylophone of his protruding ribcage. In accordance with the deal, the Koh-i-Noor spared Humayun's life, and took Babur's instead.

Humayun recovered and began his reign, but was defeated in 1540 by Sher Khan's Afghan forces, and had to flee India and wander in exile. In loneliness—having had to abandon his wives, sons, and daughter—Humayun clung to the diamond, allowed it to become his companion in displacement, his imaginary friend. He spoke to it, and it spoke to him.

When he arrived, emaciated and bloodied by the terrain, at the threshold of Shah Tahmasp, the ruler of Persia, he was received with such uncommon generosity that the vulnerable Humayun burst into tears and offered the shah the Koh-i-Noor in gratitude. When the astonished shah had the diamond appraised, he was told that it was "above all price," and could only be measured against the collective expenditures of the remainder of the world, maybe even the universe. As a result, perhaps, of giving up the Koh-i-Noor, Humayun was restored to his throne, but the damage had been done. The diamond had bewitched him, and he longed for it with such intensity that only heavy doses of opium allowed him to bear it. A mere six months after his royal restoration, as he heard the muezzin's call to prayer, he fell down the long flight of stairs to his library and died, his skull cracked at the temple, his body twisted among the spilled books.

In subsequent generations, the diamond passed through the hands of the monarchic miscellany—shahs and kings, emperors and tsars—all of whom succumbed to premature deaths as a result of the possession. Even the East India Company fought for it, after the British annexed the Punjab on March 29, 1849. One of the terms of the Treaty of Lahore decreed, "The gem called the Koh-i-Noor which was taken from Shah Shuja-ul-Mulk by Maharajah Ranjit Singh shall be surrendered by the Maharajah of Lahore to the Queen of England." The East India Company wanted the credit for presenting the gem to the Crown and, according to Lord Dalhousie, the handsome thirty-five-year-old officer responsible for acquiring the Koh-i-Noor for the Crown, "The Court of the East India Company are ruffled by my having caused the Maharajah to cede to the Queen the Koh-i-noor . . . I was fully prepared to hear that the Court chafed at my not sending the diamond to them . . . They ought not do so . . . It was more for the honor of the Queen that the Koh-i-Noor should be surrendered directly from the hand of the conquered prince into the hands of the sovereign who was his conqueror." When Queen Victoria subsequently endured a beating at the hands of a confused officer, Dalhousie was unsurprised. "The several sad or foul events in England," he wrote, "lie at my door, as I have sent the Koh-i-Noor which always brings misfortune to its possessor."

In ensuing years, various nations—India, Pakistan, Russia, Turkey, Afghanistan, Iran—have claimed ownership of the diamond and have demanded its return. The British responded that they alone have clear title, given the confused history of the diamond, based on the claim that they did not "seize" the gem but had it "presented to them," as if the maharajah had had a choice in the matter. Even Lord Ballatrae, the great-grandson of Lord Dalhousie, devised a pathetic treatise in which he named himself as the diamond's rightful owner. Jawaharlal Nehru, the first prime minister of independent India, was more diplomatic when he said, "Diamonds are for the Emperors and India does not need Emperors."

The Koh-i-Noor that resides today in the center of the Maltese Cross of the crown that was made for Queen Elizabeth, consort of George VI, in 1937 is believed to be a fake (the original having been smuggled out of the U.K. during one of the routine maintenance-and-cleaning-of-the-crown productions). Historians speculate that the real gem lies either in the bowels of the Kremlin or among the subterranean labyrinths that house the Iranian crown jewels, but these claims remain unsubstantiated. More substantial: today, Babur's revered corpse rests in a shady corner of the Bagh-e Babur Gardens in Kabul among groves of walnut, cherry, quince, and apricot trees, a garden that has been alternately decimated and rebuilt over the years of foreign occupation, unrest, civil war, devastation carried out by the Taliban, and the U.S. war in Afghanistan. Mines and other unexploded ordnance lurk in the garden's mud walls, within which sit contemporary Afghans longing for a peaceful haven from war, some kind of imagined, euphoric future among plants and ancestors, however brief.

Pilgrims to Babur's tomb believe the many pigeons that flock the courtyard to be the spirits of good-hearted humans; the pilgrims wait patiently among these birds on the adjacent bench, the muted sounds of bombs detonating in the distance, for Babur's spirit to emerge and address their traditional questions. "If you want a simple life," Babur will answer, "I can turn you back into a pigeon and you can lead the uncomplicated life of a bird." The pilgrims will respond, as they have for centuries, "I want a solution to my predicament as a human and not as a pigeon," and Babur—ever inscrutable—will disappear, as he always does, into the fog.

Chapter 10

Odyssey to Die Houthoop

"YOU'VE GOT TO STOP BEING ALONE WITH MEN LIKE THAT," LOUISA says of MacDonald. We hold hands and stare beyond the motel parking lot, watch the desert come together with the sea. Out there are bones and wings, the outlines of flamingos, green and white beaded shells, emptied by the sea of the soft bodies of the urchins. We see worthless rocks, and diamond hoses. Resisting the wind, these things whistle and gurgle and ring, but not like bells.

Louisa and I look up and into—toward the airborne and the impacted—so as not to look back. The sky hangs over us like a shroud. This, we tell ourselves, is trying again. We go inside. We close the door. We eat a supper of ketchup sandwiches. We shower with brittle blue soap.

The next morning, I wake with swollen eyes, sad but ready. Louisa and I drive to the Kleinzee Café to buy a few supplies before trying to find this Die Houthoop guesthouse. I've asked a few locals how to get there, and the directions I've received conflict. Some believe the place is no longer in existence. Some believe it never existed—that it's a mirage, a pipe dream, a way-station for fugitive spirits who wish to hide out from both the land of the living and the land of the dead. "I'm afraid," Louisa tells me, and so am I, but I keep quiet.

At the Café, the cashier and the customer with whom she was conversing give us astonished stares. Anyone not from Kleinzee incurs such wariness. I wonder if the town's narrative, as written and self-published and poorly bound with black plastic coiling, and poorly copied on a machine with low toner by De Beers, still stands. I wonder if they still feel themselves part of a "very special, but isolated community." If they still feel "that they were never treated as mere numbers."

The Café is a hoarder's version of a convenience store (not really a café at all, though one can order a cup of coffee here), hospice for the unwanted and forgotten goods of the past decade or so, the cardboard boxes stacked, still filmed in cellophane, floor to ceiling, forming a labyrinth through which the customer must snake, beneath the dim flicker of the one working fluorescent, in order to make it to the actual shelves, and the unwrapped jars and cans, themselves garnished with a veneer of dust so thick that I can (and do, on a museum-worthy tin of Koo Chakalaka) draw my initials into it. Apparently, I was here, surrounded by imperishables.

The two women watch us, and whisper. Because there are no carts or baskets, we fill our hands, and when we approach the counter, the two women straighten.

Of course, they know who we are. When the desert blows itself through the open doorway, the dust sparkles and whirls about their heads. I am dizzy. The women appear to be dancing with the cashier's counter between them, as if bound, forever sepia and strobe-lit, to some epileptic phenakistoscope. They volunteer the information that they used to work at the mine, but were retrenched by MacDonald ("but we don't blame him"). The customer, who is here more for conversation than to shop—clad in purple blouse, purple pants, and purple pillbox hat—tells us that her last name is Carstens. "As in Jack Carstens," she brags.

The Carstens family name is still often invoked in contemporary Kleinzee. On August 15, 1925, freed from the anchor of the First World War and his remote military station in British India (where he served as an officer in Queen Alexandra's Gurkha Rifles under T. E. Lawrence, a.k.a. Lawrence of Arabia), Jack Carstens returned to the Kleinzee area, and began to dig into Namaqualand in earnest. "It was Jack Carstens," the customer tells us, "who discovered the first diamond" in the sand of what was to become known as the Diamond Coast.

Carstens, during his service, had had it with Lawrence's self-obsession and slandered the man's affectation of dressing like a Bedouin and his birth as a bastard. By the time Carstens met him, Lawrence, exhausted with his own fame, had become withdrawn, given to speaking to his men of his dreams as if they were true.

Itinerant and out of sorts himself, Carstens found solace in and communion with Lawrence's habit of muttering tenderly to his beloved pet carrier pigeons, which had served him so well during his glory days in the Arab Revolt. Carstens would eavesdrop as Lawrence whispered to the birds of the heroics of their antecedents, which had been trained in coops in Palestine, telling them about the honeyed messages their progenitors had carried between Damascus and Cairo (to and from the British government officials stationed there).

Lawrence laughed as he spoke of swimming in the Mediterranean, facing on shore the warehouses full of cotton, rice, and cigarettes, and the water tank on which he saw alight one of his carriers, exhausted from its long flight, the bird grooming itself and recuperating, until Lawrence fetched a stone from the seabed and threw it at the pigeon, in order to startle it back into flight. Lawrence became wistful as he spoke of waste and karma, how the Turks had seized the wheat from Jewish farms and how, in ignorance, they had stored it in uncovered troughs, and so, when it rained, the upper level germinated and provided a feast for the journeying pigeons, who ate most of the lot, thriving while both the confiscators and confiscatees starved. And Lawrence sighed as he spoke of the necessity of killing some of his best pigeons during raids, lest they be captured and used by enemies in Ottoman Turkey; how they buried the carcasses in cotton fields and plowed over their graves.

These pigeons, and the stories Lawrence whispered to them in depression, aroused Carstens's nostalgia and empathy. Until the discovery of the fateful diamond, his father, William Carstens, would-be prospector, supported his family as a Port Nolloth shopkeeper and as the local Reuters correspondent, in the days when the press agency still used carrier pigeons to transmit information. As such, both father and son had personal relationships with pigeons, which they used to disseminate information about Jack's discovery, inspiring the influx of treasure hunters, the De Beers syndicate included. In the "Protection Reports," issued on sheets of parchment, De Beers began referring to all non-company treasure seekers as " 'out-of-works,' crooks, and undesirables . . . trespassing upon the Company's properties with the object of 'prospecting.' The precaution was taken of doubling the guards . . . The trifling punishment inflicted [by the police force and magistrate] in these cases is a direct incentive to further crimes of this nature." And so they began to take matters of punishment into their own hands.

Jack Carstens, meanwhile, fell under the spell of a charismatic Cape Town businessman who sold his diamond claims without his knowledge, forcing Carstens to work as a security guard on the very claims he had "discovered." He dreamed of writing a book and mulled incessantly over possible titles, the one he always came back to being "A Fortune Through My Fingers." Soon, a glut of diamonds was unearthed from the shells of fossilized *Ostrea prismatica* oyster beds in sites known as the Cliffs, hills known as the Twins, and a trench known as the Oyster Line, by wild-eyed, infighting men named Kennedy and Rabinowitz, Merensky and Reuning (the latter referred to diamond prospecting as his "old, true love," and bought ad space in local magazines and newspapers which he filled with his tirades against the moral fabric, illiteracy, faulty memories, and dictatorial natures of his competitors, Merensky especially).

Merensky had secured the largest claim among the men for a

total of 17,000 pounds, and, in less than a month, he extracted 2,762 diamonds, 487 of them found beneath a single flat rock (or so he bragged). "Ah, they were all a bunch of crooks," the purple-clad customer tells us, as the cashier frowns, "trespassing on what should have stayed in the Carstens family. A bunch of *gat kruipers* with the corrupt politicians." (*Gat kruipers* translates as *ass creepers*, the equivalent of brown-nosers.)

Desiring to protect his assets against what he called "the stampede to the Diamond Coast," Merensky, *gat kruiping*, traveled to Cape Town to meet with government officials (including the prime minister), to tattle on his competitors. Ears sufficiently bent, the government, effective February 22, 1927, issued an edict prohibiting all further diamond prospecting along the Namaqualand coast. Almost immediately, after stoking governmental pocketbooks, Ernest Oppenheimer and his Diamond Syndicate intervened, convincing officials that Merensky's distribution plans "could bring chaos to the market, with a total collapse in the value of diamonds." Oppenheimer was permitted to buy the entire output of the Namaqualand fields, promising to maintain a stronghold on the booty and release the diamonds very slowly onto the market, in order to fictionalize the element of rarity, and thereby value.

The newspapers, meanwhile, dubbed the Rabinowitz claim "a human story of hardship, determination, and triumph over public ridicule." The young, destitute, itinerant Jewish trader had originally come to Namaqualand to open a general store, to unwind in the desert, as he was suffering from post-traumatic stress disorder, having fought the British in the Anglo-Boer War. Until he could afford his modest business venture, he read books about diamonds, and explored what the newspapers incorrectly believed to be "inaccessible areas of Namaqualand, travelling on foot or by wagon . . . sleeping on the open veld." In this way, he became intimate with the terrain. He went bankrupt. His few friends ridiculed him, nicknamed him King Solomon.

Desperate, a mere one day after his friends saddled him with this moniker, Rabinowitz discovered his first diamond in the Buchuburg zone, which was quickly claimed by the state. All mineral rights were thereafter transferred to the Crown, and De Beers swept in and overtook the land, buying the entirety of Kleinzee for two hundred pounds sterling. Rabinowitz retreated to the settlement of Steinkopf and finally opened his store, sold bread and beans to the inpouring of De Beers officials. Due to his Jewish heritage, in spite of his discoveries, his few friends forsook him. He slept amid stock in the back of his store. In cages beneath a tarp, in the sand behind his quarters, he raised pigeons in secret, for company. He was known to mutter to his birds about faith and "the theory of diamonds." Soon, a mob the newspapers called "a syndicate of local men," likely working for De Beers, kicked Rabinowitz off his property and claimed it as their own, believing diamonds could be found there. His shop was demolished, his birds killed for sport. Some say he fled to Johannesburg. Most say he died there alone.

"A real shame," Ms. Carstens says, her purple bracelet shimmying, the cashier still frowning. "He was the only one at that time—besides Jack Carstens, of course—who knew the details of this land."

Soon, geologists in the employ of De Beers, combing the littoral, decided that the fossilized plant material in which diamonds were embedded dated back 17 million years to the Miocene Age, but had little idea as to how the diamonds had gotten there in the first place. They wondered, in exclusive articles for the *Mining and Industrial Magazine*, "Were these gems tossed from a submarine bed and cast upon the shores by the fury of Atlantic gales many centuries ago? It is 'the riddle of the sands' again, an enigma which perhaps man will never satisfactorily be able to answer." Others felt that assured wealth was its own sort of answer, a solving of the mystery. "And the fabulous wealth of Namaqualand was finally revealed!" proclaims the sepia newsletter in the Kleinzee Museum, between old, laminated photographs of hired hands hoisting pickaxes and newer ones of confiscated pigeons, one of which is having her head pinched between the thumb and forefinger of a mine security guard whose head is cut off above his smiling mouth. So, the tasks with which Carstens's Reuters pigeons were originally saddled effectively launched the diamond industry here, and, strangely, those pigeons begat this subsequent generation of pigeons who were raised by the inpouring of laborers, and used for launching the counter-industry of diamond smuggling.

In the flickering, haunted-house light of the Kleinzee Café, Ms. Carstens nods, a big diamond ringing her wedded finger, diamonds studding her earlobes and strung around her neck. Even the cashier sports an enormous diamond ring, and I feel, sans adornment, as if I'm crashing a secret society. A wormy anxiety accumulates in my belly.

"Have either of you heard of someone called Mr. Lester?" I ask. Louisa squeezes my shoulder. I'm desperate for someone beyond Johann MacDonald to humanize this man, to lend him pathos. I want someone to refer to him, simply, as "nice," or something. Instead, Ms. Carstens and the cashier only stare at each other, refuse to look at me.

"I'm trying to find Die Houthoop guesthouse . . . I'm hoping to meet him there tonight . . ."

The cashier looks to Ms. Carstens as if for approval, then returns her eyes to her register. Her fingers hover over the buttons there as if they are piano keys. "Down the main road out of town," she says, "pass through the gate, and keep driving. You'll see a road on the left, but it won't look like a road. Take it. Two rights after that, and then two lefts, and then the curves, and then it's straight for a while, and then it's right, and straight again, and soon you will see the lights."

"Thank you," I say.

I swallow hard, and buy our tins of viennas in brine, chicken-flavored Spookies (cousin to Cheetos), and an envelope of Grandpa's Headache Powder. The cashier takes my coins in silence. Louisa and I step through the doorway. Ms. Carstens mutters, "Fools."

*

JOHANN MACDONALD WAS RIGHT: DIE HOUTHOOP GUEST FARM IS indeed located deep into the desert, an hour's drive from Kleinzee proper along unnamed roads that traverse the middle of nowhere. I try to hold the cashier's directions in my head. My palms are sweaty, and my throat dry. The early evening sun lends even the roadkill a misleading silver lining.

Along the way, we stop on the road shoulder to get a closer look at the corpse of an albino camel that rots in the desert next to the withered chassis of a Tata Sierra. Next to this is a Jock of the Bushveld splash pool, childless, the water spoiled and evaporating, the color of Assam tea. Into this water, I toss what appears to be a Lower Paleozoic trilobite fossil, heaved up onto this sandy crust from the silicified gneissic beds of Namaqualand, for luck. It has the feel in my palm of one of those pressed pennies one passed through the decorative vises of the Midwestern carnivals of my childhood, until they emerged elongated and embossed with images of clowns and Ferris wheels and state flowers and state birds. Naturally, I make a wish—the same one I've been making for months—and, unnaturally, when the three-lobed arthropod hits the water, there is no splash, no sound at all, just the sinking.

As I pull into the red sand parking lot of Die Houthoop, the sun is low, angry. "Oh, God . . ." Louisa says. She sees him before I do. A man stands in the parking lot's center in a welding mask and green rubber smock, the sparks of his torch catapulting from the facemask of a diamond diving suit. The suit looks as if it should be hanging in some 1940s' superhero locker, still damp with the orris and seawater of old heroics; a collectible relic sewn when our species' bodies were slightly larger than they are today, when our fingers and toes still bore webbing between them, when we were flippered and winged.

"Do you think that's him?" Louisa asks. I have no answer, but somehow, I don't think so. I don't think Mr. Lester would feel the need to hide his face, though—if we're to believe all we've heard—he's surely confident in his power to disappear those who behold it.

The grounds of Die Houthoop are littered with the remains of armoires and hutches, metal dishes and cups tattered with rust, picture frames framing no pictures, all in the name of shabby chic décor, some high-minded conservationist aesthetic—the wreck at the center of the wreck.

The hostess, Jackie, rushes from inside the red stucco office. She wears a white lace jabot, stained by past meals, which bunches like a bib over her blouse-front. The tops of her feet burst like soufflés from blue house slippers. The waistband of her black pants is damp with sweat, and her short brown hair is dusty. She's wearing yesterday's red lipstick. Yesterday's perfume. The air smells of creosote, yeast, and acetylene. The man in the welding mask seems to be looking at us through the slot of protective glass, his retinas hot, his corneas steaming. He strikes me as some sort of muscle at the gate.

I fill out our information in the guestbook, and when Jackie briefly turns around to gather clean towels, I flip the pages, hoping to find evidence of Mr. Lester's reservation, further proof of his status as human—an address, a phone number, a full name. Two pages back, I find an entry empty of all information save for a cursive *L* in the "Name" field. Jackie turns with the towels and, heart accelerating, I fumble with the guestbook, nearly drop it to the floor, as I quickly flip back to our page.

Though I don't invoke Mr. Lester's name, and don't dare use the word *smuggle*, Jackie narrows her eyes and asks if I have a slip of paper. From my pocket, I retrieve an old supermarket receipt, printed with reasonably priced guava fruit leather and passion fruit juice, lamb neck, and Sunlight laundry soap. On it, in carmine ink, she writes, *Mr. Lester, 12-midnight.*

"How did you know?" I ask.

"Very few visit this place," she says. "And the people who still live here—we talk."

Why does it have to be midnight? Why does everything have to be so liminal out here? Jackie walks us to our room, through the twist-ing passages of the courtyard littered with donkey sculptures fash-ioned from rusted barrels and coffee cans and painted bubblegum pink, tangles of barbed wire, bleached mobiles made of animal bones and mussel shells, the sound of them in the wind horrifying, tapping some coded message on the inner side of a coffin lid; smashed oxi-dized wagon wheels, the guts—springs and levers—of old vises and presses filling the brown inch-deep sulfur water of the putrid concrete fountains, gangrenous hope chests and wash basins, dishes, cabinetry, padlocks . . .

Jackie opens the door to the room. The windows at the foot of the bed afford a view of the aviaries and coops—the African gray parrots, Namaqua doves, chickens, roosters, grouse and guinea fowl, yelping peacocks, cinnamon warblers, bustards, larks and babblers, sugarbirds and pigeons. It seems as if every confiscated and executed bird from every Diamond Coast mining village somehow has a living counter-part here in Die Houthoop's courtyard. I wonder if they are real, or if they are spirits. They confer with one another across bird languages. They kick up the dust. Beyond the birds, through the wire and mesh and bars of the enclosures, stout green water tanks and an odd rusted platform bearing the corpse of a pickup truck decompose; and beyond that, the red desert stretches. Something about the room feels pur-gatorial, as if a holding cell. On the woven mat before the bathroom, stains that resemble blood spatter. Jackie says, seemingly from some great distance, "So this will be suitable?"

I can hardly make out her words. Louisa looks at me. She forces a smile for Jackie. The windows are without curtains, and the layer of sand on the concrete floor is so thick I can see my footprints. Jackie leaves us. The bed's white sheet, crispy, crunches under my weight, smells of a long-shuttered museum. Simply by lying on it, I feel as if I'm violating the rules.

"I feel like we're awaiting trial," I say.

"We should get out of here," Louisa says, and I know she's right.

"We can't now," I say.

She sits down next to me on the bed. She does not touch me. "I know," she says through her teeth.

The birds roost in the hollow of a dead cement mixer, pace among the metal bladders—what appear to be mortar bombs from old wars. They rove among mannequin heads and dressmaker's dummies, which Jackie hollows out with a knife, fashioning small, dirty gardens from the torsos and skulls, planting blooms and herbs, cutting stalks that burst from eyes and ears, ribcages and the swell of hips. The paint of old mannequin eyebrows and the old pins of late tailors still hold fast to their repurposed skins. I wonder if Jackie uses these "mannequin planters" as scarecrows, or if she uses them, conversely, to attract birds.

Once the dummies are so groomed, Jackie threads a chain through the heads and bodies, and hangs these cadaver gardens from the ceiling of the long corridor that leads from Die Houthoop's spare office into the large attached house where she cooks, watches television, and sleeps. Closest to the threshold, as a sort of welcome, is the sole pair of fiberglass arms—one cut off at the elbow, the other at the triceps—dangling just in front of a modest chandelier, and thereby hauntingly backlit, chipped white hands offering a pubic tangle of flowering lemon thyme.

For the umpteenth and most indelible time in my life, I whistle "Hotel California." I feel as if Mr. Lester and his team of cosmic sidekicks here may be hatching some punishment for our trailing of him to his desert lair. On the bed, Louisa's eyes are closed, though I know she is not sleeping. I wonder if she's envisioning what I'm envisioning—our bodies being buried out in this desert later tonight. In the courtyard, the man in the welding mask, frightening and fatherly, nurtures his sparks toward conflagration, his torch beaked with feathery flame. Beneath his helmet, surely, a skull outsized and orphic, perhaps even

the decapitated head of Orpheus himself having found a new body in
the heat of the Namaqua desert and its slim resource of oxy-fuel.

*

HERE, IN DIE HOUTHOOP'S INNER SANCTUM, IS THE IDEA OF DECENT
and resurfacing made manifest, Orpheus having trailed his betrothed,
Eurydice, to the underworld, after she was bitten by a poisonous snake
while escaping from the clutches of Aristaeus, the lecherous, cheese-
making, beekeeping Lothario-god.

Frantic, Orpheus searches for his bride in the underworld, combing the alluvial beds of its five sleepy rivers (flowing with woe, lam-
entation, vow, fire, and forgetfulness), the diamond gate guarded by
that three-headed dog Cerberus and the kingdom that lies beyond,
the Tartarus abyss—that torture dungeon of the wicked, black hole of
the Titans—its adamantine gate comprised of diamonds so hard that
no soul can cut through it and flee. Orpheus survives on the cuisine of
the fairies—toasted ant heads and fetid dewdrops—before moving on
to the more substantial breasts of the underworld doves, which he eats
in desperation, doves being in this realm the birds of eternal sorrow,
thus predicting their prominent place—still today—in Greek funerary
sculpture.

As Orpheus navigates the diamonds and doves of the underworld, he keeps sane by playing his lyre, the beauty of his grieving
music compelling the doomed ghosts to weep. For a brief moment,
the business of the underworld ceases. Sisyphus—forever doomed to
roll his boulder uphill, only to have it roll back down—is granted brief
respite, as he squats on his rock and eavesdrops on the song. Even the
innumerable Furies—those infernal goddesses and chthonic deities of
retribution—take the time to listen and, for the only instant in their
execrable existence, sob.

This sobbing allows Orpheus not only momentary artistic satisfaction, but also a sad aural pathway, which he tracks all the way to his

beloved Eurydice, who crouches against a pillar of diamonds with two pigeons of sorrow playing in her hair. Because his music is so beautiful, the underworld powers-that-be grant Orpheus permission to smuggle his bride back to the upper world, but his desire for reassurance undoes him. Just as the two lovers come to the diamond portal, daylight beginning to show itself, he turns around to make sure she's still there with him, and as he gazes finally on her face, she extends her arms toward him in a foiled last embrace as she's dragged back into the depths, now irretrievably dead. Their final communal act—akin to their final act before they wed—was the feeding of two would-be escapist pigeons.

This is certainly not the only time pigeons were used as symbols for the faulty human soul, for its penchant to sin. In *The Odyssey*, after Odysseus and Telemachus sleep with maidens who then prove themselves disloyal, Homer recounts:

> With that, taking a cable used on a dark-prowed ship, [Odysseus] coiled it over the roundhouse, lashed it fast to a tall column, hoisting it up so high no toes could touch the ground. Then, as doves beating their spread wings against some snare rigged up in the thickets—flying in for a cozy nest, but a gristly bed receives them—so the women's heads were trapped in a line, nooses yanking their heads up one by one, so all might die a pitiful ghastly death . . . They kicked up their heels for a little—not for long.

Once again, the pigeon-as-simile appears in the lexicon of punishment.

And so, doubly heartbroken by losing Eurydice for the second time, Orpheus returns to the surface and plays his music only for inanimate objects, trying in vain to wring tears from the trees and rocks. He swears off the love of other women, becomes an unrepentant misogynist, and takes any further sexual act in the form of pederasty. Angered by the destructive ways in which he fetishizes his grief, an all-female mob of Thracian bacchantes attacks Orpheus and tears his body apart, as if the carcass of a beast in the amphitheater. The women toss his still stubbornly singing head into the Hebrus River, and heave his lyre to the heavens, where it now plays for the satellites, Bartholomew, the deaf ears of the *Voyager* Golden Records which silently imprison so much sound.

Bacchus, enraged at the vigilanteism of his murderous female constituents, turns them into trees, doomed to be forever rooted in one place, their branches adorned only by pigeons weak enough to be tempted by the bait traps of the cunning fowlers of the world.

Strange how our narratives turn our very human need for reassurance of love in the face of tragically intense (or even just vaguely unique) circumstances into a punishable offense: Orpheus and Eurydice, Izanagi and Izanami, Lot and his wife, all of which carry auxiliary dogmas about creation, birth, rebirth, metamorphosis . . . In these stories, doubt is punished, but in life, doubt is paramount, the essential, if ephemeral, counterpart to food, water, and air in the survival game.

"An impossible repetition," Mehdi Belhaj Kacem might have called these narrative tropes in *Transgression and the Inexistent*. "To begin with, event *is* repetition: mimesis . . . *instituted* repetition becomes a 'second nature' of our daily life"; the sort of redundancy—chained to a suffocating hindsight—that characterized the fate of Sisyphus, and made of him a technomimetic animal: a rotor, a gear, a gyroscope, a tweezers.

"It is indeed the incompletion of his love story," says Sophie Chiari of Orpheus in *Renaissance Tales of Desire*, "which seems to him totally unbearable . . . [and he becomes] a dangerous and irrational creature. Love, thus, cannot be reduced to a spiritual form of desire. Its consummation is what makes it real."

So, we put up decorations, and feign interest in them until the interest bears the dimensions of reality; hang art on our walls, diamonds from our fingers; stuff pigeons into our coops and our lunch-bins, fix them onto our rafters and our trees, and alternately use them and worship them, love them and hate them—all to serve the kind of myth we birthed from our boredom, to keep busy, until the stories with which we've laden them bear such an overwhelming and conflicting epochal arc that they can stand in for ourselves. Even the secrets stymied in our hearts are doomed—by way of heartbeat—to the underworld redundancy that so plagued the souls of Tartarus; the heart ever looking back on itself for that next known hiccup, reassurance made electric and innate inside of us.

But unlike Sisyphus, we are not entombed in myth to the point at which evolution ceases. We can better bear our burden by affixing it to something exterior—the feet of the birds we've so judiciously complicated—and setting it into the air, the upper world, where things are free to love one another and to tear one another apart in a more forward-moving sort of way. The most we can hope for is to be like those things—to have our best instruments tossed skyward after the terrestrial world has ripped our heads off for our transgressions. At least Orpheus knew what his best instrument was.

In this way, we can make of the pigeons, and the diamonds tied to them, beasts who straddle both worlds (if there's nothing to fall from, one can't fall from grace), and who can deliver to us answers from one that the other cannot offer. Of course, we try to believe this against the strong odds of our realizing that they're just birds and rocks with which we happen to be sharing the planet right now; realizing that the ways in which they navigate and throw their light are unanswerable except in this reductive sort of way, and in this sort of way, bathed in soft mystery, we tell ourselves we can commune with them, *communion* being just another moving part of *appropriation*. Redundancy is the mask we pull over silence.

In the myth, Orpheus's head floated downriver, and though his soul was reunited with Eurydice in the underworld, the fate of his head remains debated. If De Beers's "forever" myths are any indication, it still sings, having fallen through space, time, story, and landscape, the river emptying into a plain rife with diamonds, the head descending and descending some shaft until it landed here, on the shoulders of this man welding something to something in the Namaqualand abyss—itself guarded by a diamond gate of sorts—doomed to be concealed for all eternity behind this mask, its song sung now only for itself, reverberating against the helmet walls, never again reaching the ears of an audience who, as a result, will know less of rapture.

*

"ORPHEUS?" I ASK THE MAN IN THE MASK. NO ANSWER. BEHIND him, the pigeons of Die Houthoop resist the temptation of his sparks and live, if not in the heavens, then in all unlikelihood on this corner of ruined earth where their species is corporately hunted.

Since Mr. Lester is due to arrive only at midnight, I decide to take a nap, ready myself for the encounter. I lie down next to Louisa and doze for an hour or so. When I wake, there's no man in the welding helmet. Jackie's presence is testified to only by the sound of dripping water in the house, of a fork colliding with a knife. In the aviaries, the shivering of wings. In the coops, low, ground-level flops. It's late, but still too hot. The piles of junk—decorative and otherwise—seem overcooked, strung out. Hordes of lizards scramble into the loneliness, each one damaged, missing a body part. In the house, a plant sprouting from a composite pelvis is watered. A tine comes together with a blade.

Chapter 11

Champagne and Death at Dark

The Origins of a Pigeon Obsession

A FEW YEARS AGO, WHEN RUMMAGING THROUGH THE STORAGE closet at my parents' house, I found my old baby book—a scrapbook my mom compiled of my toddlerhood interests. It was filled with Post-it note addendums, marginalia, paper clips, and staples. My own desire to fetishize the artifact pointed to a disturbed and disturbing self-absorption, and as I squatted in the shadows of the closet, smelling the sweet rankness of old sleeping bags, and opened the cover (which had an orange pterodactyl on it), I felt a measure of shame wedge into the crevices of my excitement. According to my mom's evenhanded documentation, I was, at four years old, prone to disappear among the stacks of local libraries, seeking out books on ghosts. In 1980, under "Interests," my mom wrote, in blue script, "Anything ghoulish."

It would take another five years for me to marry said interest with birds. I was in fifth grade in 1985, and my English teacher, Mrs. Bircheim, as evidenced in the yearbook pictures, bore the most robust perm in the whole of Aptakisic Junior High—even more so than head cheerleader Joelle Manewith, more so than Spanish 1 teacher Mrs. Lipcott. Mrs. Bircheim was built like a stork, if not a pigeon, and when she swallowed her spit amid lectures on climaxes and participles and *Johnny Tremain*, she swallowed with her whole body.

Portions of the junior high school were still under construction and walled off with Visqueen, those thick sheets of translucent plastic, behind which we would watch ghostly men in ghostly blue jeans and yellow hard hats bolt together the rafters in which pigeons began to roost. Occasionally, a pigeon would find its way beyond the construction curtain and into the locker rooms and classrooms, staff lounge and cafeteria, where its cries would commune with those of the bird-fearing students and teachers, until Mr. Dino, the resident janitor, stalked the hallways brandishing his mop like a lance.

In 1985, smuggling allowed many world economies to survive—cocoa from Ghana to Togo, peanuts from Senegal to Gambia, onions from Nigeria to Niger, diamonds from South Africa to the United States. Protected from all of this illicit trade by the humid green cinderblock of the junior high classroom, its smells of pencil shavings and pigeon shit, its communal-use protractors and compasses and art-gum erasers, I thought of escape, and of blood, and of anything more dangerous than agreements—subject–verb, or otherwise.

My friend Ryan and I began meeting after school, lying on our bellies on my bedroom's beige carpeting, notebooks split open before us. We decided to collaborate on a serial—linked gross-out stories called "Death at Dark" (II, III, IV . . .), which featured an anonymous serial killer and an ever-fresh set of victims. We sensed in these stories the beginning of a conversation, and we wanted it to be more than one-sided. We decided to show our extracurricular work to Mrs. Bircheim, who—in spite of the derivative subject matter—was so excited that Ryan and I were inspired to write beyond the parameters of her syllabus that she allowed us to present each new installment aloud to the class. Mondays began with our readings, and soon we realized that to keep our audience riveted, we needed to ratchet up the gruesomeness with every installment.

It was "Death at Dark XXI," I think, that culminated with the killer forcing a man's hand into a sink drain and turning on the garbage disposal. I remember the description (it was mine) of the man's stump as he removed it from the drain, the blood "running like egg yolk down his wrist." Just as the victim was about to run from the kitchen, a pigeon flew through the open window into the house. With one hand, the killer grabbed the man by the collar, and with the other, he snatched the bird out of the air, mid-flight, and in a movement like modern dance, stabbed the man in the heart with the bird's head, the pigeon asphyxiating in the chest cavity, wings madly flapping. In the story, man and bird die simultaneously, their spirits braiding and ascending like DNA; and, as we read this to our rapt classmates, Shannon Everly—the cheerleader on whom I had a serious crush—started to cry. Duke Lee, the class clown, began to mock-wail, ridiculing Shannon, and I didn't know what to do, how to feel about this.

Mrs. Bircheim banned us from reading any further installments. We had gone overboard. I was confused, but electrically so: our writing had power. I sensed some kind of potential energy in this—a little delicious, a little malign, and wholly addictive.

Later that year, at the Spring Fling dance, I sipped magenta punch, checked my zipper, and smiled at the adult chaperones, until I worked up the courage to ask Shannon—who wore a pink, poofy-sleeved dress—to dance. And this was not just any dance, but the famed and nerve-racking Champagne Snowball dance, wherein the DJ, a middle-aged man in a white button-down shirt and white button-fly jeans, would lean into his microphone at various intervals during the song (it was Whitney Houston's "Saving All My Love for You"), and, mustering the sort of vocal inflection that depended on the creepiest kind of lechery, the spittle glowing disco-ball silver on his lips, his blond mustache rustling breathily and too-loud on the grille, croon, "Champaaaagnnne." At this directive, we young dancers were supposed to express some sort of affection for each other, be it the quick hug, or smile, or hand squeeze, or—for the courageous few—a kiss on the cheek, and then part ways, searching in the half-dark like bemused electrons for another dance partner with whom to finish the song.

I was shocked when Shannon said yes, and she said yes within earshot of Mr. Morteo, the balding social studies teacher with a toothbrush mustache, who nodded at me and winked in that *Attaboy* sort of way, in spite of my failing his class. Shannon's bangs were bigger than ever that night, and above her ears, her hair was laudably feathered. The DJ cranked the volume. Whitney sang her heart out. Shannon's hands twined around my neck, bunched my garage-sale sport coat. She smelled like hairspray and *herbes de Provence*—predominantly chervil and lavender. This was clearly a soap more expensive than the purloined motel soaps my parents supplied. She wore stud earrings that looked like real diamonds.

I had the sentence in my head for a full thirty seconds before I spoke it, and I knew time was limited. I knew the DJ was about to say, "Champagne." It was still a full decade before the Revolutionary United Front began their reign of terror in Sierra Leone, commandeering the local diamond mines; still a full decade before they began amputating the limbs and lips, ears and tongues of farmers and families who kept pigeons, before emptying their AKs into the birds themselves.

"I'm sorry I made you cry," I said to Shannon, and she finally looked at me. I felt as if I would tip over like a tree. We were shadows among shadows.

"It was the bird," Shannon said. "That the killer stabbed that man with that poor bird."

I didn't know what to say. I think I was confused, or concerned that Shannon lent her heart to the dead bird over the dead man.

I said, "Oh."

Her fingers adjusted on my shoulders. They tightened, and so did I.

"I have a mynah," she said. "She's my best friend. My parents had her before I was born. I've known her my whole life."

I didn't want to admit it, but I admitted it. "I don't know what that is."

"It's like a parrot. She's yellow and black. She talks."

"I'm sorry," I said.

She told me that the mynah would talk her to sleep as an infant, though, of course, she had no memory of that. For no good reason, or for all good reason, I said it again: "I'm sorry."

Shannon looked down, and I realized that there was not only a power in writing, but in birds too. I was going to ask the mynah's name. I promise I was. But beyond Shannon, within the cage of disco-ball light—the thousands of facets—I saw one of Aptakisic's stowaway pigeons fly into the gymnasium from the construction zone. Alarmed whispers punctuated Whitney.

But that's just an old fantasy
I've got to get ready, just a few minutes more

As if anticipating what was to happen next, Shannon pushed her face in between my neck and shoulder, and it was hot there, and it was wet there, and I could feel her body bounce, as I watched Mr. Morteo put down his cup of punch, put down his oatmeal-raisin cookie, and with a shoe that in my memory was huge, out of proportion with the rest of him, kick the pigeon along the length of the refreshments table. The first blow stunned it so that it couldn't take off, merely flap as it tried to walk away. Its sounds weren't audible above the song. The shadows danced, and Shannon hid her face, and I briefly thought she was clairvoyant, and I couldn't believe that no one else was seeing this. Behind the drape of the paper tablecloth, I watched Mr. Morteo, social studies specialist, bend his right knee, lift his foot into the air, and stomp, finally, down. His thin hair, once combed-over, hung in strings over his face. He looked surprised, and guilty, as if he had just meant to shoo it away, not kill it, but his body overtook him. For that moment, he looked like a boy, not a teacher. He dragged the sole of his shoe over the elastomeric floor.

"Cham-paaaagnnne," said the DJ.

Shannon lifted her head. She looked startled, but certain.

In the scattered light, Mr. Dino squatted, rose, dustpanned the carcass into a rubber trashcan on wheels. I took my hands from Shannon's hips, the cloth there having made my palms itch. She leaned in, and I didn't know what to do. My hands hovered in the air. Disco-ball light spilled over my fingers. Shannon breathed out through her nose. Lavender, lemon peel, rosemary, salt. The pigeon thumped the can bottom and, in this way, I was, for the first time by anyone outside my family, kissed on the lips.

Shannon walked into the dark, and I stood there, not wanting to search for another partner, not wanting to be standing up at all. I wanted to follow her, but I couldn't move, something futuristic and feathery opening up in my chest. The desire to lift off, the desire to keep secrets, or something even more ephemeral than that. I didn't know it then, or couldn't attach words to it, but I think I desperately wanted to say *I love you* to someone.

Bartholomew Variation #5

MSIZI'S MOTHER ALWAYS UNPACKS THE BAGS AT THE BIRD'S FEET indelicately.

Bartholomew flies toward some vision of her, in her threadbare pink bathrobe, tough bare feet on the concrete kitchen floor, her belly pressed to the oven, stirring cornmeal porridge.

Below, a shirtless man roasts a donkey leg over a fire built of desiccated cactus paddles. The smoke rises, and the bird is sandwiched in.

Bartholomew is neither here nor there, flying toward neither here nor there. He can be the pigeon that the early Dutch and British colonists here believed him to be, dependent as they were for their medicinal cures on Francis Bacon's *Sylva Sylvarum*. He can be the sort of pigeon whose head can be cut open and bled out onto the soles of the feet of men and women suffering from headaches ("The Soales of the feet have great Affinity with the Head"). His brain, when smeared onto the feet of the afflicted colonists, was said to have cured "Frenzy, Melancholy, and Madness." He can be the pigeon whose blood failed to cure the sick infant of one of the early diamond mine bosses in Kleinzee, who painted the baby's chest in vain with a red cross. He can be that same pigeon eaten by the grieving mine boss and his wife, in pie form, after they buried their child in the dust. He can most certainly be the pigeon that, if found perched on the edge of a diamond mine, the early colonists believed to be an "Aderyn y Corff," or "corpse bird," a prognosticator of death by collapse. If Bartholomew's belly feathers were even whiter than they are, these early colonists would have been even more frightened of him, associating as they did the color white—the color of their own skin—with vengeful ghosts.

Bartholomew's wings belong now to so many past and future birds, hatching and living, eating and mating, rearing, migrating, carrying and dying inside of him. And still, he somehow senses that he is forty-five minutes away from Msizi's mother's hands, and his coop.

There is water, or a mirage of water beneath him. He decides to land, take a much-needed drink. Unlike most birds, who tip their heads backward for the water to run down their gullets, pigeons can drink with their heads down, bowed, as if in mourning, or deference.

Chapter 12

This Security Thing

ABOVE DIE HOUTHOOP, A FISH-SHAPED STAR FALLS AND DIES. THE
birds squabble in their cages. I sit at the courtyard's picnic table—the
junkyard's inner circle—waiting for the enigmatic, venerable, perhaps
murderous, and perhaps mythological Mr. Lester to arrive. Filamen-
tous things thread the sky, insectile or hallucinatory, and everything
up there, in the face of this bird-sound, seems desperate to declare
some kind of fiercely independent identity, jockey for position. Louisa
remains in the room. In the dark, the desert opens up, extends itself,
the manifest destiny of reddish barrenness. The dunes and pans rush
at each other, and at their end, the Atlantic nurtures its nighttime
mist, reclaims the crispiest of the seaweed, makes it pliable again. I
think of Orpheus, and wonder which ghosts are turning back toward
Louisa and me. With the toe of my shoe, I test the elasticity of a fish
spine. It fails.

It's midnight. A car door slams. Right on time. My face is wet with
mist or drool. It's 12:01. I stand and follow the newly arrived Mr. Lester, the lumpy back of his tucked-in white button-down, losing itself
and reemerging in the murk.

Soon, we are sitting at Die Houthoop's de facto bar, another piece
of wood with bottles behind it. Mr. Lester is frumpish, and his jowl
shudders as he rounds the bar and—since it is otherwise unmanned—

pours us two deep glasses of Richelieu brandy. He has so far brandished no weapon, has not cut me open lengthwise. He looks tired, but it could be a ruse.

Mr. Lester is, in fact, Lester Le Roux, former director of De Beers mine security. Currently, he goes by various titles, each of them vague in a way appropriate to someone in the espionage trade: Top-Level Security Specialist, Top-Level Crime Investigations Analyst, Top-Level Law Enforcement Intelligence and Risk Management Assessor, Tactical Assessor of Threat and Vulnerability, Expert Operations Analyst, Expert Investigation Analyst, Top-Secret Security Military Intelligence, Psychometrics Expert, Polygraph Expert, Counter-Strategist, Director of Precision and Accuracy, Mitigator.

I try to decipher the hieroglyphs of his sweat stains, his white curly hair. He smells sour, mildewy, and familiar, as if ferreted out from the nethers of a forebear's storage closet. Jackie's mannequin heads and dummy torsos hover over us, gutted satyresses dripping with herbs, giving the bar the feel of some deserted inner sanctum, the naos in the waste. Half-dead white Christmas lights blink like surveillance cameras, and the desert guards the door. Lester match-lights a Camel unfiltered, slides the pack to me, and I light one too. Together, we cough, give off exhaust.

Lester wanted so badly to be a chemist, to unstitch the riddles of epigenetics, but instead, he followed the path of his friends, who joined the military to pay off their debts and then, he says, "I got into this security thing." We sip from our brandies and drag from our cigarettes, and when I set my glass down, I allow my pinky to brush his arm hair.

Given their perception of Lester's personality, the military beadledom pushed him toward a covert suborganization in counterintelligence, where he studied criminology, industrial psychology, information science, strategic thinking, and tacit knowledge management, ever feeling estranged from these disciplines at which he excelled.

"I had to force this distance," he says. "And always looked at security—the police—as a subculture. It's a sociological thing. Policing as a science. Police act differently than other people—they're constantly exposed to the negative aspects of society. They don't have many friends who are not police, and they talk about police work, which doesn't involve strawberries and cream and tea parties, but gore and guts. And this fuels aggression."

When De Beers attained an 85 percent share of the diamond market, they also faced the expected backlash, and so hired Lester to study the size and impact of the "illicit" diamond industry, and that's when his chronic sleeplessness began. De Beers briefly (and deliberately) decreased their market share to 50 percent, as they tired of their image as an evil monopolistic syndicate, and wanted to change public opinion.

"We're not miners," Lester says, speaking as De Beers. "We're just earth movers. We're strippers. Our biggest fear is diamonds traded for drugs, diamond mines that fund the huge cartels and international terrorism that fueled 9/11. De Beers has to manage that rhetoric, keep an eye on things, so they contract out satellites, flyovers."

Lester first came to Kleinzee in 2009 and found that "the entire of the local population was used as a medium in illicit trade."

He sips and sighs. He becomes MacDonald's warning from the future, parroting MacDonald's edicts. "Legitimate diamond dealers have to buy in to what is known as the Kimberley Certification—a regulatory thing, to assure the diamonds aren't illicit. The Ivory Coast was banned for years because of the terrible stuff going on there, but we've readmitted them. They have to accept the vision, you see? But, it's flawed as hell in any case. The certificates are issued by the country, so if you have a corrupt official somewhere in the process, they can demand a high price for the certificate and go ahead and issue it, and no one will know the difference. As a guarantee, you have only the integrity of people, and the human race is corrupt. We're driven by greed. Big Mr. G. De Beers's whole vision—the Diamond Dream . . . It has no intrinsic value. Its value comes from the foolishness of man. Even talking about this, I've got the fear of God in me for even thinking that there's value in that thing. I'm not allowed to say that. As being part of the company, one of the values is being passionate about the product, so I need to just see the longevity and foreverness of the stone. But the fear . . ."

I watch Lester glimpse himself in the mirrored glass behind the bottles. He can likely see only a portion of his face between them, a cheek, or one eye, but still he averts his gaze quickly, as if afraid of inspiring the aggression of his own reflection.

"We've already found the main diamond deposits in the world, and now the business is to control them," Lester says. "Diamond formation depends on lava and eruption, and that happens only so often. In Mozambique, I've seen trucks filled with Zimbabwean diamonds as if gravel. But most people can't control themselves. Around a diamond—like a beautiful woman—people lose control of their cerebellum. The illicit diamond trading is still good and well in Port Nolloth. After 1994 [and the fall of apartheid], and the change in dispensation, all of these police forces were disbanded. And they became services. We didn't *enforce* anything anymore, but *served* the people. The Diamond Squad was replaced by the Scorpions, who were more or less general crime investigators. Diamond investigations had to be funded by the industry itself—by De Beers. If they catch someone with diamonds, they know more than the police how to get them to talk.

"I just picked up a pigeon yesterday in Alex Bay. It was exhausted, a leather container around its neck. They have pictures of it at the security gate at Oranjemund. How long has this been going on? How long have pigeons been around? They have a number of uses other than being eaten. When I was a kid, the caretaker's son used to hunt pigeons off the school roof because they make a terrible mess, and he sold pigeon pies. Here, private companies are employed to eradicate the pigeons in town. I mean, the poor thing: a diamond can't steal itself. The sweepers develop special tricks where they flick a diamond into their mouth, or even kill another sweeper's pigeon. A carcass can be used as a conduit. And there are definitely on-site consequences if you are caught with a diamond."

Miles down the road, beyond the Kleinzee boom gates, in the shuttered museum, two crossed assegai spears—once the tools of mine security here—lurk in their closet of glass. I think of Msizi's lame pinky. And I think of how, in 1991, a digger caught trying to smuggle a rough diamond was shot through the head. Two years later, mine security discovered—by means redacted from their report—the "highest number of rough diamonds secreted in a bodily orifice": 475 of them with a mass of 431.56 carats "found in a condom retrieved from the suspect's anus" (which De Beers, in their report, referred to as "in the vicinity of the subject's lower stomach"), prompting the random cavity searches. In this bar, in this light, even stories of violence take on a soft glow. I sip. Lester sighs, woolly, a big sheep.

"But how'd it come to pigeons?" Lester says. "If you got hold of a diamond, you have to get it out of the area. You can't walk out the gate, because you'd get searched. And we have the X-rays, so if it was in an alimentary canal, or concealed in the foreskin or behind the scrotum, we would see it. One woman was caught hiding diamonds in the socket behind her glass eye. So the natural criminal instinct is to put it through the fence. Then we put in a second fence, made the distance between them greater, so they can't throw it over the second fence. Then, they got really clever with the bows and arrows, until we added even more fences and increased the distances even more. Something had to get over these fences, and it was a pigeon.

"So you train homing pigeons. Security would often follow the pigeons home, and wait for [the smugglers] there. From a risk management perspective, it was determined that we should not have pigeons in the mining areas, which included then the towns, this town of

Kleinzee—a closed-off town. And if you saw a pigeon, you would shoot it. You couldn't even bring in your own furniture. You got a house with furniture already inside. Those garages you see outside the security gates? Workers park there, walk through the gates, and then take the company buses wherever they needed to go—to the mine, shopping. Vehicles from inside town would never go outside town, and vehicles from outside town would never go inside town. You're removing a conduit. Believe you me, the smugglers know more than I do. That's why they still smuggle."

Outside, I hear the pigeons. Lester swirls his glass.

"Some people get away with it and some don't. I had a mine collapse here in 2012. I've got photographs of the boards that I put up on the fence that said, NO ENTRY, MINING AREA, KEEP OUT, WARNING, TRESPASSERS WILL BE PROSECUTED, which they actually took off the fence and used to keep the backflow of dirt from running into the little tunnel. The first photo I took was of that. I've confronted illegal diggers in the act and told them they'd have to cease what they were doing or I had to arrest them. I told them to just go home. And they say to me, 'We will cut your throat now and it will be days before your bosses know about it.' I'm quite afraid of what's happening. I'm there alone. I once had to get ninety people out of this mine by myself. Without security. We didn't have the staff to do it. And they swear at me, and curse at me, and say things like I won't see my wife by Christmas, because they've seen my eyes, and a spell has been cast. And I don't carry a firearm. Actually, I'm shit-scared of carrying a firearm, because then I'd be had up for murder.

"I worked a case with border police recently," he says. "In South Africa, we have a church [the Apostolic Faith Mission of South Africa, the country's largest Pentecostal church, which conducted most of its early missionary activity in mining compounds]—we call them the Blourokkies because they all wear that light blue dress. Extremely conservative. The ladies always have their hair in this little ball. We interrogated some of them and said, 'We know you smuggle diamonds, but how did you manage to get the diamonds across the border?' They admitted the ladies actually stuck it in their *bolla* [hair bun]. Can you imagine? You're being searched, and someone wants to undo your *bolla* . . . No, not if you're a Blourokkie . . ."

In the Christmas bar-lights reflected from the rheum in Lester's eyes, I can see them, muddied, pious bluebirds traipsing through the morning fog coming off the Orange River, their mouths tight, chins dimpled, approaching the Namibia–South Africa border, dragging behind them their children, their babies strapped to their breasts and their backs, their supplies heaped onto pulks sewn of the branches of scorched quiver trees, smuggling diamonds in their hair. They smuggle also the rotten edicts responsible for the success of their denomination, namely, their shunning of medical treatment in favor of divine healing through prayer, their enforced racial segregation within the religion and creation of an all-white executive council who controlled an all-white subcommittee, who in turn dictated what was to be the denomination's "black work"—building their churches, for instance—making of their black constituents an indentured labor force who would be expelled from the cloister should they defy the "holy" edicts laid down by that all-white executive council. Dressed in their blue cloaks, they cross the border, speaking in tongues or holding their tongues, their hands raised in the orant posture, their blue sleeves sagging like the secondary feathers of the underwing, retaining their gems, just as their version of Jesus—perhaps also veiled in blue, judge of the living and the dead—predicted.

"One of the guys," Lester continues, "took a baby and undid the nappy and put the diamonds in the nappy of the baby and then closed it up. Who is going to think of undressing a baby, thinking that there's diamonds in there?" (And clearly one border guard did think of doing this, as Lester has the story to tell.)

"A Bic pen," he says, and takes the pen from my hand, pinches the plastic bottom from it. "You take this off, and you have a canister for a diamond. Boot heels! Hollow them out!" he says, and leans back in his stool, shows me that his own boots are made of ostrich skin. "These impulses! The human brain is a fascinating machine. But we've taken new measures, too. We embed the floor of the X-ray rooms with wedges, so the floor tilts slightly, so these things show up more easily in shoes. You take a new vulnerability, and you put in a new control."

Lester passes me another cigarette and lights it for me. The bar lights are blinking, and Jackie's thyme is growing slowly and silently from the skull of a strung-up mannequin.

I wonder to what lengths De Beers may be willing to go to deploy Lester to implement these "new controls." In the book *Cross Currents: The Promise of Electromedicine, the Perils of Electropollution*, orthopedic surgeon and electrophysiologist Dr. Robert O. Becker cites research that proves that the human brain contains magnetite, a crystalline iron, which we share with whales, salmon, honeybees, and homing pigeons, the chemical component which, we believe, allows them to detect the vibrations in the earth's magnetic field responsible for their navigational prowess. In manipulating the magnetite, we can manipulate thought, some psychologists believe. Our telephone poles and our power lines, the whispers and hums emitted by our own brains, affect those of the pigeon; allow our homes to be their homes in a way we can't entirely call deliberate, but can't quite call generous either.

Perhaps this space shared by our brains can help explain B. F. Skinner's 1947 finding that pigeons are susceptible to what was believed to be an element strictly of the human condition: superstition. According to *Psychologist World*, "Skinner conducted his research on a group of hungry pigeons whose body weights had been reduced ... For a few minutes each day, a mechanism fed the birds at regular intervals. ... [T]he birds develop[ed] superstitious behaviour, believing that by acting in a particular way, or committing a certain action, food would arrive." One pigeon came to believe that if it turned around three times in succession counterclockwise, that would yield a feeding. Another was compelled to swing its head like a pendulum six times, three to the right, three to the left. And another nodded in bursts of five. *Yes-yes-yes-yes-yes*, it seemed to be saying before pausing, staring plaintively through the bars at the macrocephalic forehead of Burrhus Frederic, and then nodding again, five times fast, the magnetite in its brain confused, as if asking, as I am now, *How in the world did I end up here, with this man?*

I think of purposely starving pigeons. Of weighing them down. I think of how hunger, like the lobotomy, like carriage, changes the ways in which we perceive and traverse sound. The absence of it, or the intensity of it. The blood beating into our ears, or draining from them. How we make our way across this phonic pandemonium and back, as if along one of those saggy suspended jungle gym nets, toward some kind of home, or a memory of home, or simply a homey memory. I think of desperately wanting to land, even if at random. Funny, how I remember the miscarriages in sounds, as sounds; the first one in that Mexican restaurant in Mt. Pleasant, Michigan—the tortilla chips sweeping through the variable viscosities of the salsa and the guacamole, cracking in our teeth; the tamarind sodas burbling up through the straw as they passed over ice from glass to mouth, the horrible medical nature of the roomful of silverware ringing and screeching against the earthenware plates. And the absence of sound—the music Louisa and I missed, the sounds we chose to cut out of our lives from then on; how, even though we had second-row tickets, we skipped the Loretta Lynn concert at the Mt. Pleasant casino to go to the emergency room; how, even though we didn't see the show, and couldn't associate any specific songs with this first particular sadness of many, we still to this day cannot listen to Loretta Lynn's music.

"When I was driving in today," Lester says, "I saw this bird. It wasn't a vulture, but another kind of raptor. It had caught like a little rabbit thing. As I was coming over the Garies road, I saw it in the middle of the road there, and wondered what it was, and as I got closer, she flew up with this thing between her legs, and she could hardly get over the fence. It was too heavy for her. She was going to have to eat only some of it, and leave another piece of the kill. Strangely enough, I thought, they're built to move themselves. To carry only themselves. They're not built to carry a small lamb, although they'd enjoy eating it. And I thought about the pigeons who have actually collapsed in front of security buses, because the bags are too heavy for them."

I'm having trouble picturing Lester out of this bar, raptor-spotting; picturing him in the backseat of a car, or the front seat, eating a sandwich or petting a dog, dressing a salad or lighting a candle. Out there, so many hooded wayfarers mine the old abandoned dumps illegally, looking for diamonds. Lester cocks his head as if listening for their sneezes, the clearing of their throats. Or perhaps Lester is envisioning himself at the chalkboard of a chemistry classroom in the same way that I see myself as a father-to-be with my ear listening for tiny hiccups at Louisa's belly—as an ash drawing smudged with a thumb, the angles that once defined the shapes there rubbed out.

"In spite of all these ruthless things you hear about De Beers, I actually do care, and have a high regard for human rights," Lester says. "I'm heading up a division on voluntary principles of security in regard to human rights, and I'm even questioning our search procedures," and he sighs, sips, "because you can't search for a diamond by holding your hands inches away from the body. You need to touch the body. Human rights make it very difficult for security and easy for the criminals."

Lester hangs his head in silence, and I wonder if he's interrogating what he just said. I feel at a loss too. I no longer know what the best route is, how it is we should get from one place to another, but I do know that the pigeons' bones are conduits. That the air they navigate is rife with conduits. Lester's eyes are downcast, and so soft-looking it seems as if he's trying to call upon some wisdom that doesn't quite belong to him but he's inherited anyhow from some earlier version of ourselves, winged and preserved in the humid amber of the Jurassic.

Into this, Louisa walks. I've never seen her walk this way—shoulders back, neck extended, careful and confident, as if over ice. She's never looked so tall. Lester lifts his head. Louisa walks right past me, and right up to him. She towers over him. She holds up the first two fingers of her right hand, and somehow, he knows to slip a cigarette between them. She introduces herself and doesn't allow him to reciprocate. I can't believe what I'm seeing. She recounts to Lester the Namaqua legend of the eland, whose bones, when they run, are said to clap together like bells, the sound standing in for their bragging that they are the biggest and most beautiful of the antelopes, and therefore, they are cursed.

"Because you can hear them," Louisa says, her mouth not six inches from Lester's, "a mile away." She begins to cry, and Lester rises from his stool. He takes her in his arms, and she him, and they embrace like that for a while, and I can't believe this.

Eventually, as they must, they let each other go. When she can speak again, Louisa tells Lester the story I already know, of how her aunt bought a condemned hospital and turned it into her house; of how when Louisa and her brothers went to visit as children, they slept in beds in the old morgue wing. She tells Lester that against all presumptions, her nights spent there were blissfully dreamless. Lester is not confused by any of this.

Finally, Louisa sits, takes a stool between, and a little behind, Lester and me.

"I'm sorry," Lester says. "I'm sorry," he says, and retrieves his lighter, ignites her cigarette. She inhales. She exhales. She touches his leg. He calls her "my child . . ."

Lester opens his mouth again, and for a while, nothing comes out, and this is the sort of silence—one only enlarged by this landscape's wild infertility, and by the shutting down of the mine, and the resultant hypoperfusion that wipes out a community, and by the distance between beakers and human rights violations, sludge tests and the atom bomb, his childhood bed and tonight's barstool, and other gulfs between here and Port Nolloth; and the gulf between this barstool and the bed back in Michigan with the green sheets we called Sea of Green or the Jelly Green Sea on which Louisa and I decided—yes, yes—to make what we believed would be a baby—this is this sort of silence that Lester seems to inhabit, white-haired and lost, a silence indicative, it seems, of many people in positions of power after you've gotten them alone, and after hours, in a bar.

Without turning from Lester, Louisa takes my hand, squeezes it, and lets it go. The wind outside models the last stage of idleness before atrophy.

"Trust me," Lester says. He looks neither at Louisa nor at me. His lips are brandy-sheened. I want to see him out of this deserted bar, out of this light, but know I never will, and this knowledge, which Lester certainly shares, frees us to treat each other as momentary Namaqualand nighttime receptacles for the unburdening of our hearts. "If I told Johann MacDonald all that I know," he says, "he wouldn't be able to sleep at night. Such regrets. There's a hell to what I do. I would far sooner go and plant daisies. I want to get out of this." He briefly makes eye contact with me, then with Louisa. He picks at his thumbnails.

"I don't want to do this with the rest of my life," he says. "It's been fourteen years of hell. People know that I know these things. People don't like me because I know these things. I don't want people to think of me like this. Ten people killed in that mine collapse in 2012—some of them were underage, but at least one man was over sixty . . . Everything I know is intellectual property of the company, so I can't write books about what I know. I'm looking at what I'm going to do now. And when I'm done, I don't want to be paranoid. I don't want pigeons, for instance, to have that [smuggling] connotation. I want them to just be birds again."

Bartholomew Variation #6

THE IMPACT OF LANDING SENDS SHOCKWAVES THROUGH A PIGEON'S body.

Here is a bird, alone with a hallucination of water. Still, Bartholomew drinks, scoops beakfuls of sand, which, in small doses, acts as an abrasive digestive aid, but, in these quantities, becomes a cement-like paste, clogs his networks. Above, the amorous altocumulus clouds couple with the loftier and aloof cirrostratus. They dance, draw all sorts of ligatures onto the sky. Soon, like the bird, the sky is too congested.

Does Bartholomew really carry within him the longings and adventures of his progenitors, across epoch and biome? At a time like this, does he suddenly recall lily pads and damselflies, the mildew of a creaky brig-sloop, drippy seasick lamplight; the loamy lowlands of French forests, the flying over them in pain, and against pain; old storms, welding sparks jumping from skyscraper shells, cages and sequins and popcorn and jazz? The smell of every hand that feeds?

Before the species evolved to bear hollow bones, three toes, and such a buxom figure, they flew over the earth's quaking kimberlitic pipes as they began to disgorge their first diamonds, well before the hands of men began to stir their feed, keep them as pets, cinch these stones to their feet . . .

Who knows what horrible and heroic lives lie ahead of these birds? Maybe they'll even see Antarctica, adapt and fatten to build nests there, and live amid glaciers, feast on the ice-worms. Bartholomew never tasted an invertebrate so cold, fresh. But he knows what oats taste like from a child's hands in the Kalahari, his scattered mother screaming about diamonds from the kitchen. He knows what jazz sounds like, hummed from Msizi's mouth, that song about machetes and eel-shaped scars that swim over bellies.

Tonight, in bars called Diamond Hunters, and bars called Fortune's, the knife fights of the world stop short of the stabbing. No one and nothing wants any more blood, except the pigeon's throat, and Msizi's throat. The locusts, or something like the locusts, bounce so beautifully from Bartholomew's body.

But, oh, if this pigeon still had a voice, it would howl like some wolf, finally converse directly with everything magnetic and invisible by which he once navigated, and the South Atlantic would talk back in waves—white, then blue-white—itself howling in defiance tonight. Like each animal, their stories long ago carved into some crawlspace of the planet, pigeons die, a lunchbox finally closing. And if Bartholomew's last song is the crooked announcement of our continental scars, no one will listen. No one ever listens.

*

"BARTHOLOMEW? HE'S SOMEWHERE IN THE DESERT, DEAD OF course," Msizi, nonplussed, will tell me when we meet again in a little park across from an unnamed café. We will sit on the concrete, lean against the park's sole attraction—an elongated and rusty four-person rocking horse. As usual, he will hang his head, cough his blood, put his lame pinky to his lips and breathe warmly onto it, as if trying to reanimate it. He will use words like *feathers* and *remains* and *very worried*. I will wait for him to use the word *love*, but he will not. I will nod, and do my best to remember what he's saying. The sky will purple, and the wind off the ocean will turn cold. He will have had a long day, unearthing diamonds for much bigger men. He will be very tired.

When I will ask him if he will replace Bartholomew, he will shrug, force a smile.

From the café, before leaving, I will buy him a chicken mayonnaise sandwich. He will take it from me quickly, look around as if we're being watched. "Don't tell my mother you bought me this," he will say. He will hold the sandwich in his hands, leaning against the toy horse. He will assess its weight, pick nervously or impatiently at the cling wrap with his thumbnails. He will wait until I am gone to eat it.

Epilogue

We wake the morning after our Lester encounter, thick-headed and parched. The peacocks are arguing, and the air smells of scorched aloe. Lester's car is gone, and Jackie is sweeping up broken glass from the courtyard. I remember dreaming something about being a parent. My knees crack as I bend. I consider the intensity and crispness of dreams in the desert—the ways in which landscape plays with the tracking on our subconscious—dated and too-bright and ingrained with something of childhood, like Technicolor.

The doves of Die Houthoop are the last things I see as we drag our duffels through the dust to the rental car, and pull from the parking lot, traversing, it seems, the road from one underworld to another. On the side of the road, the mine dumps sprout their mutant grass. The shacks, mills, and clubs disintegrate in the middle of these dumps, their ripped-open flanks painted with messages that no longer make sense: SNOWFLAKE, says one, as if the final pleading clue of some lost colony; PLS CONTACT MR. TATA, says another. The black wattle acacia trees, feral and aggressively invasive, have found a way to grow here, choking out the other species, sucking up water. They are beautiful, though. The pigeons love them.

To get to Louisa's family's home from Kleinzee, we have an eighteen-hour drive ahead of us, across South Africa, and we plan to do it straight, without spending the night on the road. We are ready to arrive someplace that's intimate, but not-quite-home, and we are ready to drive through the dark to get there. As I drive, I try not to think about Orpheus anymore, about his turning-around head. I try not to imagine Bartholomew on his doomed flight, turning back toward Msizi and the mine. I try not to think of Louisa in pain, struggling to sit still in the passenger seat. I try not to wonder if, on their journeys, our babies are still looking back at us.

I drive, and I know: Louisa's parents will be happy to see us together, and will be sad to see us together. I know this is unfair, but their expressions of sympathy will be a drain. For the next week, Louisa and I will spend hours on their brown couch, climbed over by so many nieces and nephews. They will be annoying and they will be wonderful, overweight and too skinny. On medication, or perfectly healthy. They will wear glasses, or they will not, and they will sit on Louisa's lap, and play rock–paper–scissors, and braid her hair, and interrupt her on the toilet and in the bathtub, and watch cartoons and cooking shows on TV, and eat leftovers out of the fridge, and play with cell phones, and sleep. All of this will seem to take place on one long couch-bound afternoon, and within it, and among them, I hope I will see, however briefly, some alternative future with us as parents. I hope I can feel the weather there. But for now, still driving away from the Diamond Coast, this future seems, in turn, to drive away from me, as if running downstream along with Orpheus's stupidly still-singing head, petering out into some beach fan with the diamonds, where it joins so many other deposits into a bajada convergence, forms one big apron.

Louisa points out the window to a grove of infamous fever trees with their powdery jaundice bark, the smell of which attracts anopheles mosquitoes, making the tree inadvertently responsible for the spread of malaria. Beneath the branches, an eland and a donkey drink from the same trough. We pass a giant church complex called Spirit World; a provisional barbershop housed in a converted telephone booth, tufts of hair marooned in the cacti; a mortuary truck with a cooling fan on its roof; a ghost town called Big Grave Water; a dying village named Hopetown.

The sun is setting, and we're hungry and low on fuel, and so pull over at a rest area along a meander in the Orange River. "Do not urinate here," says the handwritten paper sign on the outside wall of the Engen gas station, just above the concrete in which a baby's feet were commemoratively sunk when it was still soft and wet. Two pigeons— mates for life, perhaps—dip their beaks to the dirty water that has collected in the small, sole-shaped depressions.

We purchase our supper from the gas station's counter—sandwiches called the AK-47, limp French fries, and a Russian sausage, and eat it at the picnic table on the riverbank. Vagrant pigeons comb for crumbs. The sun goes down, and silhouettes of Brahma bulls move like phantoms in the tallgrass. The river flows under the barbed wire a butternut and cabbage farmer has strung across the water. Beyond his farm is a graveyard, the headstones tipping in the pillowy sand. And beyond that, radio towers blink to warn no planes. There is not, overhead, any kind of flight pattern besides that of the birds. I toss the last bit of bun to them.

Fire smoke curls from the distant mountains—a wild burn, or a controlled one. We and the birds will soon be gone, as geologic time does what it does. But for now, it's night, and we walk back to the rental car. We have a long drive ahead of us, too much to mull over. Beyond us, the cabbages, the squash. We put on our seat belts. I will use my turn signals, drive the speed limit, follow from safe distances. I will brake well in advance. Louisa takes, then releases my hand. She sighs, and gestures to the windshield—to the horizon or the darkness or the moths. To all the people out there who love us, who are waiting for us to catch up. As we pull onto the road, I can see, in the rearview mirror and red of the taillights, the seemingly weightless husks of so many dung beetles blow up from their hiding places, lift into the wind, seed the savanna. As it should be: nothing worthwhile to us will grow from them.

Acknowledgments

THANK YOU:

To all those on the ground and in the air who were willing to endure my interloper presence and, sometimes even, to speak or coo to me for the sake of this book.

To all at the archives and libraries at the University of Cape Town, Stellenbosch University, the Niven Library at the Percy FitzPatrick Institute of African Ornithology, the National Library of Cape Verde, Durham University, the University of Paris–Nanterre, and University of Amsterdam, for your openness and access.

To all at the Kleinzee Museum, Port Nolloth Museum, Kimberley Mine Museum, Museu Municipal Lagos, Diamond Museum Amsterdam, and South African National Pigeon Organization for your guidance.

To Northern Michigan University, especially Rob Winn and Lynn Domina, for their generous support of this project.

To the writers/editors who saw something in, and featured early excerpts from, this book: Dinty W. Moore, Zoë Bossiere, Lee Martin, and Leslie Jamison—in, respectively, *Brevity, The Best of Brevity: Twenty Groundbreaking Years of Flash Nonfiction* (Rose Metal Press), *1966: A Journal of Creative Nonfiction,* and *The Best American Essays 2017* (as a Notable selection; Houghton Mifflin Harcourt).

To Johan and Bokkie for your sweet-and-sour meatballs, your reliable vehicles, and your conversation.

To my friends and colleagues who contributed support, feedback, and the occasional whisky to this endeavor: Elena Passarello, Ander

Monson, Jenny Boully, Cynthia Hogue, Norman Dubie, Rigoberto González, Doug Jones, Elizabyth Hiscox, Matt Bell, Timston Johnston, Jen Howard, Russ Prather, Carol Phillips, Jaspal Singh, Mike Madonick, Rafael Naranjo, Armando Santamaria, and many others I'm probably and regrettably forgetting at the moment . . .

To Bob Weil and Katie Henderson-Adams for their generous support and invaluable advice.

To the marmalade cat who kept that puff adder from biting me.

To Kathy Daneman, Cordelia Calvert, and Nick Curley for your PR and marketing prowess and rock-stardom.

To the continued support of my family: Mom, Noely, The Rub, Brian, Only Avery, Ella the Lizard.

To my amazingly wonderful and wonderfully amazing agent, Rayhané Sanders, and my brilliant editor, Gina Iaquinta. Without your essential voices, this book wouldn't be what it is. Also, it would be 1,000 pages long.

And to you, Louisa—goodness gracious, you.

Notes

PROLOGUE

2 **"important historical relics":** "The Big Hole Kimberley," brochure, Kimberley Mine Museum.

4 **in 1998, a local lawmaker:** Dean E. Murphy, "Pigeons Take Rap for Stolen African Diamonds," *Los Angeles Times*, April 19, 1998 ("'The law now is to shoot all pigeons on sight,' Mandla Msomi, the chairman of the parliamentary committee that oversees Alexkor's operations, told his fellow lawmakers after visiting the mine"); and Dean E. Murphy, "Pigeons Smuggle Gems—S. African Diamond Town Threatens to Shoot Birds," *Seattle Times*, April 20, 1998. I confirmed this information when on site.

CHAPTER 1: MSIZI AND HIS BIRD

7 **This is the dust:** E. J. King, M. Yoganathan, and G. Nagelschmidt, "The Effect of Diamond Dust Alone and Mixed with Quartz on the Lungs of Rats," *British Journal of Industrial Medicine* 15, no. 2 (April 1958): 92–95. This report deduced that similar symptoms would likely occur in humans.

10 **One recent survey found:** Cited by the Bureau of International Labor Affairs in "South Africa: Prevalence and Sectoral Distribution of Child Labor," 2016.

10 **a harvest that can exceed 176 million carats:** Statistics throughout the book are taken from Yury Spektorov, Olya Linde, Bart Cornelissen, and Rostislav Khomenko, "The Global Diamond Report 2013: Journey Through the Value Chain," Bain and Company, August 27, 2013, as well as similar reports from other years, and the World Diamond Council's "Diamond Industry Fact Sheet" for 2011, as well as similar reports from other years.

14 **"important vestige of . . .":** Dr. Jeff Birdsley, "Internal Anatomy," in *Ornithology*, edited by Frank B. Gill (London: W. H. Freeman, 2006). Birdsley was a professor of ornithology at the University of Illinois at Urbana–Champaign. His office was in a building called the Shelford Vivarium, a climate-controlled greenhouse once fronted by two duck and turtle ponds (now drained). Birdsley's Ornithology 461 course featured subunits such as "Eggs and Nests," "Bird Song," and "Feathers." Though he is something of an expert on pigeons, his real passions are for the evolution of prey capture behaviors in the tyrant flycatcher family, and the field collection of fruit flies.

CHAPTER 2: ISAAC NEWTON & CO.

17 **according to University of Virginia physicist Michael Fowler:** Michael Fowler, "Newton's Life," in *Isaac Newton* (Charlottesville: University of Virginia, Physics Department, 2015,

http://galileoandeinstein.physics.virginia.edu/lectures/newton.html). My favorite published lecture of Fowler's—however, mostly inscrutable to me—remains "Time Dilation from a Lightclock," a title I plan on stealing for a poem.

17 **Newton was captivated by pigeons:** Much of the information in this paragraph, and elsewhere in this chapter, was derived from William Stukeley, *Memoirs of Sir Isaac Newton's Life* (presented to the Royal Society by Mr. A. W. White, 1752).

18 **"the first autonomous volatile machine of antiquity":** Kotsanas Museum of Ancient Greek Technology, "The Flight Machines of the Ancient Greeks," kotsanas.com.

18 **Soon, he became so obsessed with bones:** As cited in Alejandro Jenkins, "Isaac Newton's Sinister Heraldry," Escuela de Física, Universidad de Costa Rica, 11501–2060, San José, Costa Rica, August 1, 2014. Available at: arxiv.org/pdf/1310.7494.pdf.

20 **She wants to calm her 600 heartbeats:** I found these numbers, as they pertain to a pigeon's anatomy and biological function, in a number of sources, including Eugene P. Odum, "Variations in the Heart Rate of Birds: A Study in Physiological Ecology," *Ecological Monographs* 11, no. 3 (July 1941): 299–326; Bob Doneley, *Avian Medicine and Surgery in Practice: Companion and Aviary Birds*, 2nd ed. (Boca Raton, FL: CRC Press, 2016); and "Pigeon Facts" at himalayanpigeon.com). I used these numbers as the bases from which to spin out and scratch at the implications (however ephemeral) lurking within these numbers, and in the pigeon's capacity for such rigors. The subsequent math (though mine, and I am no mathematician) is accurate.

21 **"inherited spatiotemporal vector-navigation program":** P. Berthold, "Spatiotemporal Programmes and the Genetics of Orientation," in *Orientation in Birds*, edited by P. Berthold (Basel: Birkhäuser, 1991).

21 **In 2005, in order to agitate:** H. G. Wallraff, "Ratios Among Atmospheric Trace Gases Together with Winds Imply Exploitable Information for Bird Navigation: A Model Elucidating Experimental Results," *Biogeosciences* 10, no. 11 (2013): 6929.

22 **All of these mangled, overloaded, electrocuted birds:** W. T. Keeton, "Effects of Magnets on Pigeon Homing," in *Animal Orientation and Navigation*, edited by S. R. Galler et al. (Washington, DC: NASA, 1972).

22 **They chalked up the pigeon's ability . . . even principles of Newtonian alchemy:** Rupert Sheldrake, *Seven Experiments That Could Change the World* (New York: Riverhead, 1994).

23 **"This philosophy . . . the world":** Estefania Wenger, *Isaac Newton: A Biography* (London: Alpha Editions, 2017).

24 **"Pigeons normally keep their bodies":** "Pigeons in Space," video by Bioastronautics Research: Aerospace Medical Division HQ 6570th Aerospace Medical Research Laboratories, posted February 4, 2011, at YouTube.com.

BARTHOLOMEW VARIATION #1

29 **The bird refuses—given:** Martha Romeskie and Dean Yager, "Psychophysical Studies of Pigeon Color Vision—I. Photopic Spectral Sensitivity," *Vision Research* 16, no. 5 (1976): 501–05.

29 **Though mineworkers have to pass:** This information was relayed to me (from very different perspectives) by both Msizi and Johann MacDonald.

30 **1,300 kilometers away:** "Minister Ngoako Ramatlhodi: Mineral Resources Dept. Budget Vote 2015/16," May 7, 2015, https://www.gov.za/speeches/minister-ngoako-abel-ramatlhodi-occasion-budget-vote-29-7-may-2015-0000.

30 **"the malign ingenuity of the poor . . .":** From a clipped article tacked to the wall of the Kleinzee Museum. The top of the article (headline included) had been cut off. The clipping was grouped with a few others from the *Cape Argus*, a Cape Town–based newspaper first published in 1857. The *Argus* (as it's colloquially known) was founded by Saul Solomon, a liberal Jewish politician who advocated for a multiracial democracy, religious equality, and women's rights in South Africa. His pro-imperialist cofounders soon abandoned the paper due to Solomon's liberal views.

CHAPTER 3: BEYOND THE PITS OF ALEXANDER BAY

32 **"The tape attaching the diamonds . . . a fearless smuggler's teasing":** Dean E. Murphy, "Pigeons Take Rap for Stolen African Diamonds," *Los Angeles Times*, April 19, 1998. I confirmed and clarified this story, and a subsequent similar instance, when on site.

33 **When a pigeon explodes:** Andrew D. Blechman, *Pigeons* (New York: Grove/Atlantic, 2006).

35 **The long-closed tourist lodge:** Gleaned from personal observation and Bobby Jordan, "They Call Us the Poor Millionaires," *Cape Argus*, October 7, 2013.

37 **a sting using police-trained homing pigeons:** Estelle Ellis, "Undercover Operation Busts Diamond Racket," *Cape Argus.* Clipped article, Port Nolloth Museum.

38 **Rumor has it also:** Estelle Randall, "State Diamond Mine Slap-Bang in Middle of Smuggling Scam." Clipped article, Port Nolloth Museum.

38 **"If you get too close to the truth":** Ranjeni Munusamy, "Secret Agents Bust Diamond Dealers." Clipped article, Port Nolloth Museum. The sentiments expressed in this article are confirmed by various others, including, for instance, "Murders Focus Attention on Organized Crime in South African Diamond Industry," Voice of America News, October 30, 2009, voanews.com.

CHAPTER 4: PORT NOLLOTH AND THE HALFWAY DESERT

40 **"Bloom hunters" will descend:** Northern Cape Tourism Authority, "Namakwa and West Coast Flower Route," map and brochure, 2015. The brochure is a great, if adjective-heavy, read. Adjectives applied to various flower species include *stunning, charming, delightful, proud, showy, star-like,* and (my favorite) *pensive.*

41 **"Where the Water Took the Old Man Away":** a rough English translation of the Khoi name Aukotowa.

42 **"We don't want to be part of a legacy of ghost towns" . . . until the ship dies:** Nelendhre Moodley, "De Beers Sets Up Key Marine-Mining Hub in Impoverished Port Nolloth," *Mining Weekly*, April 26, 2007. I confirmed and clarified this when on site.

44 **In the mythologies:** Hukam Chand Patyal, "Pigeon in the Vedic Mythology and Ritual," *Annals of the Bhandarkar Oriental Research Institute* 71, no. 1/4 (1990): 310–17; Radhika Ravi Rajan, "The Biggest Curses in Hindu Mythology," *Speaking Tree*, April 25, 2013, available at speakingtree.in; "Native American Dove and Pigeon Mythology," Native Languages of the Americas, native-languages.org. 2015; and Debra Kelly, "10 Truly Crazy Birds from World Mythology." Listverse: History, February 22, 2014, listverse. com.

44 **they are body-hoppers:** Edward Dwight Walker, *Reincarnation: A Study of Forgotten Truth* (New York: John W. Lovell, 1888); and News Elliott Wood, ed., *Star of the Magi: An Exponent*

of Occult Science, Art, and Philosophy (Chicago: N. E. Wood, 1899). I found the latter in the library of the University of Illinois; when I accessed it in 2016, I saw that it had previously been checked out on November 11, 1974, the same date that saw the mass flooding of the U.S. Virgin Islands, eliciting extreme mosquito breeding and a subsequent mosquito "plague," as well as the birth of Leonardo DiCaprio (who, in 2009, bought an island off Belize on which he plans to open a "sea-cooled eco-resort that's nearly mosquito-free").

45 **The average mosquito weighs:** "Mosquitoes," Animals/Reference, National Geographic, nationalgeographic.com; and Thomas Gaffigan and James Pecor, "Collecting, Rearing, Mounting, and Shipping Mosquitoes," Walter Reed Biosystematics Unit (Washington, DC: Smithsonian Institution, 1997).

47 **These trees—the date palms:** Much of the information in this section comes from Ashley T. Brenner, *The Dutch Have Made Slaves of Them All . . . And They Are Called Free* (Saarbrücken: Lambert Academic Publishing, 2009).

48 **This: the desperate passing on of any sweetness:** Mohamed Al-Farsi and Chang Yong Lee, "Nutritional and Functional Properties of Dates: A Review," *Critical Reviews in Food Science and Nutrition* 48, no. 10 (December 2008): 877–87.

48 **to increase their levels of serotonin:** Claire Sissons, "How to Boost Serotonin and Improve Mood," *Medical News Today*, July 10, 2018; Philip J. Cowen and Michael Browning, "What Has Serotonin to Do with Depression?," *World Psychiatry* 14, no. 2 (June 2015): 158–60; Simon N. Young, "How to Increase Serotonin in the Human Brain Without Drugs," *Journal of Psychiatry and Neuroscience* 32, no. 6 (November 2007): 394–99.

49 **psychologists say that the literal carrying of weight:** Meng Zhang and Xiuping Li, "From Physical Weight to Psychological Significance: The Contribution of Semantic Activations," *Journal of Consumer Research* 38, no. 6 (April 1, 2012): 1063–75.

49 **alive via flood irrigation:** P. J. Leibenberg and A. Zaid, "Date Palm Irrigation," Food and Agriculture Organization of the United Nations Corporate Document Repository, 2002, fao.org.

50 **The divers believe that such practices:** Melanie Gosling, "Divers Who Risk Their Lives for 'Women's Vanity.' " Clipped article, Port Nolloth Museum.

50 **it's the moral imperative of the divers:** Ben Trovato, "It Should Be Legal to Pursue Diamonds as Long as You Never Do it in a Speedo." Clipped article, Port Nolloth Museum.

52 **"Sabotaging boats in this community":** Peter De Ionno, "Sea Treasure Splits Town." Clipped article, Port Nolloth Museum.

52 **"Don't look at me . . . gravel under our feet":** De Ionno, "Sea Treasure Splits Town."

52 **"a once vibrant" . . . consortium of smugglers:** Melanie Gosling, "Call to Break Up West Coast Marine Diamond Monopoly," *Cape Argus.* Clipped article, Port Nolloth Museum.

55 **one sheepish local informer:** Sivuyile Mangxamba, "Smuggling, the Pulse of Port Nolloth," *Sunday Argus*, June 23, 2002.

57 **He does not tell me:** But this article did tell me: Estelle Ellis, "Undercover Operation Busts Diamond Racket," *Cape Argus.* Clipped article, Port Nolloth Museum.

57 **"Port Nolloth looked like an opium smoker's den":** Chris Marais, "The Diamond Men of Port Nolloth," *Scope*, October 4, 1985.

58 **the chefs were able to purchase:** Information gleaned from a badly creased food-ordering form dated October 17, 1960, found in the Kleinzee Museum, the disclaimer at the bottom of which reads: "All prices have been increased due to a substantial loss in the Butchery."

58 **the tailings heaps . . . the stables:** Much of the information in this paragraph was gleaned

from captioned photographs in the Port Nolloth Museum, the Kleinzee Museum, and the Big Hole Museum (part of the Kimberley Mine Museum), and in Kokkie Duminy and Dr. R. J. L. Sabatini, *Fifty Years on the Diamond Fields: 1870–1920* (Kimberley: Africana Library Trust, 2013).

59 **"If I have to die":** Alex Duval Smith, "Refugees Defy Crocodiles to Cross Border," *ObserverZimbabwe*, July 6, 2008.

60 **At about the same time:** David Fleminger, *Richtersveld: Cultural and Botanical Landscape: Including Namaqualand* (Johannesburg: Southbound, 2008).

CHAPTER 5: RIDING WITH THE FACELESS

64 **a pair of marked terns:** I confirmed this story with the hosts at the Kleinzee Museum, which had a small display about it, including the (quoting the museum's placard) "rings retrieved from two terns found . . . They are marked Museum Zoology Helsinki Finland."

67 **Illicit pigeon shoots:** Some of this information was gleaned from Simon J. Bronner, "Contesting Tradition: The Deep Play and Protest of Pigeon Shoots," *Journal of American Folklore* 118, no. 470 (Autumn 2005): 409–52.

69 **I'm desperate to stylize this whole scene:** Information on Canaletto comes from the wonderful essay "Capricci" in Thomas Mira y Lopez, *The Book of Resting Places: A Personal History of Where We Lay the Dead* (Berkeley, CA: Counterpoint Press, 2017).

69 **what Marie Curie might have called its seemingly "spontaneous luminosity":** Lauren Redniss, *Radioactive* (New York: Dey Street Books, 2015). It stands to mention that Canaletto's coveted Prussian blue once served to assuage the nightmares of so many, once it was discovered that capsules of the stuff, when taken orally, alleviated the symptoms of certain types of radioactive contamination. In fact, following the nuclear disaster at Chernobyl, various countries began spraying their grasslands with a solution of Prussian blue in order to keep grazing animals alive. In this way, to the planes and pigeons passing overhead, the earth itself resembled a dreamscape, an odd patchwork of Canaletto skies stitched together against further calamity.

70 **In ancient Egypt, pigeon excrement:** Andrew D. Blechman, *Pigeons* (New York: Grove/Atlantic, 2006).

72 **As the Tokoloshe is said:** Nhlanhla Mkhize (University of Natal, Pietermaritzburg), "Mind, Gender, and Culture: A Critical Evaluation of the Phenomenon of Tokoloshe 'Sightings' Among Prepubescent Girls in Kwazulu-Natal," paper presented to the 2nd Annual Qualitative Methods Conference: "The Body Politic," Johannesburg, South Africa, September 3–4, 1996. In this fascinating article, Mkhize also discusses the ways in which the "'sightings' of this creature are accompanied by fainting spells, deterioration from previous level of (scholastic) performance, fearfulness, and other psychosomatic type symptoms . . . The process of ideological becoming (or identity, moral development) therefore entails claiming responsibility for one's feelings, emotions, and acts. The Tokoloshe narrative, therefore, could be seen as an intense struggle against authoritative discourse . . . The Tokoloshe narrative is clearly authoritative. He instructs the children 'not to tell anyone' that they have seen him (Thou shall not!). He makes several threats, and those who disobey him are punished (slapped on the face). He also offers rewards (money, apples) to those who obey him. Thus, his is a voice of authority with the powers to reward or punish." As Louisa had numerous times discussed with me the role of the Tokoloshe in her life, and as I had therefore done quite a

bit of reading up on the myth before this "ride with the faceless," such thoughts (of the Tokoloshe narrative and subsequent analysis thereof) were going through my head in real time, there in the back of that Land Rover.

CHAPTER 6: DRIVING TO KLEINZEE AMID SHIPWRECKS AND SNAKES

75 **Deep below the surface:** Lourens Myburgh, "Re: Baie Danke," September 2, 2004, email correspondence, Kleinzee Museum. I'm not sure what elicited this email response (to someone named Jackie), but Myburgh writes, in part (and, yes, in all caps), "THIS FOSSIL REPRESENTS CLAY CONTAINING FOSSIL PLANT MATERIAL. IT WAS FOUND IN AN ABANDONED MEANDER OF THE BUFFELS RIVER, CLOSE TO KLEINZEE . . . THIS SAMPLE IS +/- 17 MILLION YEARS OLD AND DATES BACK TO THE MIOCENE AGE. THE WEATHER WAS QUITE WARM DURING THIS PERIOD WITH HIGH RAINFALL. THE BUFFELS RIVER PROBABLY FLOWED THE WHOLE YEAR ROUND . . . DIAMONDS WERE CARRIED DOWN THE RIVERS TOWARDS THE SEA DURING THIS PERIOD." In trying to find out who this Lourens Myburgh is, I came up dry. I found a Lourens Myburgh who died in 1986 and who was nicknamed "Daan." I found a Lourens Myburgh who has too many pictures of boats and airplanes on his Facebook page, and who shares a disproportionate number of links titled "Food Coma." I found a Lourens Myburgh who is a world archery "champion," though I wonder as to the nature of this definition, as statistics show that he has lost as many matches as he's won. And, finally, I found a Lourens Myburgh whose last Twitter contribution (as of this writing) is a retweet asking, "How much fried chicken does one municipality need?"

75 **"very cautious, very wary":** From my early email correspondence with "Adele Wickens," dated April 24, 2015.

77 **I thumbed through my book:** Details of this story were gleaned from G. W. Mullins and C. L. Hause, *Cherokee: A Collection of American Indian Legends, Stories, and Fables* (Colorado: Light of the Moon Publishing, 2016); and "Uktena and the Ulunsuti," exhibit: plaque and article, Kimberley Mine Museum.

80 **In 1985, the 1,400-ton:** Keith Grieve, "All 26 Crew of the Diamond Dredger *Poseidon Cape* Were Hoisted to Safety," *Cape Argus*, July 30, 1985; and Dick Usher, "Diamond Rig Runs Aground," *Cape Argus*, July 28, 1985.

80 **The sign once necklaced:** I found this sign—understandably a little worse for wear—prominently displayed in the Kleinzee Museum.

80 **Thirty kilometers south:** "Rare find donated to Kleinzee Museum." Clipped article, Kleinzee Museum. There are, in fact, so many clipped articles pertaining to shipwrecks in the Kleinzee Museum that they could be said to have their own wing. Next to this one, for instance, was "Shipwreck at Port Nolloth," *Cape Argus*, February 9, 1886. (On February 8, 1886, a Port Nolloth correspondent reported the loss of the *Veronica*, "a sad catastrophe," which took place on the same night of "heavy gales and rough seas" that also saw the wreck of the *Taunton*, the wreck of the *Maxima*, the wreck of the *Esempio*, and the wreck of the *Marquis of Worcester*. Bowsprits were carried away into the sea, and "a chopping battle commenced between the bows of one and the sterns of the other, which ended up in the eventual slipping and sinking," and no birds were reported circling overhead. "Great sympathy is expressed here," said the unidentified correspondent, "for Captain Kite [of the *Veronica*], who is well known as an industrious man, and one who studies the interests

of his owners. He is a very heavy loser . . ." In the absence of any auctioneer, the *Veronica* was sold as-is, underwater, for four British pounds.

80 **Down the shore, plants:** "Steamer Wrecked." Clipped article, Kleinzee Museum.

80 **the vigilant diamond police . . . The tinned sardines:** Tara Turkington, "Diamond of the Desert," *Cape Times*, November 5, 2013.

81 **Wrecks beget wrecks:** Shipwreck log (filled out in beautiful handwritten script), Kleinzee Museum. Tacked to the wall, over the log, was a clipped article, "Wreck of Gertrude Woerman," reporting the 1903 wreck of the 1,743-ton steamer *Gertrud Woermann* (named for a Hamburg art patron and first owner of Karl Schmidt-Rottluff's chimerically elongated cityscape *Houses at Night*, which now hangs in a shadowy couloir of New York's MoMA), which once transported a sickly group of German merchants to Liberia—a voyage which saw the burial at sea of a man, a chimpanzee, and a gray parrot (the latter killed by rats). One of the passengers, E. F. Cronin, photographed the wreck as it occurred, producing, according to the illustrated supplement of the *Cape Argus* weekly edition, "the first recollection of seeing the actual incidents of a shipwreck reproduced." He and the rest of the crew were transferred to a boat named the *Nautilus*, which turned into the same fog that destroyed *Gertrud*, and disappeared.

81 **vessels chartered by the East India Company:** Information in this paragraph was gleaned from William Dalrymple, "The East India Company: The Original Corporate Raiders," *Guardian*, March 4, 2015.

82 **they adapted to the habitat:** Hillary Mayell, "Extinct Dodo Related to Pigeons, DNA Shows," *National Geographic*, March 14, 2002.

82 **Also off the Diamond Coast:** H. V. Bowen, Margarette Lincoln, and Nigel Rigby, eds., *The Worlds of the East India Company* (Woodbridge, UK: Boydell Press, 2003).

82 **There, in 1900, one such gun:** Mark Avery, *A Message from Martha: The Extinction of the Passenger Pigeon and Its Relevance Today* (London: Bloomsbury, 2014).

BARTHOLOMEW VARIATION #3

83 **noses of curious basking sharks:** George Moyses, *Diamond Diving* (Cape Town: Port Nolloth Museum, 2011).

83 **The experiences of their forebears—Darwin's pigeons:** This references the ocean voyages of HMS *Beagle* (the ten-gun brig sloop of the Royal Navy on which Darwin was reputed to have brought at least one pigeon companion); the First World War (during which the heroic pigeon Cher Ami, trained by the U.S. Army pigeoneers, saved the lives of the U.S. Army's "Lost Battalion" in the Argonne forest of France (Cher Ami flew 25 miles, successfully carrying what would be a lifesaving secret message from one division to another, even though a significant portion of her body had been mutilated by German bullets); and the final days of Martha, the world's last passenger pigeon (who perished in a cage at the Cincinnati Zoo).

84 ***"Vrouw, ek het hom!":*** Kokkie Duminy and Dr. R. J. L. Sabatini, *Fifty Years on the Diamond Fields: 1870–1920* (Kimberley: Africana Library Trust, 2013).

84 **a tame zebra foal:** Duminy and Sabatini, *Fifty Years on the Diamond Fields.*

85 **He hums his favorite tunes:** Information on the Jazz Epistles comes from John Edwin Mason, "Mannenberg: Notes on the Making of an Icon and Anthem," *African Studies Quarterly* 9, no. 4 (Fall 2007); and Carol A. Muller, *South African Music: A Century of Traditions in Transformation* (Oxford: ABC-CLIO, 2004).

86 **This local superstition has many variations:** Iona Opie and Moira Tatum, eds., *A Dictionary of Superstitions* (Oxford: Oxford University Press, 1989). Another variation, from Old Provence: The pigeon's carcass was medically prescribed for bringing the dead back to life. If a poor French villager succumbed to typhoid fever, after the corpse was sprinkled with holy water, family members would trap frogs in a burlap sack, which was then laid over the torso of the corpse. It was believed that the desperate hopping of the frogs, their wild attempts at escape, would recharge the heart. If this method failed (as it often did), one last-ditch effort was made. A family member was to take a pillowcase (silk, preferably) from the sickbed and with it trap a live pigeon feeding in the lavender fields, wild thyme, canola. In one instance, recounted in M. F. K. Fisher, *A Cordiall Water: A Garland of Odd and Old Receipts to Assuage the Ills of Man and Beast* (New York: Little, Brown, 1961), the sickbed belonged to a little girl who was two days dead. It took that long to trap the pigeon. The girl's grandmother reached into the pillowcase, took the bird by the throat and, with a *laguiole* knife, cut it open lengthwise, unfolded the pigeon's breast from its heart, and scrolled the bird's body back doubly toward its wings. She slapped the pigeon's body onto the dead girl's forehead, and, though it could no longer bob its head forward, it reportedly saw its own blood gush down the girl's chilled face. It seemed to steam there. Slowly, painting the girl with the red stripe, the grandmother—her own hand gnarled and in a different kind of pain, which she differently expressed—ran the pigeon's body downward, and pressed its heart—still pumping—to the flesh over the girl's heart. The pigeon's heart had six beats left in it, and at the sixth beat, as the bird faded into the ether, waiting to be reborn, perhaps, as Darwin's muse, the girl came back to life, sucked air, and sat up in the sour bed. The grandmother, and the rest of the family, celebrated by weeping and pouring cups of mead, and the old corporeal pigeon was a shell of feathers on the hardwood.

Chapter 7: New Rush and Kimberley

88 **in spite of the initiative:** Blake's initiative is cited in Martinique Stilwell, "Diamond Mines Are Not Forever," *Mail & Guardian*, November 18, 2011.

89 **Rhodes, seventeen years old, anemic:** "Cecil John Rhodes, 1853–1902," South African History Online, sahistory.org.za.

89 **the De Beer brothers had been raising karakul sheep:** Dawid W. De Beer and Jaleen De Beer, *The De Beer Family: Three Centuries in South Africa*, CD-ROM (South Africa: De Beer Family Register, 2000).

89 **Rhodes soon exchanged:** Information on Rhodes comes from Ian Duncan Colvin, *Cecil John Rhodes, 1853–1902* (Los Angeles: Hardpress, 2012).

90 **their code of signals:** Displayed, in an abridged form as approved by the government mining engineer, at the Kimberley Mine Museum.

90 **the spell of a South African legend:** Pricillia Meintjies, "Kimberley: The City of Diamonds," *Discover South Africa*, February 9, 2012.

90 **the place now called Kimberley:** "Diamond Fields of Kimberley," exhibit: plaque and article, Kimberley Mine Museum.

91 **Digging rules ... "and pointed out by a Committee":** Committee of the Dorstfontein Executive Council, "Rules and Regulations for the Diggings," 1871. Article 10, Ordinance 3.

91 **He came of age motherless:** Information on Barnato's childhood comes from Stephen Inwood, *City of Cities: The Birth of Modern London* (London: Pan Books, 2005).

91 "... and Barnet too": M. B. Leavitt, *Fifty Years in Theatrical Management* (New York: Broadway, 1912).

92 Barnato's portion of the Kimberley Mine equaled Rhodes's portion of the De Beers mine: Information on Barnato and Rhodes comes from Brian Roberts, *The Diamond Magnates* (London: Hamish Hamilton, 1972).

92 The miners slated for the underground work: Information in these three paragraphs comes from "A Day in the Life of a Miner," *Kimberley Times* (clipped article, Kimberley Mine Museum); "Chambering: An Early Underground Mining Technique," *Kimberley Times* (clipped article, Kimberley Mine Museum); and "From Open Cast to Underground Mining," *Kimberley Times* (clipped article, Kimberley Mine Museum).

93 the new "stripping clause": "De Beers Mine Company, Searching for Diamonds," exhibit: plaque and article, Kimberley Mine Museum.

93 "Unless this evil is crushed": Martin Meredith, *Diamonds, Gold, and War* (London: Simon and Schuster, 2007).

93 "the madness and mayhem of Kimberley": "The Diamond Route Pledge," February 2, 2010, document from De Beers Consolidated Mines, Ltd., reproduced on a plaque at the Big Hole (part of the Kimberley Mine Museum).

94 "should the fields be thrown open to everyone": "De Beers Consolidated Mines, Ltd., First Annual Report," July 1889. Kleinzee Museum.

94 "There cannot be any doubt": Phillipe Mellier, "Dear Colleagues," August 18, 2012. De Beers correspondence displayed in the Kleinzee Museum.

94 energetic renditions: These numbers were among the most popular songs of the day, and would have likely featured in the brothers' stage performances. See Benjamin Robert Tubb, "Music from 1800–1860," Public Domain Music, dirkncl.github.io/pdmusic_org/1800s.html, updated October 24, 2016.

95 The derelict mining village: Paul Burkhardt, "Blyvooruitzicht: The Fallout from a Gold Mine's Closure," *Moneyweb Investor*, December 18, 2013.

95 "Water is the most precious thing ... deliver services there": Sheree Bega, "The Town Where No Water Runs," *Saturday Star*, June 6, 2015.

97 "Gentlemen! This is the rock": Quoted in Greg Campbell, *Blood Diamonds* (New York: Perseus, 2004).

98 Historians have described: Chris Marais, "Recapturing the Heady Days of the Diamond Rush," Kimberley Mine Museum page, southafrica.net.

98 "allowing labourers [to be] free": "The only way to stamp out IDB." Clipped article, Kimberley Mine Museum.

98 stories of malarial camp fever: Much of the information in this paragraph was gleaned from the brochures and informational video (2015) at the Kimberley Mine Museum.

99 "soul searching in South Africa": David Smith, "Students' Attack on Cecil Rhodes Statue Leads to Soul Searching in South Africa," *Guardian*, March 20, 2015.

99 variously interpreted as freak accident or suicide: Scott Balson, "The Story Behind 'Barney' Barnato," tokencoins.com, 1997.

CHAPTER 8: BEYOND THE BOOM GATE, TOURING THE ERASURE

101 hotshot twenty-two-year-old diamond buyer: Anthony Hocking, *Oppenheimer and Son* (New York: McGraw-Hill, 1973).

101 He used his position to further foster: David Pallister, Sarah Stewart, and Ian Lepper,

South Africa Inc. The Oppenheimer Empire (Sandton, South Africa: Media House Publications, 1987).

102 **"They are unsophisticated":** DAP Pifer (Manager Kleinzee) to Consulting Engineers, Kimberley (quoting the 1938 Kleinzee Mine Manager, Drury Pifer), "General Manager, NMK Collection, File 6," September 27, 1938. De Beers Archives (Kimberley), temporarily displayed in the Kimberley Mine Museum.

102 **Soon, the workers' ...** *jukskei*: Manager, Kleinzee, to Manager, South Finance Corporation, Cape Town, "Golden Jubilee, 1926–1976." December 10, 1930, p. 31. De Beers Consolidated Mines, Ltd., Kleinzee Mine, GM, NMK 2, temporarily displayed in the Kleinzee Museum.

104 **the compacted carbon:** Information in this paragraph and the next was gleaned from World Diamond Council, "Diamond Producing Countries in Africa Fact Sheet," 2011; "Diamonds," U.S. Library of Congress, countrystudies.us/south-africa (accessed October 16, 2015); William F. Gardner, "Discovery of Diamonds in Africa (1867)," History World International, history-world.org; and Diamond Fields International, "History of Marine Diamonds," diamondfields.com.

104 **Having formed as the Earth itself formed:** W. Barnett et al., "How Structure and Stress Influence Kimberlite Emplacement," in *Proceedings of the 10th International Kimberlite Conference*, edited by D. G. Pearson et al. (New York: Springer, 2013).

105 **Ostriches occasionally swallowed diamonds:** "Deformed Ostrich Eggs." Exhibit (donated by the Farms Department), Kleinzee Museum. The eggs are displayed beneath the deformed shells of tortoises.

117 **"We understand that diamonds are different":** Cynthia Carroll (Chief Executive, Anglo American Corporate Office), "Dear All," November 4, 2011. Written correspondence displayed in the Kleinzee Museum.

118 **"We have spent decades exalting anniversaries":** Nicky Oppenheimer and Jonathan Oppenheimer, "Dear Colleagues," August 16, 2012. Written De Beers correspondence displayed in the Kleinzee Museum.

119 **when taken together ... luxury retailers:** Janine F. Roberts, "Masters of Illusion," *Ecologist*, September 1, 2003.

119 **treated as an organized crime group:** Janine F. Roberts, *Glitter and Greed: The Secret World of the Diamond Cartel* (New York: Disinformation, 2007).

119 **"You reinforce our brand":** Oppenheimer and Oppenheimer, "Dear Colleagues."

119 **"the magic people ... the best kind of people on earth":** "The Magic People," July 2, 1997. De Beers correspondence to employees at the Namaqualand Mines. Kleinzee Museum archives.

120 **In the old days, the Lashing Gang:** S. H. Badenhorst, "The Unique Namdeb Trilogy— Our Past, Present, and Future Mining Applications in This Unique Deposit," *Journal of the South African Institute of Mining and Metallurgy* (November 2003): 539–50.

121 **mine security carried sharp assegai spears:** "Assegais Were Carried by Security Guards." Exhibit (donated by the Security Department, Koingnaas), Kleinzee Museum.

122 **"The first find" ... five hundred years old:** Much of this information was gleaned from "Bushman Burial (Excavation Report, Research Findings, Other Skeletal Finds, Historical Material and the Law)," document in the Kleinzee Museum archives.

123 **"If you travel from here to Cape Town":** These burial grounds got me thinking of the strange holes we make into the earth, and the strange hills we leave behind in the doing so, and of larger-than-life dead things; of the giant human skeleton unearthed during a gas

exploration in the Rub' al Khali, the Empty Quarter of the Arabian Desert, the phenomenal size of which was the result of either archaeological anomaly or photographic exaggeration; of the giant human skeleton found in the bottom silt of the Black Sea outside Varna, Bulgaria, in the ancient city of Odessos, the posture of the remains indicating that the massive man died while praying; of "Goliath," the giant skeleton of a warrior found in Santa Mare, Romania, the trachea of which was ample enough to be a vambrace, the huge skull of which seemed to be screaming next to a ceremonial dagger; of the coal miners of Moberly, Missouri, who, in 1885, tunneled 360 feet into the earth, only to break through the ceiling of a bygone underground city that housed a network of roads enclosed in stone arches and a stratum of lava, and the interred remains of yet another human giant—three times the size of a contemporary human, the head bones split, the sagittal and coronal sutures crushed—adjacent to a stone fountain that still gushed pure water impregnated with lime. "The story, if true, is singular," reported the *St. Paul Daily Globe* in 1885, "and if not true is a yarn that would have done credit to Missouri in the palmiest days of her romancing." Kristan T. Harris, "City Found 360 Feet Below Missouri City, Giant Human Skeleton Found," *St. Paul Daily Globe*, April 14, 1885; "A Missouri Wonder: A Buried City Discovered," *Semi-Weekly South Kentuckian*, April 17, 1885.

124 **"a pure state, pure Namaqualand":** "Environment," 2008. De Beers Family of Companies, Report to Society, 82–95.

125 **"One of the strongest predictors of conservation behavior":** Richard Osbaldiston, "Synthesizing the Experiments and Theories of Conservation Psychology," *Sustainability* 5, no. 6 (June 2013): 2770–95.

125 **"The reasons that the passenger pigeon was unable to recover":** Craig Kasnoff, "The Passenger Pigeon: Extinct," bagheera.com.

127 **"Moving forward, we will be out of the diamond business":** Oppenheimer and Oppenheimer, "Dear Colleagues."

BARTHOLOMEW VARIATION #4

129 **oracular priests known as the Augurs:** "Augury (Divination)," *Encyclopaedia Britannica*, 1998.

CHAPTER 9: PILGRIMS AND THE MOUNTAIN OF LIGHT

131 **the famed Koh-i-Noor, the *Mountain of Light*:** William Dalrymple and Anita Anand, *Koh-i-Noor: The History of the World's Most Infamous Diamond* (New York: Bloomsbury, 2017); Anil Dhir, "Why the Kohinoor Should Be Restored to Its Rightful Place at Jagannath Temple Puri," *Odisha News*, October 18, 2018; "Koh-i-Noor Curse," exhibit: plaque and article, Kimberley Mine Museum; and Ayesha L. Sethi, "A Brief History of the Kohinoor Diamond, and What All the Fuss Is About," *Citizen*, April 19, 2016.

133 **Babur hypnotized Lodi's squad of 150 war elephants:** Babur, *Baburnama: A Memoir*, translated by Annette Susannah Beveridge (New Delhi: Rupa Publications India, 2017).

134 **"The gem called the Koh-i-Noor":** George Anderson and Manilal Bhagwandas Subedar, *The Last Days of the Company: A Source Book of Indian History, 1818–1858* (Bombay: A. H. Wheeler, 1918).

135 **"The Court of the East India Company are ruffled":** Edward Hollis, *The Memory Palace: A Book of Lost Interiors* (Berkeley, CA: Counterpoint, 2014).

135 **"The several sad or foul events":** Dalrymple and Anand, *Koh-i-Noor.*

135 **they did not "seize" the gem, but it was "presented to them":** Dalrymple and Anand, *Koh-i-Noor.*

135 **"Diamonds are for the Emperors":** Balaji Sadasivan, *The Dancing Girl: A History of Early India* (Pasir Panjang, Singapore: Institute of Southeast Asian Studies, 2011).

136 **unexploded ordnance lurk in the gardens' mud walls:** Lalage Snow, "Kabul's Hidden Gardens Offer Afghans Haven from War," *Financial Times,* September 13, 2013.

136 **Pilgrims to Babur's tomb:** Ursula Sims-Williams, "Pigeon-Keeping: A Popular Mughal Pastime," *Asian and African Studies,* British Library, February 23, 2013, bl.uk.

136 **"If you want a simple life":** Babur, *Baburnama.*

CHAPTER 10: ODYSSEY TO DIE HOUTHOOP

138 **"very special, but isolated . . . treated as mere numbers":** De Beers document "Kleinzee," chapter 1, "Introduction." Kleinzee Museum archives. The photocopied and bound document is full of diamond-loving, company-loving propaganda. The quotes used here were apparently taken from an anonymous De Beers operative's interview with a Kleinzee local named Wessel Olivier on July 5, 1997, but the citation states that Olivier lives in Joubertina, which is a twelve-hour, 1,052-kilometer drive from Kleinzee, so who knows.

139 **Jack Carstens:** Jack Carstens, *A Fortune Through My Fingers* (Cape Town: Howard Timmins, 1962); Patrick Richard Carstens, *Port Nolloth: The Making of a South African Seaport* (Cape Town: South African Library, 2011); Peter Carstens, *In the Company of Diamonds: De Beers, Kleinzee, and the Control of a Town* (Athens: Ohio University Press, 2001); and "Die Ontdekkers: The Discoverers," exhibit: series of clipped articles and captioned photographs, Kleinzee Museum.

139 **Lawrence's habit of muttering tenderly:** Information on Lawrence comes from T. E. Lawrence, *Seven Pillars of Wisdom* (1926; Adelaide: University of Adelaide Library, 2014, ebooks .adelaide.edu.au); Philip Walker, *Behind the Lawrence Legend: The Forgotten Few Who Shaped the Arab Revolt* (Oxford: Oxford University Press, 2018); and Jeremy Wilson, *Lawrence of Arabia: The Authorized Biography of T. E. Lawrence* (New York: Atheneum, 1990).

139 **the honeyed messages their progenitors had carried:** Marius Kociejowski, *The Pigeon Wars of Damascus* (London: Biblioasis, 2010).

139 **seized the wheat . . . starved:** Ronald Florence, *Lawrence and Aaronsohn: T. E. Lawrence, Aaron Aaronsohn, and the Seeds of the Arab-Israeli Conflict* (New York: Penguin, 2007).

140 **"'out-of-works,' crooks, and undesirables":** De Beers, "Protection Report," November 1930. Kleinzee Museum archives.

140 **and a trench known:** "Picking Out Diamonds by Hand Along the Oyster Line." Exhibit: series of clipped articles and photographs, Kleinzee Museum.

140 **"old, true love":** E. Reuning, "The Discovery of Namaqualand Diamonds: An Answer to Dr. H. Merensky's Reply Published in January, 1929," displayed in the Kleinzee Museum.

141 **"the stampede to the Diamond Coast":** Dr. Merensky, "How I Found the Richest Diamond Fields in the World," *Mining and Industrial Magazine,* May 18, 1927.

141 **Ears sufficiently bent:** Union of South Africa, Magistrate's Office, Springbok, Namaqualand, "Certificate in terms of Section 62 of Act no. 11 of 1899," October 7, 1927.

141 **"could bring chaos to the market":** "Merensky and Reuning." Exhibit: series of clipped articles and photographs, Kleinzee Museum.

141 **promising to maintain:** And thereby devising and instituting such notices as "Notice: Every Digger Shall Enter into This Register," January 15, 1927. Kleinzee Museum archives.

141 **"a human story of hardship" . . . he died there alone:** "Mr. Schlesinger Buys a Farm" (from Our Special Representative). Clipped article, Kleinzee Museum.

142 **"Were these gems tossed from a submarine . . .":** "Full Story of the Namaqualand Diamond Discoveries," *Mining and Industrial Magazine*, May 18, 1927.

148 **Orpheus having trailed:** Details of the Orpheus myth come from Robert Graves, *The Greek Myths: The Complete and Definitive Edition* (New York: Viking, 2018); Ovid, *Metamorphoses*, translated by David Raeburn (New York: Penguin Classics, 2004); and Virgil, *The Georgics of Virgil*, translated by David Ferry (New York: Farrar, Straus and Giroux, 2006).

148 **toasted ant heads and fetid dewdrops:** The cuisine of the fairies also included the legs of mites, the brains of butterflies, and the thighs of fleas, a creampuff made of rainbows, and barleycorn beer.

148 **Greek funerary sculpture:** Brittany Garcia, "The Symbolism of Birds on Ancient Greek Grave Steles," classicsnewsneedsandnow.blogspot.com, November 5, 2013; and Janet Burnett Grossman, *Greek Funerary Sculpture: Catalog of the Collections at the Getty Villa* (Los Angeles: J. Paul Getty Trust, 2001).

148 **Even the innumerable Furies:** The Furies' origins variously lie in the immaculate conception of Night herself, the miscarriages of the fetuses forged by Air and Mother Earth, and the coupling of the blood of Uranus's castrated genitalia with the silt at the bottom of the sea into which the sky-godly bits were tossed.

149 **"With that, taking a cable":** Homer, *The Odyssey*, translated by Robert Fagles (London: Penguin, 1996).

150 **the bait traps of the cunning fowlers of the world:** Prudentius, *The Origin of Sin: An English Translation of the Hamartigenia*, translated by Martha A. Malamud (Ithaca, NY: Cornell University Press, 2011). In the *Hamartigenia*, a cunning fowler sets his bait traps and "Some of the doves are attracted to the tempting food and are caught in the snares: they are strangled by cords or their wings are gripped by the sticky glue . . . The birds that refrain from turning their eyes toward the food fly off to the heavens, clapping their wings as they go; those trapped in the snares are captive, helplessly beating their wounded wings as they gaze in vain at the swift breezes."

150 **"An impossible repetition":** Mehdi Belhaj Kacem, *Transgression and the Inexistent* (New York: Bloomsbury, 2014).

150 **the sort of redundancy—chained to a suffocating hindsight:** Such redundancy also plagued many other souls in the Tartarus abyss, but, when Orpheus plays his music, for a brief moment, the business of the underworld ceases. Tantalus—doomed to stand forever in a pool of water beneath the branches of a fruit tree that ever eludes his grasp, the water retreating whenever he stoops to sip from it—forgets, if only for a few seconds, his hunger and thirst. Sisyphus, forever doomed to roll his boulder uphill only to have it roll back down, is granted a brief respite, as he squats on his rock and eavesdrops on the song. Ixion, mad with guilt at having murdered his father-in-law, chained to a fiery solar wheel set to spin ad nauseam and infinitum in the corridors of Tartarus, sees, if only for the duration of Orpheus's song, the horrible revolutions cease.

150 **"It is indeed the incompletion":** Sophie Chiari, *Renaissance Tales of Desire* (Cambridge: Cambridge Scholars Publishing, 2009).

Notes

BARTHOLOMEW VARIATION #5

159 **"The Soales of the feet ... Madness":** Francis Bacon, *Sylva Sylvarum, or, A Natural History, in Ten Centuries* (London, 1670). Available at archive.org.
159 **failed to cure ... vengeful ghosts:** *Notes and Queries: A Medium of Intercommunication for Literary Men, General Readers, Etc.* (London: Bream's Buildings, 1901).

CHAPTER 12: THIS SECURITY THING

165 **shot through the head:** "Diamond Deals Gone Wrong, 1991." Exhibit: plaque and article, Port Nolloth Museum.
165 **"highest number of rough diamonds secreted ... suspect's anus":** "Avoiding the X-Rays, Stealing Diamonds." Exhibit: plaque and article, Port Nolloth Museum.
165 **"in the vicinity of the subject's lower stomach":** "With Criminal Intent." Exhibit: plaque and article, Port Nolloth Museum. The report also justified further invasive search policies: "over the years diamond thieves have repeatedly attempted to secrete [sic] contraband in every bodily crevice or orifice, including ears, mouths, foreskins, rectums, and even behind testicles."
167 **They smuggle also the rotten edicts:** Allan Anderson, "Pentecostals and Apartheid in South Africa During Ninety Years, 1908–1998," *Cyberjournal for Pentecostal-Charismatic Research*, September 11, 2000; and David Maxwell, "Historicizing Christian Independency: The South African Pentecostal Movement c. 1908–1960," *Journal of African History* 40, no. 2 (July 1999): 243–64.
168 **the human brain contains magnetite:** Robert O. Becker, *Cross Currents: The Promise of Electromedicine, the Perils of Electropollution* (New York: Penguin, 1990).
168 **"Skinner conducted his research on a group of hungry pigeons":** "Superstition: How Skinner's Pigeon Experiment Revealed Signs of Superstition in Pigeons," psychologistworld.com.

BARTHOLOMEW VARIATION #6

173 **At a time like this, does he suddenly recall lily pads:** As earlier in the text, this references the ocean voyages of HMS *Beagle* and the imagined lamplight of Darwin's (and his pigeon companion's) cabin; the First World War, during which the heroic pigeon Cher Ami, trained by the U.S. Army pigeoneers, saved the lives of the U.S. Army's "Lost Battalion" in the loamy Argonne forest of France; and Martha, the world's last passenger pigeon (who reportedly spent some of her early days in the University of Chicago office of Professor Charles Otis Whitman, who doted on her and gave her comfort, especially during the great Chicago thunderstorm of 1885, which not only shook Professor Whitman's office building, but also rattled the windows of the newly erected Home Insurance Building—the world's first skyscraper, its iron skeleton initially drawing ridicule from the architectural community who dismissed it as "impractical" and "ludicrous"—and flushed the sewage of the Chicago River deep into Lake Michigan, all the way out to the city's drinking water intake cribs). Martha spent her final days in a cage at the Cincinnati Zoo, under the scant care of head zookeeper and former circus elephant handler Salvator "Sol" Stephans, who, in the company of the dancers of the nearby Empress Burlesque Theater (where the G-string was invented), often stood drunk before Martha's cage late

at night, after hours, tossing sequins that had loosed themselves from the Empress dancers' bustiers into the pagoda-shaped cage, which, at first, Martha would confuse for seed. As Martha tried to sleep, Sol and the dancers would routinely revel deep into the night at the Zoo Club restaurant, laughing amid the columns of the wraparound porch as the resident musicians, forced to work overtime, took their places beneath the bandstand, lifted their horns to their lips, and played their jazz amid the low groans of Pheasant Yard, the Monkey House, and the Carnivora Building. At some point during Martha's last days in 1914, she had an apoplectic stroke. When visitors to the zoo came to see her, she was so slack that they often decided to throw sand and concessions—typically popcorn—at her in order to make her more interesting to them. Oftentimes, she appeared dead, flat on her back, until that thrown thing struck her breast and she was, once again, as the *Cincinnati Enquirer* reported, "shocked . . . into" feeble "activity" ("The Days of the Last Passenger Pigeon," August 18, 1914).

Sources

"18th- and 19th-Century Traveller's Journals and Other Early Views of Africa." Africana Collection, Stellenbosch University Library.

Able, K. T. "The Effects of Overcast Skies on the Orientation of Free-Flying Nocturnal Migrants." In F. Papi and H. G. Wallraff, eds., *Avian Navigation*. Berlin: Springer, 1982.

Abs, Michael. *Physiology and Behaviour of the Pigeon*. London: Academic Press, 1983.

Adams, Cecil. "Where Are All the Dead Pigeons?" *The Straight Dope*, May 20, 1988.

Addison, Henry Robert, Charles Henry Oakes, William John Lawson, Douglas Brooke, and Wheelton Sladen, eds. *Who's Who*. Vol. 55, part 2. New York: Macmillan, 1903.

Allatt, Captain H. T. W. "The Use of Pigeons as Messengers in War and the Military Pigeon Systems of Europe." *Royal United Service Institution* 30, no. 133 (1886): 107–48.

American Pigeon Museum and Library. "Real History of Pigeons." theamericanpigeon museum.org.

Anderson, George, and Manilal Bhagwandas Subedar. *The Last Days of the Company: A Source Book of Indian History, 1818–1858*. Bombay: A. H. Wheeler, 1918.

Army and Navy Register. Vol. 1, no. 1645. Washington, DC: U.S. Marine Corps, July 1, 1911.

Arrian. *The Campaigns of Alexander*. London: Penguin Classics, 1976.

Avery, Mark. *A Message from Martha: The Extinction of the Passenger Pigeon and Its Relevance Today*. London: Bloomsbury, 2014.

Babur. *Baburnama: A Memoir*. Translated by Annette Susannah Beveridge. New Delhi: Rupa Publications India, 2017.

Badenhorst, S. H. "The Unique Namdeb Trilogy—Our Past, Present, and Future Mining Applications in This Unique Deposit." *Journal of the South African Institute of Mining and Metallurgy* (November 2003): 539–50.

Baker, Robin. *Human Navigation and Magneto-Reception*. Manchester, UK: Manchester University Press, 1989.

———. *The Mystery of Migration*. New York: Viking, 1981.

Barnett, W., et al. "How Structure and Stress Influence Kimberlite Emplacement." In D. G. Pearson et al., eds., *Proceedings of the 10th International Kimberlite Conference*. New York: Springer, 2013.

Basu, Saurab. "Murshidabad—The Land of the Legendary 'Siraj-ud-dullah' Unveiled." Last revised 2007. historyofbengal.com.

Basu, Tanya. "Cape Verde Gets a New Name: 5 Things to Know About How Maps Change." *National Geographic*, December 14, 2013.

Beauty of Birds. "Heavy Metal Poisoning in Pet Birds." 2011. beautyofbirds.com.

Beck, Sam. *Manny Almeida's Ringside Lounge: The Cape Verdeans' Struggle for Their Neighborhood*. Providence: Gávea–Brown Publications, 1992.

Becker, Robert O. *Cross Currents: The Promise of Electromedicine, the Perils of Electropollution.* New York: Penguin, 1990.

Bega, Sheree. "The Town Where No Water Runs." *Saturday Star,* June 6, 2015.

Bejan, A. "The Constructal Law Of Organization in Nature: Tree-Shaped Flows and Body Size." *Journal of Experimental Biology* 208 (2005): 1677–86.

Bengali, Shashank. "Toll of Zimbabwe's Election Yet to Come." McClatchy Newspapers, July 5, 2008.

Benson, Tom. "A Brief History of Rockets." National Aeronautics and Space Administration. grc.nasa.gov.

Berthold, P. "Spatiotemporal Programmes and the Genetics of Orientation." In P. Berthold, ed., *Orientation in Birds.* Basel: Birkhaüser, 1991.

Birdsley, Jeff. "Internal Anatomy." In Frank B. Gill, ed., *Ornithology.* London: W. H. Freeman, 2006.

Blechman, Andrew D. *Pigeons.* New York: Grove/Atlantic, 2006.

Bose, Purnima, and Laura E. Lyons, eds. *Cultural Critique and the Global Corporation.* Bloomington: Indiana University Press, 2010.

Bowen, H. V., Margarette Lincoln, and Nigel Rigby, eds. *The Worlds of the East India Company.* Woodbridge, UK: Boydell Press, 2003.

Branom, Mike. "Arpaio's Ploys Can't Keep Jailbirds out of Tent City." *East Valley Tribune,* March 16, 2006.

Brenner, Ashley T. *The Dutch Have Made Slaves of Them All...And They Are Called Free.* Saarbrücken: Lambert Academic, 2009.

Brenner, Robert. *Merchants and Revolution: Commercial Change, Political Conflict, and London's Overseas Traders.* Princeton: Princeton University Press, 1993.

Bronner, Simon J. "Contesting Tradition: The Deep Play and Protest of Pigeon Shoots." *Journal of American Folklore* 118, no. 470 (Autumn 2005): 409–52.

Bureau of International Labor Affairs. "Cape Verde," in "Findings on the Worst Forms of Child Labor." 2002.

——. "South Africa: Prevalence and Sectoral Distribution of Child Labor." 2016.

Burkhardt, Paul. "Blyvooruitzicht: The Fallout from a Gold Mine's Closure." *Moneyweb Investor,* December 18, 2013.

Cahill, Petra. "A Diamond's Journey: Grim Reality Tarnishes Glitter." NBC News, June 26, 2009. nbcnews.com.

Campbell, Greg. *Blood Diamonds.* New York: Perseus, 2004.

Cape Town Diamond Museum. Exhibits. Cape Town, South Africa.

Carling, Jorgen. "Emigration, Return and Development in Cape Verde: The Impact of Closing Borders." *Population, Space, and Place* 10, no. 2 (March 2004): 113–32.

"Carrier Pigeons as Smugglers." *Popular Science News* 30, no. 1 (September 1896): 216.

Carstens, Jack. *A Fortune Through My Fingers.* Cape Town: Howard Timmins, 1962.

Carstens, Patrick Richard. *Port Nolloth: The Making of a South African Seaport.* Cape Town: South African Library, 2011.

Carstens, Peter. *In the Company of Diamonds: De Beers, Kleinzee, and the Control of a Town.* Athens: Ohio University Press, 2001.

Carter, D. E., and D. A. Eckerman. "Symbolic Matching by Pigeons: Rate of Learning Complex Discriminations Predicted from Simple Discriminations." *Science* 187 (1975): 662–64.

Carthy, J. D. *Animal Navigation.* London: Unwin, 1963.

Chudler, Eric H. "Brain Facts and Figures." Center for Sensorimotor Neural Engineering, University of Washington, 2015.

Coemans, M., and J. J. Vos. "On the Perception of Polarized Light by the Homing Pigeon." Utrecht: University of Utrecht, 1992.

Cokinos, Christopher. *Hope Is the Thing with Feathers*. New York: Penguin–Putnam, 2000.

Colvin, Ian Duncan. *Cecil John Rhodes, 1853–1902*. Los Angeles: Hardpress, 2012.

"Constitution of the Republic of Cape Verde." 1992, amended 1999. Available at the University of Richmond website, richmond.edu.

Cook, Robert. *Avian Visual Cognition*. Medford, MA: Tufts University Department of Psychology/Comparative Cognition Press, 2001.

Corbett, Alison. *Diamond Beaches: A History of Oranjemund*. Oranjemund: Namdeb Diamond Corporation, 2002.

Cornell Lab of Ornithology. "Rock Pigeon." Ithaca, NY: Cornell University, 2015. Available at allaboutbirds.org.

Creola Genealogist. "The Question of Slavery in Cape Verde." April 2, 2013. https://thecreolagenealogist.com/2013/04/02/the-question-of-slavery-in-cape-verde/.

Dalrymple, William. *The Anarchy: The East India Company, Corporate Violence, and the Pillage of an Empire*. London: Bloomsbury, 2019.

——. "The East India Company: The Original Corporate Raiders." *Guardian*, March 4, 2015.

Dalrymple, William, and Anita Anand. *Koh-i-Noor: The History of the World's Most Infamous Diamond*. New York: Bloomsbury, 2017.

D'Ambrosio, Charles. *Loitering: New and Collected Essays*. Portland, OR: Tin House Books, 2014.

Darwin, Charles. "Notes on Rhea americana and Rhea darwinii." *Proceedings of the Zoological Society of London* 5, no. 51 (1837): 35–36.

——. *On the Origin of Species*. London: Murray, 1859.

——. "Origin of Certain Instincts." *Nature* 7 (1873): 417–18.

——. *The Variation of Animals and Plants Under Domestication*. London: Murray, 1881.

Darwin, Charles, et al. The Darwin Correspondence Project, University of Cambridge. darwinproject.ac.uk.

"Data Transfer? Forget Email, Send for the Pigeon Post." *Daily Mail*, September 10, 2009.

De Beer, Dawid W., and Jaleen De Beer. *The De Beer Family: Three Centuries in South Africa*. CD-ROM. South Africa: De Beer Family Register, 2000.

De Beers Group of Companies. Archives, Kimberley, South Africa, and online at debeers.com.

Defender Bird Spikes. "21 Amazing Facts You Didn't Know About Pigeons." 2015. deterapigeon.com.

de Greef, Kimon. "Inside South Africa's Abandoned Mining Town." *Vice*, March 28, 2016.

Dewar, Genevieve Isabel. *The Archaeology of the Coastal Desert of Namaqualand, South Africa: A Regional Synthesis*. D.Phil. thesis, Department of Archaeology, University of Cape Town, February 2007.

Dhir, Anil. "Why the Kohinoor Should Be Restored to Its Rightful Place at Jagannath Temple Puri." *Odisha News*, October 18, 2018.

Dial, K. P., A. A. Biewener, B. W. Tobalske, and D. R. Warrick. "Mechanical Power Output of Bird Flight." *Science* 390 (1997): 67–70.

Diamcor Mining, Inc. "World Diamond Retail." diamcormining.com.

Diamond Fields International, Ltd. "History of Marine Diamonds." diamondfields.com.

"Diamond Smugglers Make Use of Many Clever Tricks." *Free Lance-Star*, September 10, 1948.

"Diamonds." U.S. Library of Congress, countrystudies.us/south-africa. Accessed October 16, 2015.

Dinman, Bertram D., and Frank G. Standaert. *A Review of the Toxicology Research Program of the 6570th Aerospace Medical Research Laboratory, Wright-Patterson Air Force Base, Ohio.* National Research Council, U.S. Committee on Toxicology. Springfield, VA: National Academy of Sciences, June 1974.

Diski, Chloe. "Famous Foodies: Charles Darwin." *Guardian*, March 9, 2003.

Doneley, Bob. *Avian Medicine and Surgery in Practice: Companion and Aviary Birds.* 2nd ed. Boca Raton, FL: CRC Press, 2016.

Dop, Henk, and Phillip T. Robinson, eds. *Travel Sketches from Liberia: Johann Büttikofer's 19th Century Rainforest Explorations in West Africa.* Boston: Brill, 2013.

Dorstfontein Executive Council. "Rules and Regulations for the Diggings." Article 10, Ordinance 3. 1871. Kleinzee Museum, Kleinzee, South Africa.

Duminy, Kokkie, and Dr. R. J. L. Sabatini. *Fifty Years on the Diamond Fields: 1870-1920.* Kimberley: Africana Library Trust, 2013.

Duncan, Gillian. "Dubai to Make Blood-Diamond Smuggling Harder." *National*, May 6, 2012.

Elliott, Andrew. "Lesser Rhea." In Josep del Hoyo, Andrew Elliott, and Jordi Sargatal, eds., *Handbook of the Birds of the World*, vol. 1. Barcelona: Lynx Edicions, 1992.

Emery, Nathan J. "Cognitive Ornithology: The Evolution of Avian Intelligence." *Philosophical Transactions of the Royal Society of Biological Sciences* 361, no. 1465 (January 2006): 23–43.

Epstein, Edward Jay. *The Rise and Fall of Diamonds.* New York: Simon and Schuster, 1982.

European Geosciences Union. "How Pigeons May Smell Their Way Home." November 5, 2013. Available at sciencedaily.com.

"Falling Pigeons in New York Force Shutdown at Hospital." *Orlando Sentinel*, July 29, 2006.

Farrand, John, Jr. *An Audubon Handbook: Eastern Birds.* New York: McGraw–Hill, 1988.

Fauvel, John, Raymond Flood, Michael Shortland, and Robin Wilson, eds. *Let Newton Be!* Oxford: Oxford University Press, 1989.

Fisher, M. F. K. *A Cordiall Water: A Garland of Odd and Old Receipts to Assuage the Ills of Man and Beast.* New York: Little, Brown, 1961.

FitzRoy, Robert. *Narrative of the surveying voyages of His Majesty's Ships Adventure and Beagle between the years 1826 and 1836, describing their examination of the southern shores of South America, and the Beagle's circumnavigation of the globe. Proceedings of the second expedition, 1831–36, under the command of Captain Robert Fitz-Roy, R.N.* London: Henry Colburn, 1839.

Fleminger, David. *Richtersveld: Cultural and Botanical Landscape: Including Namaqualand.* Johannesburg: Southbound, 2008.

"FLIGHT: The Genius of Birds – Embryonic Development." Video. Illustra Media. Posted May 21, 2013, at YouTube.com.

Florence, Ronald. *Lawrence and Aaronsohn: T. E. Lawrence, Aaron Aaronsohn, and the Seeds of the Arab-Israeli Conflict.* New York: Penguin, 2007.

"For Heaven's Sake, Stop It." Letter from Major Charles Whittlesey to friendly-firing allies during the Meuse–Argonne offensive, September 1918. Available at lettersofnote.com.

Fraser, Maryna. "International Archives in South Africa." *Business and Economic History* 16 (1987): 163–73.

Freeman, Philip. *Alexander the Great.* New York: Simon and Schuster, 2011.

"Full Story of the Namaqualand Diamond Discoveries." *Mining and Industrial Magazine*, May 18, 1927.

Fuller, Errol. *The Passenger Pigeon.* Princeton: Princeton University Press, 2014.

Gaille, Brandon. "56 Diamond Industry Statistics and Trends." January 28, 2019. brandon gaille.com.

Gallagher, James. "'Memories' Pass Between Generations." BBC News, December 1, 2013. bbc news.com.

Gardiner, Robert. *The Naval War of 1812*. London: Chatham, 1998.

Gayle, Damien. "Near-Death Experiences Occur When the Soul Leaves the Nervous System and Enters the Universe, Claim Two Quantum Physics Experts." *Daily Mail*, October 30, 2012.

Geldenhuys, Henriette. "Diggers Trapped in Mine Dead, Say Police." IOL, May 26, 2012. iol.co.za.

Gerlin, Andrea. "Pigeons Fit Bill to Detect Poisons." *Orlando Sentinel*, March 15, 2003.

Gibbs, David, Eustace Barnes, and John Cox. *Pigeons and Doves: A Guide to the Pigeons and Doves of the World*. London: Pica Press, 2010.

Gibson, Alan G. S. *Eight Years in Kaffraria (1882–1890)*. London: Wells Gardner, Darton and Co., 1891.

"Gold and Diamond Mines of South Africa." U.S. Library of Congress, 1917. https://www.loc .gov/item/00694217/.

Gooley, Lawrence. "The Homing Pigeon in NY History." *New York History*, August 7, 2012.

Gotch, A. F. *Latin Names Explained: A Guide to the Scientific Classifications of Reptiles, Birds & Mammals*. London: Facts on File, 1995.

Gould, J. L. "The Map Sense of Pigeons." *Nature* 296 (1982): 205–11.

Gould, John. *Birds*. London: Smith Elder, 1839.

Govender, Peroshni. "Pigeon Transfers Data Faster Than South Africa's Telkom." Reuters, September 9, 2009. reuters.com.

Graber, Richard R., and Jean W. Graber. "Variation in Avian Brain Weights with Special Reference to Age." *Condor* 67, no. 4 (July 1965): 300–18.

Grant, K. Thalia, and Gregory B. Estes. *Darwin in Galapagos: Footsteps to a New World*. Princeton: Princeton University Press, 2009.

Graves, Robert. *The Greek Myths: The Complete and Definitive Edition*. New York: Viking, 2018.

Greelis, Jim. "Pigeons in Military History." World of Wings. pigeoncenter.org.

Green, Lawrence G. *Eight Bells at Salamander: The Unwritten Story of Ships and Men in South African Waters*. Cape Town: Howard Timmins, 1960.

Greenberg, Joel. *A Feathered River Across the Sky: The Passenger Pigeon's Flight to Extinction*. New York: Bloomsbury, 2014.

Hagstrum, Jonathan T. "Infrasound and the Avian Navigational Map." *Journal of Experimental Biology* 203 (2000): 1103–11.

Hansell, Dr. Jean. "The Pigeon in History." pigeoncontrolresourcecentre.com.

Harlow, George E. *The Nature of Diamonds*. Cambridge, UK: Cambridge University Press, 1997.

Hart, Matthew. *Diamonds: A Journey to the Heart of an Obsession*. London: Walker, 2001.

——. "How to Steal a Diamond." *Atlantic Monthly*, March 1999.

Haupt, Lyanda Lynn. *Pilgrim on the Great Bird Continent*. New York: Little, Brown, 2006.

Hausheer, Justine E. "How Do Pigeons Find Their Way Home?" *Audubon*, September–October 2012.

Hawkins, Michelle. "Avian Pain and Analgesia." Lecture, Association of Avian Veterinarians conference and expo, Davis, CA, 2004. Available at thebirdclinic.com.

Hayden, Robert C. *African Americans and Cape Verdean-Americans in New Bedford: A History of Community and Achievement*. Pernambuco, Brazil: Federal University, 1993.

Heinrich, Bernd. *The Homing Instinct: Meaning and Mystery in Animal Migration*. New York: Mariner, 2015.

"Hemingway's Suicide Gun." *Garden and Gun*, October 20, 2010. gardenandgun.com.

Hill, C. "Boomerang Flying." *Racing Pigeon Pictorial* 15 (1985): 116–18.

Hill, John. *A History of the Materia Medica*. London: Longman, 1751.

Himalayan Pigeon. "Pigeon Facts." https://www.himalayanpigeon.com/pigeon-facts/.

Hocking, Anthony. *Oppenheimer and Son*. New York: McGraw-Hill, 1973.

Hollis, Edward. *The Memory Palace: A Book of Lost Interiors*. Berkeley, CA: Counterpoint, 2014.

Homer. *The Odyssey*. Translated by Robert Fagles. London: Penguin, 1996.

"Homing Pigeons in France During WWI, 1918." OHS Film and Video Archives. Posted March 21, 2014, at YouTube.com.

Howard, G. S. "Culture Tales: A Narrative Approach to Thinking, Crosscultural Psychology, and Psychotherapy." *American Psychologist* 46, no. 3 (1991): 187–97.

Hurford, James. *The Origins of Meaning: Language in the Light of Evolution*. New York: Oxford University Press, 2007.

Hutton, Andrew N. *Pigeon Lore*. London: Faber and Faber, 1978.

Ingram, Joseph Forsyth. *The Land of Gold, Diamonds, and Ivory*. London: W. B. Whittingham, 1893.

International Programme on the Elimination of Child Labour. "Good Practices and Lessons Learned on the Elimination of the Worst Forms of Child Labour in Namibia." International Labour Organization, June 2012.

Iwaniuk, A. N., and J. E. Nelson. "Developmental Differences Are Correlated with Relative Brain Size in Birds: A Comparative Analysis." *Canadian Journal of Zoology* 81, no. 12 (December 2003): 1913–28.

Johnson, George B. "The Great Pigeon Race Disaster of 97 Suggests an Answer to an Enduring Mystery." 2015. biologywriter.com.

Josiah, Barbara P. *Migration, Mining, and the African Diaspora*. Basingstoke, UK: Palgrave Macmillan, 2011.

Karmali, Faisel, and Mark Shelhamer. "The Dynamics of Parabolic Flight: Flight Characteristics and Passenger Percepts." *Acta Astronautica* 63, nos. 5–6 (September 2008): 594–602.

Kasnoff, Craig. "The Passenger Pigeon: Extinct." bagheera.com.

Keeton, W. T. "Effects of Magnets on Pigeon Homing." In S. R. Galler et al., eds., *Animal Orientation and Navigation*. Washington, DC: NASA, 1972.

Keynes, Richard, ed. *Charles Darwin's Beagle Diary*. Cambridge, UK: Cambridge University Press, 1988.

——. *Charles Darwin's Zoology Notes and Specimen Lists from H.M.S. Beagle*. Cambridge, UK: Cambridge University Press, 2000.

Kimberley Mine Museum. Exhibits, archives, and website. Kimberley, South Africa.

King, E. J., M. Yoganathan, and G. Nagelschmidt. "The Effect of Diamond Dust Alone and Mixed with Quartz on the Lungs of Rats." *British Journal of Industrial Medicine* 15, no. 2 (April 1958): 92–95.

Kleinzee Museum. Exhibits and archives. Kleinzee, South Africa.

Klopfleisch, R., O. Werner, E. Mundt, T. Harder, and J. P. Teifke. "Neurotropism of Highly Pathogenic Avian Influenza Virus A/chicken/Indonesia/2003 (H5N1) in Experimentally Infected Pigeons (Columbia livia f. domestica)." *Journal of General Virology* 43, no. 4, November 2007: 463–70.

Kociejowski, Marius. *The Pigeon Wars of Damascus*. London: Biblioasis, 2010.

Lee, Jane J. "New Theory on How Homing Pigeons Find Home." *National Geographic*, January 30, 2013.

Levi, Wendell. *The Pigeon.* Sumter, SC: Levi, 1977.

"Limpopo." *Soon News,* December 6, 2017. soon.news/limpopo.

Liu, Y., J. Zhou, and H. Yang. "Susceptibility and Transmissibility of Pigeons to Asian Lineage Highly Pathogenic Avian Influenza Virus Subtype H5N1." *Avian Pathology* 36, no. 6 (March 2007): 461–65.

Lobban, Dr. Richard A. *Cape Verde–Crioulo Colony to Independent Nation.* Boulder, CO: Westview Press, 1998.

———. "Jews in Cape Verde and on the Guinea Coast." Paper presented at the University of Massachusetts–Dartmouth, February 11, 1996. www1.umassd.edu/SpecialPrograms/CaboVerde/jewslobban.html.

Long, W. J. *How Animals Talk.* New York: Harper, 1919.

Maillard, Robert. *Diamonds: Myth, Magic, and Reality.* New York: Crown, 1988.

Mangile's Pigeon Pages. "Pigeon Endocrine Glands" and "Pigeon Skeleton." mangile-pigeons.sperry-galligar.com.

Mann, Richard P. *Prediction of Homing Pigeon Flight Paths Using Gaussian Processes.* D.Phil. thesis, Oriel College, University of Oxford, 2009.

Marais, Chris. "Diamond Legends of Alexander Bay." *Karoo Space: At the Heart of South Africa,* Spring 2005. karoospace.co.za.

"Marine Casualty Database Southern African Coast (1552–1984)." OoCities.org. http://www.oocities.org/heartland/ridge/2216/text/MARITIME.TXT.

Marshall, Sarah. "All the Presidents' Menus." *Awl,* June 29, 2012.

Mason, John Edwin. "Mannenberg: Notes on the Making of an Icon and Anthem." *African Studies Quarterly* 9, no. 4 (Fall 2007).

Matthews, G. V. T. *Bird Navigation.* Cambridge, UK: Cambridge University Press, 1968.

Maxwell, David. "Historicizing Christian Independency: The South African Pentecostal Movement c. 1908–1960." *Journal of African History* 40, no. 2 (July 1999): 243–64.

Mayell, Hillary. "Extinct Dodo Related to Pigeons, DNA Shows." *National Geographic,* March 14, 2002.

McAtee, James J. "How the Navy Air Service Breeds Homers." *American Pigeon Journal,* July 1920: 300–05.

McClary, Douglas. *Pigeons for Everyone.* London: Winckley Press, 1999.

McFarland, D. "Homing." In D. McFarland, ed., *The Oxford Companion to Animal Behaviour.* Oxford: Oxford University Press, 1981.

Meintjies, Pricillia. "Kimberley: The City of Diamonds." *Discover South Africa,* February 9, 2012.

Meredith, Martin. *Diamonds, Gold, and War.* London: Simon and Schuster, 2007.

Merensky, Dr. "How I Found the Richest Diamond Fields in the World." *Mining and Industrial Magazine,* May 18, 1927.

Meriwether, Colyer. *Raphael Semmes.* American Crisis Biographies. Philadelphia: George W. Jacobs, 1913.

Miklian, Jason. "'Let's Deal': A Conversation with a Diamond Smuggler." *Words Without Borders,* September 2013.

Mira y Lopez, Thomas. *The Book of Resting Places: A Personal History of Where We Lay the Dead.* Berkeley, CA: Counterpoint Press, 2017.

Moore, B. R., K. J. Stanhope, and D. Wilcox. "Pigeons Fail to Detect Low-Frequency Magnetic Fields." *Animal Learning and Behavior* 15 (1987): 115–17.

Mora, C. V., M. Davison, J. M. Wild, and M. M. Walker. "Magnetoreception and Its Trigeminal Mediation in the Homing Pigeon." *Nature* 432 (2004): 508–11.

Morris, Ronnie. "Alexkor Sparkles over Discovery of 111-Carat Diamond in Alexander Bay." *Cape Archives*, January 2003.

Moyses, George. *Diamond Diving*. Cape Town: Port Nolloth Museum, 2011.

Muller, Carol A. *South African Music: A Century of Traditions in Transformation*. Oxford: ABC-CLIO, 2004.

Mullin, Molly, and Rebecca Cassidy. *Where the Wild Things Are Now: Domestication Reconsidered*. New York: Bloomsbury Academic, 2007.

Murphy, J. J. "Instinct: A Mechanical Analogy." *Nature* 7 (1873): 483.

Naidoo, Dr. Rajen, Prof. Thomas Robins, and Prof. Noah Seixas. "Respiratory Diseases Among South African Coalminers." SIMHEALTH 607. University of Natal/University of Michigan, March 2002.

Native Languages of the Americas. "Native American Dove and Pigeon Mythology." 2015. native-languages.org.

Nayar, Usha, Priya Nayar, and Nidhi Mishra. "Child Labor." In *Encyclopedia of Social Work*, edited by Terry Mizrahi and Larry E. Davis. Oxford: Oxford University Press, 2014.

Neto, Octavio Amorim, and Marina Costa Lobo. "Between Constitutional Diffusion and Local Politics: Semi-Presidentialism in Portuguese-Speaking Countries." Social Science Research Network, July 19, 2010. ssrn.com.

"Next Serving of French Pate May Include Dutch Pigeon." *Orlando Sentinel*, December 14, 1995.

"Nigel Clive." Obituary. *Telegraph*, May 18, 2001.

"Not Enough People Left Alive to Bury the Dead." *Oxford Journal*, March 23, 1771.

Nunes, Maria Luisa. *A Portuguese Colonial in America: Belmira Nunes Lopes*. Pittsburgh: Latin American Literary Review Press, 1982.

Odum, Eugene P. "Variations in the Heart Rate of Birds: A Study in Physiological Ecology." *Ecological Monographs* 11, no. 3 (July 1941): 299–326.

"One of the Biggest Diamonds Ever Found Discovered in South Africa." *Telegraph*, September 29, 2009.

"One Section of Amsterdam Bans Feeding of Pigeons." *Orlando Sentinel*, December 23, 1998.

Opie, Iona, and Moira Tatum, eds. *A Dictionary of Superstitions*. Oxford: Oxford University Press, 1989.

Osbaldiston, Richard. "Synthesizing the Experiments and Theories of Conservation Psychology." *Sustainability* 5, no. 6 (June 2013): 2770–95.

Osman, A. H., and W. H. Osman. *Pigeons in Two World Wars*. London: Racing Pigeon Publishing Company, 1976.

Pack, Todd. "Disney Halts Pigeons' Show as Sitting Ducks for Hungry Hawks." *Orlando Sentinel*, July 19, 2002.

Pallister, David, Sarah Stewart, and Ian Lepper. *South Africa Inc.: The Oppenheimer Empire*. Sandton, South Africa: Media House, 1987.

Papi, F. *Animal Homing*. Chapman and Hall Animal Behaviour Series. Berlin: Springer, 2012.

Parker, W. Kitchen. "On the Morphology of the Duck and Auk Tribes." *Nature* 43, no. 1117 (March 26, 1891): 486–87.

Passarello, Elena. "Harriet (1830–2006)." *Passages North*, no. 34 (Winter 2013): 222–28.

Pigeon and Dove Rescue. "Pigeon Paramyxovirus: PPMV, Twisted Neck Disease." 2010. pigeonrescue.co.uk.

Pigeonweb. "Pigeon Food," "The Intense Life of the 'Carrier Pigeon.'" pigeonweb.net.

"Pigeons in Space." Video. Bioastronautics Research: Aerospace Medical Division HQ 6570th Aerospace Medical Research Laboratories. Posted February 4, 2011, at YouTube.com.

"Pigeon in the Sky with Diamonds." BBC News. June 18, 1998. news.bbc.co.uk.

Sources

"Pigeons Reveal Map-Reading Secret." BBC News, February 5, 2004. news.bbc.co.uk.

"Poisoned Pigeons Falling From Sky, Dying at Annual Festival." *USA Today*, September 13, 2006.

Port Nolloth Info. "Diamonds Are Not Forever." 2015. portnollothinfo.co.za.

Port Nolloth Museum. Exhibits. Port Nolloth, South Africa.

Ports and Ships: Port News and Shipping Movements in African and Southern African Ports and Harbours. "Port Nolloth." 2003. ports.co.za.

Primm, Arallyn. "A History of the Pigeon." *Mental Floss*, February 3, 2014.

Richa, Sami, and Nathalie Richa. "Pigeon Cave: A Legendary Place of Suicide in Lebanon." *American Journal of Psychiatry* 172, no. 1 (January 2015): 16.

Rickard, Bob, and John Michell. *The Rough Guide to Unexplained Phenomena*. 2nd ed. London: Penguin, 2007.

Ritchison, Gary. "Ornithology—Lecture Notes 3, Bird Flight II." Department of Biological Sciences, Eastern Kentucky University. people.eku.edu/ritchisong/ornitholsyl.htm.

Roberts, Brian. *The Diamond Magnates*. London: Hamish Hamilton, 1972.

Roberts, Janine F. *Glitter and Greed: The Secret World of the Diamond Cartel*. New York: Disinformation, 2007.

——. "Masters of Illusion." *Ecologist*, September 1, 2003.

——. "Working Conditions in De Beers Diamond Mines—Koffiefontein." Web Inquirer, 2002. http://www.sparkle.plus.com/koffie.html.

Rockstroh, Christina. "The Incredible Cape to Namibia Route." *Frankfurter Allgemeine Zeitung*, April 1, 2010.

Romeskie, Martha, and Dean Yager. "Psychophysical Studies of Pigeon Color Vision—I. Photopic Spectral Sensitivity." *Vision Research* 16, no. 5 (1976): 501–05.

Rosen, Jonathan. "The Birds." *New Yorker*, January 6, 2014.

Roth, Patti. "Pigeons with Notes Under Wings Puzzle Investigators." *Fort Lauderdale Sun-Sentinel*, April 19, 1993.

Ruthven, John A. "Martha, the Last Passenger Pigeon." Pamphlet. ArtWorks Cincinnati, 2013.

Sabar, Ariel. "Making a French Connection." *Baltimore Sun*, October 17, 2003.

"SA Pigeon 'Faster Than Broadband.'" BBC News, September 10, 2009. news.bbc.co.uk.

Schatz, Dennis. "Why Should We Care About Exploding Stars?" *Publications of the Astronomical Society of the Pacific*, no. 8 (Spring 1987).

Schmidt-Koenig, Klaus, and J. U. Ganzhorn. "On the Problem of Bird Navigation." In P. P. G. Bateson, ed., *Perspectives in Ethology*. New York: Plenum, 1991.

Schmidt-Koenig, Klaus, and H. J. Schlichte. "Homing in Pigeons with Impaired Vision." *Proceedings of the National Academy of Sciences* 69 (1972): 2446–47.

Schultz, Duane P., and Sydney Ellen Schultz. *A History of Modern Psychology*. Boston: Wadsworth, 2007.

Scott, John P. *Animal Behavior*. Chicago: University of Chicago Press, 1972.

Sebald, W. G. *The Rings of Saturn*. New York: New Directions, 1999.

Selinger, Ilan. "Top Ten Crazy Secrets of Isaac Newton." *People: Science*, January 17, 2014.

Sen, Sudipta. *Empire of Free Trade: The East India Company and the Making of the Colonial Marketplace*. Philadelphia: University of Pennsylvania Press, 1998.

Sethi, Ayesha L. "A Brief History of the Kohinoor Diamond, and What All the Fuss Is About." *Citizen*, April 19, 2016.

Shalev, Meir. *A Pigeon and a Boy*. New York: Random House, 2009.

Sherry, John F. *Contemporary Marketing and Consumer Behavior: An Anthropological Sourcebook*. London: Sage, 1995.

Siddiqui, Shahid. *The Golden Pigeon*. Noida, Uttar Pradesh: HarperCollins India, 2014.

"Slave Trade in the 18th and 19th Centuries and the Exploitation and Development of African Natural Resources." n.d. Grey Papers, Durham University Library and Heritage Collections.

Smithsonian Institution. "Cher Ami—World War I Carrier Pigeon." Updated 2015. si.edu.

Smithsonian National Museum of Natural History. "'Martha,' The Last Passenger Pigeon." Collections overview. naturalhistory.si.edu.

Spear, Jane E. "Cape Verdean Americans: History, Modern Era, The First Cape Verdeans in America." World Culture Encyclopedia. everyculture.com.

Spektorov, Yury, Olya Linde, Bart Cornelissen, and Rostislav Khomenko. "The Global Diamond Report 2013: Journey Through the Value Chain." Bain and Company, August 27, 2013. https://www.bain.com/insights/global-diamond-report-2013/.

Spencer, Lee. "A Trip Down Memory Lane." *NM Chronicle*, April 1998.

Spurling, K. D. "The Passenger Pigeon: A Lost Race." Columbarian Preservational Society, June 2001.

Stanford Solar Center. "Solar Activity Effects on Pigeons." 2008. solar-center.stanford.edu.

Stockton, Nick. "What's Up with That: Birds Bob Their Heads When They Walk." *Wired*, January 20, 2015.

Swiecki, Rafal. "Diamonds in South Africa." Alluvial Exploration and Mining, March 2011.

Tappan, M. B., and L. M. Brown. "Stories Told and Lessons Learned: Toward a Narrative Approach to Moral Development and Moral Education." *Harvard Educational Review* 59, no. 2 (1989): 182–205.

Taylor, James. *Voyage of the Beagle: Darwin's Extraordinary Adventure in Fitzroy's Famous Survey Ship*. New York: Conway Maritime Press, 2008.

Teale, Edwin. "Mile-a-Minute Pigeons." *Popular Science Monthly* 128, no. 6 (June 1936).

"Their Sphere Enlarging: Homing Pigeons Demonstrate Their Usefulness in Many Ways." *New York Times*, November 28, 1896.

"Timeline South Africa." Timelines of History. timelines.ws.

"Tricks of Smugglers." *Los Angeles Herald* 26, no. 150 (March 21, 1887).

Turkington, Tara. "Soul-Searching in Namaqualand." South African Tourism, October 29, 2013. southafrica.net.

"UK Pondered Suicide Pigeon Attacks." BBC News, May 21, 2004. news.bbc.co.uk.

Universities Federation for Animal Welfare. "Rolling Tumbling Pigeons." ufaw.org.uk.

U.S. Forest Service. "Weeks Act." foresthistory.org.

U.S. Naval Institute Staff. "A Brief Illustrated History of the Naval Goat." *USNI News*, December 12, 2014.

Usherwood, James R., Marinos Stavrou, John C. Lowe, Kyle Roskilly, and Alan M. Wilson. "Flying in a Flock Comes at a Cost in Pigeons." *Nature* 474, no. 7352 (June 23, 2011): 494–97.

Varley, Douglas. *Adventures in Africana*. Cape Town: University of Cape Town, 1949.

van Wyhe, John, ed. *Darwin's Journal (1809–1881)*. Darwin-online.org.uk.

Verchot, Manon. "The Pigeon Was a Biological Storm. He Was the Lightning That Played Between Two Opposing Potentials of Intolerable Intensity." *Treehugger*, September 2, 2014.

Walcott, C. "Magnetic Maps in Pigeons." In P. Berthold, ed., *Orientation in Birds*. Basel: Birkhäuser, 1991.

Walcott, C., and R. P. Green. "Orientation of Homing Pigeons Altered by a Change in the Direction of an Applied Magnetic Field." *Science* 184 (1974): 180–82.

Sources

Walcott, Charles. "Pigeon Homing: Observations, Experiments, and Confusions." *Journal of Experimental Biology* 199 (1996): 21–27.

Waldvogel, J. A. "Olfactory Navigation in Homing Pigeons: Are the Current Models Atmospherically Realistic?" *Auk* 104 (1987): 369–79.

Wallraff, H. G. "Navigation by Homing Pigeons." *Ethology, Ecology, and Evolution* 2 (1990): 81–115.

——. "Ratios Among Atmospheric Trace Gases Together with Winds Imply Exploitable Information for Bird Navigation: A Model Elucidating Experimental Results." *Biogeosciences* 10, no. 11 (2013): 6929.

Waterbury, Sally. "Taft Senior, 17, Trains Winning Pigeon Flock." *Chicago Tribune*, November 7, 1948.

Weimerskirch, H., J. Martin, Y. Clerquin, P. Alexandre, and S. Jiraskova. "Energy Saving in Flight Formation." *Nature* 413 (2001): 697–98.

Wenger, Estefania. *Isaac Newton: A Biography*. London: Alpha Editions, 2017.

Werlin, Louise. "Jews in Cape Verde." n.d. www1.umassd.edu/specialprograms/caboverde/jews werlin.html. Archived April 8, 2015.

Whan, Bill. "Passenger Pigeons in Your State/Province." Project Passenger Pigeon. Chicago Academy of Sciences and its Peggy Notebaert Nature Museum, 2012. passengerpigeon.org.

Wilkins, Alasdair. "Pigeons Are Completely Incapable of Forgetting a Human Face." *io9*, July 4, 2011.

Wilson, Jeremy. *Lawrence of Arabia: The Authorized Biography of T. E. Lawrence*. New York: Atheneum, 1990.

Wilson, M. G. C., G. Henry, and T. R. Marshall. "A Review of the Alluvial Diamond Industry and the Gravels of the North West Province, South Africa." *South African Journal of Geology* 109, no. 3 (September 2006): 301–14.

Wiltschko, W. "Magnetic Compass Orientation in Birds and Other Animals." *Orientation and Navigation: Birds, Humans, and Other Animals*. London: Royal Institution of Navigation, 1993.

Wiltschko, W., R. Wiltschko, and C. Walcott. "Pigeon Homing: Different Aspects of Olfactory Deprivation in Different Countries." *Behavioral Ecology and Sociobiology* 21 (1987): 333–42.

"Winston the Pigeon Wings It." IOL, September 9, 2009. iol.co.za.

Wood, News Elliott, ed. *Star of the Magi: An Exponent of Occult Science, Art, and Philosophy*. Chicago: N. E. Wood, 1899.

World Diamond Council. "Alluvial Diamond Mining Fact Sheet." http://www.diamondfacts .org/fact-sheets/.

——. "Conflict Diamonds and the Kimberley Process Fact Sheet." http://www.diamondfacts .org/fact-sheets/.

——. "The Diamond Industry Fact Sheet." http://www.diamondfacts.org/fact-sheets/.

——. "Diamond Producing Countries in Africa Fact Sheet." http://www.diamondfacts.org /fact-sheets/.

Yeoman, Barry. "Why the Passenger Pigeon Went Extinct." *Audubon*, May–June 2014.

Yodlowski, Marilyn, Melvin R. Kreithen, and William T. Keeton. "Pigeons Seeing with Sound: The Perception of Infrasound." *Nature* 265 (February 24, 1977): 725–26.

Zborowski, Mark. "Cultural Components in Responses to Pain." *Journal of Social Issues* 8, no. 4 (Fall 1952): 16–30.

Zhang, Meng, and Xiuping Li. "From Physical Weight to Psychological Significance: The Contribution of Semantic Activations." *Journal of Consumer Research* 38, no. 6 (April 1, 2012): 1063–75.

Zoellner, Tom. *The Heartless Stone: A Journey Through the World of Diamonds, Deceit, and Desire*. New York: St. Martin's Press, 2006.